MOVEABLE MARGINS

The Shifting Spaces of Canadian Literature

We acknowledge the support of the Canada Council for the Arts for our publishing program.
We also acknowledge support from the Ontario Arts Council.

Canada Council for the Arts   Conseil des Arts du Canada

Cover design by Heng Wee Tan

Library and Archives Canada Cataloguing in Publication

Moveable margins : the shifting spaces of Canadian literature / edited by Chelva Kanaganayakam.

Includes bibliographical references.
ISBN 1-894770-28-5

1. Canadian literature (English)—Minority authors—History and criticism.
2. Immigrants' writings, Canadian (English)—History and criticism.
3. Community in literature.
4. Canadian literature (English)—History and criticism.
I. Kanaganayakam, C. (Chelvanayakam), date

PS8071.4.M68 2005   C810.9'8   C2005-907102-8

Printed in Canada by Coach House Printing

TSAR Publications
P. O. Box 6996, Station A
Toronto, Ontario M5W 1X7
Canada

www.tsarbooks.com

Contents

Introduction

More than thirty years ago, Margaret Atwood, in her important and influential work, *Survival* (1972), made a sustained attempt to find a trope that would reveal the basic impulse that shapes Canadian literature. Her intention was not so much to suggest markers that would identify all literature written in the country; it was not even to write a literary history of Canada; rather, it was to define the contours of "Canadian literature" – a term that implies a symbiotic relation between the nation and a varied body of writing. The shadow of the nation, conceptualized as land and landscape, thus inevitably falls on literature, and it is hardly surprising that the trope she offers is one of survival. As she looks for ways to fit a heterogeneous body of material into this mold, the term expands to include even works whose relation to survival is at best tangential. Nonetheless, the basic argument still holds one's attention. Space and land are crucial to literature, and in Canada the land hardly allows for utopian dreams. Atwood's method is spatial rather than temporal in that it brings together disparate material in order to establish patterns of repetition, reiterate instances of continuity, and demonstrate an overall centripetal focus.

Atwood does not offer a sustained poetics that historicizes Canadian literature. The grid she offers is selective, but it is a necessary one in that it seeks ways of establishing unity in a literature that grew substantially in the previous few decades. Northrop Frye, writing a conclusion to the third volume of *Literary History of Canada*, begins by justifying the need for a new edition by drawing attention to the burgeoning of literature in Canada. This edition appeared in 1976, four years after Atwood's book, and Frye is aware of both the need for unity, and the danger of creating margins that would alienate a whole body of literature. Frye's theoretical stance allows for diversity, but he is aware that abstract positions have a tendency to blur significant distinctions. All narratives may share similar impulses, but to ignore specificities might well amount to a form of appropriation.

As part of his conclusion, he maintains a necessary and even crucial dichotomy between referential conditions that constitute the subject matter of literature and the artifice and play of representation. It is all too easy to confuse literary worth with documentary accuracy, with the consequence that one is led to conclusions that are not necessarily accurate. The text, even at its most realistic, might well be a construct, intended to probe realities that agitate a writer's consciousness. To ignore this dimension could lead to a form of "sociological" criticism which refuses to acknowledge that many writers are more concerned with the constructedness of their work than with demonstrating their political or cultural stances.

The two dimensions of writing – referent and artifice – are not mutually exclusive. W.H. New tries to find a middle ground in *A History of Canadian Literature* (1989) that recognizes both "social attitudes held in common" (2) and "cultural plurality" (2). The title is significant; the author wants a history of literature rather than literary history. Locating historical conditions that made a certain kind of literature possible and necessary is central to his undertaking. And yet he realizes that such a yardstick is only one out of many. First Nations writing, for instance, insists on its orality, its tales, its fables, and its *weltanschauung*. Immigrant or multicultural literature, for the most part, asserts its own niche by moving away from Canadian referents, but always gestures towards its Canadian origins. Whatever margins that were established over a period of time have shifted in multiple ways over the last several decades as the corpus of Canadian literature insisted on being redefined and reformulated.

Recent Canadian writing, particularly by authors whose origins lie outside Canada, invokes the much abused idea of hyphenation. Whether one thinks of the hyphen as a state of limbo and indeterminacy or as a site of empowerment, the term and what it implies has remained in academic and cultural discourse with considerable stubbornness. The term is useful in that it acknowledges heterogeneity, but it also refuses to grant a sense of stable location. In a very personal and comprehensive essay titled "Canada and Me: Finding Ourselves" M.G. Vassanji writes candidly about his itinerant path, from Africa to America, and then to Canada, and the various countries, including India, that inhabit his mind. Chalk River, Ontario, becomes his point of entry in Canada, and he records how, after a period of several months, the Canadian landscape was no longer alien; "I walked back home with my skis on my shoulders and, tropical boy that I was, removed my hat because I was feeling hot" (16-17). The lure of Canada continues, and he asserts: "I believe I have seen the country as few Canadians have" (20).

Vassanji realizes that this is in some senses a satisfying story about adjusting to a new world, absorbing its influences and reiterating a feeling of oneness with it. To end the story here would be to turn away from the memory of Africa, its "music, the sight of its grasslands, its red earth, or its mighty Kilimanjaro" (20-21). The memory of a different land is integral to the consciousness of Vassanji, as it is to all immigrant writers, even when they do not respond to the new landscape as intimately as Vassanji does. The duality is not nostalgia, not posturing, but a challenge and a reality that writers must confront and resolve in their own ways. Curiously enough, the language that Vassanji uses to describe his ambivalence is reminiscent of the words of Atwood: "What I am describing, however, is a state of being, the guilt of the one who got away, the guilt of the *survivor*, if you will" (23, italics mine).

The guilt of the survivor is also the source of inspiration, a kind of "gild" to put it differently, and his writing is indebted to that pervasive chasm. "It is history and memory that living in Toronto has nurtured to inspire the novels and stories I write. And, ironically, it is a history and memory of nomad life and exile" (24). Vassanji's trajectory, then, moves from Gujarat to Nairobi, Dar es Salaam, several cities in the States and rural and urban centres in Canada. The discontinuities, fragments, and fractures become the implied substance of his short stories and novels. Multiplicity and contradiction, rather than totality and harmony, become constitutive aspects of identity. A story with a clear point of origin and a neat ending would falsify the "field of felt tensions" (29) that Vassanji claims as his own.

Vassanji quite rightly refrains from discussing his own writing in relation to his essay. To relate the two would be to engage with the problem of hermeneutics, a task best left to readers and critics. How, then, does one respond to the several novels and collections of short stories that Vassanji has written? The most recent collection, titled, *When She Was Queen* (2005) continues the tradition of moving across time and space, invoking multiple communities, in ways that subvert "national" readings of literature.

There is the story "The Sky to Stop Us" in *When She Was Queen*, a tale about a successful businessman called Nazir and his wife Almas, their fairy tale rags-to-riches life in Toronto, and their sudden, almost inexplicable misery when Almas, rather unexpectedly, decides to leave him. The story moves back and forth in time and space, recording events in the past, shifting from Africa to Canada, from Toronto to Montreal. Each transition is an attempt to explain the past and present, to uncover the various layers that lead to the present life of luxury and misery. If Nazir has difficulty in relating to his father who lives in a senior citizen's apartment in Victoria Park, it has to do with the memory of growing up in Africa. Nazir has worked his way to the top in Toronto, but to remain there in isolation would be to disown the Indian community of which he is a part. His dreams – given in italics in the story – are both satisfying as fantasies and are a source of torment. He is a hero in the success he has achieved, but to remain a hero he must acknowledge the downtrodden in his community, which he no longer cares about.

This is clearly a story about guilt, about survival and success. Does Canada intervene in any meaningful way, except as an example of the possibilities inherent in the "new world"? Would it have made any difference to the reader if the story had been set in London or New York rather than in Toronto? Admittedly, the referent is crucial, as in any fiction that works within the conventions of realism. More important, however, is the notion of artifice that Frye so astutely identifies in his essay. The urban landscape that serves as the background to Vassanji's story underscores the range of possibilities available in Canada, and the price that immigrants must pay to overcome impediments and still retain a sense of community. But the background also emphasizes the artifice of the story, the struggle to offer a context that would explain the fear of failure, the constant quest, and the persistent sense of exile. This story, like many others in this collection, emphasizes the importance of temporal and spatial coordinates, and the centrality of community, but in ways that are profoundly different. While Vassanji's story, like so much contemporary writing, might defy conventional taxonomies, its claim to be Canadian can no longer be a matter of dispute.

The essays that are included in this collection are all, in some ways, about margins, and about the function of community and space in relation to changing perceptions of boundaries. Donna Bennett's essay deals with the limits and limitations of binary constructs in Canadian literary criticism, even as it flaunts multiplicity as its preferred vision. As she analyzes the work of several authors, she also coins the term "polybridity" in order to circumvent the hierarchical relationship implied by binarisms. Diana Brydon and Jessica Schagerl look at Maud Graham's *A Canadian Girl in South Africa* (1905) and Larissa Lai's *Saltfish Girl* (2002) to examine the relation between time and the construction of gender. Predictably, much has changed during the century that separates the two texts, but asserting an uncritical binarism, Brydon and Schagerl argue, would amount to ignoring the ways in which identities are policed and regulated in contemporary times. George Elliott Clarke in his essay shifts the emphasis to pedagogy and demonstrates how there is an urgent need to introduce racial minority literatures in the curriculum and also teach them in ways that allow for the emergence of counter-histories and alternative narratives.

Paulo Horta discusses Michael Ondaatje's *The English Patient* (1993) as a text that borrows liberally from the *Geographical Journal* of the Royal Geographical Society. The intertextual links are a way of understanding Ondaatje's deep engagement with spaces and landscapes, with boundaries, community and cosmopolitanism. The exploration of desert cultures may not have an immediate bearing on Canadian realities, but it certainly suggests the insistent claims of borders and nations. For writers from New Zealand and the Caribbean, the sea has been a potent metaphor and presence, recalling historical origins, journeys of hope and despair, amnesia and empowerment. Caribbean writers in particular have often turned to *Robinson Crusoe* as a text that foregrounds the sea as a multifaceted trope. John Clement Ball's essay focuses on Douglas Glover's *Elle* (2003) and Yann Martel's *Life of Pi* (2001) as Canadian retellings of *Robinson Crusoe* – a strategy that underscores the idea of arrival as a necessary aspect of contemporary Canadian life. The sea, as Ball puts it, is now a "relational, conjoining space" bringing together multiple and fluid identities.

Christopher Levenson looks at North American poetry and Indian poetry in English to seek out ways in which poets such as Dennis Lee and Daphne Marlatt have tried to depict a sense of community that is distinctive. A comparative approach, such as the one that Levenson adopts, establishes parallels and distinctions, underscoring in the process what it means to assert a sense of community in Canada. Stephanie McKenzie looks at First Nations writing, particularly the poetry of Chief Dan George, together with the poetry of Al Pittman, to examine the role of speech and silence in poetry. What she suggests is a particular poetics that inevitably forces the reader to think of other Canadian literatures and their aesthetic stances. Along similar lines, Daniel Heath Justice's essay begins with the assertion that the relation between Aboriginal literatures and the Canadian literary canon is, for the most part, vexed. Autonomy is a central concern in First Nations writing, together with the idea of a nation. Canadian literature too is haunted by the idea of a nation. The presence of the nation in both is, at some level, both problematic and paradoxical, unless one were to conceptualize the term in alternative ways. Justice considers both assimilation and tokenism as untenable options and argues for a more inclusive framework of understanding and acceptance.

Cynthia Sugars discusses the obsessive concern with origins in Canadian cultural history and offers a variety of reasons for this "anxiety of origins." Monolithic constructs are inherently hegemonic, and Sugars looks at several authors, including Dionne Brand, Warren Cariou, Wayson Choy, Wayne Johnston, and Thomas King, all of whom interrogate the politics of genealogy in multiple ways.

Each essay in this collection offers a new perspective on how to read, interpret, and comprehend Canadian literature. The essays imply that definitive answers might be difficult to arrive at and are, in the final analysis, probably less important than a willingness to question and a desire to embrace new stances and perspectives. Notions of space have changed over the years, and the sense of community that is evident today is a far cry from what was available forty years ago. Now more than ever there is an urgent need to reexamine the scope and significance of literary production in Canada, but with a deep awareness of the fluidity of boundaries and margins.

— Chelva Kanaganayakam

WORKS CITED

Atwood, Margaret. *Survival.* Toronto: Anansi, 1972.

Klinck, Carl F. *Literary History of Canada*. 2nd ed. Toronto: University of Toronto Press, 1976.

New, W.H. *A History of Canadian Literature*. New York: New Amsterdam, 1989.

Vassanji, M.G. "Canada and Me: Finding Ourselves." *Passages*. Toronto: Doubleday, 2002: 15-33.

Vassanji, M.G. *When She Was Queen*. Toronto: Doubleday, 2005.

Donna Bennett

Getting Beyond Binaries: Polybridity in Contemporary Canadian Literature

i. a brief polemic

> French Canada was … deprived by the accidents of history of revolutionary tradition other than that of struggle to survive under English domination.
>
> Great Britain guaranteed to this compact French community the continuance of its religion and laws by the Quebec Act of 1774. That important statute, enacted to immunize the new colony against the growing spirit of independence and revolt in the American colonies, made a duality of culture the essential basis of Canadian resistance to American absorption. F.R. SCOTT, 55

The concept of hybridity has been a touchstone of contemporary cultural theory and (more recently) an occasional object of debate. In postcolonial theory, hybridity became important as a result of Homi Bhabha's arguments that it displaces hierarchical binaries by affirming *both-and* rather than *either-or*, thereby escaping into a "Third Space."[1] More recently, hybridity has been central in discussions of diasporic cultures – so much so that, Smaro Kamboureli argues, it becomes "part of the diasporic critic's task to foreground hybridity" (23).[2]

It was perhaps inevitable that in Canada some version of hybridity would seem attractive to our cultural and literary critics because similar concepts have long been invoked as particularly apt to our national doubleness, with its preexisting history of the "cultural dualism" that F.R. Scott and others of his generation described as the outcome of the Quebec Act (56). Well before contemporary theories of hybridity entered circulation, Malcolm Ross wrote: "Ours is not, can never be, the '100 per cent' kind of nationalism. We always have to think in terms of 50-50" (24).

The general sense that Canada was a place of an innately doubled consciousness – a "violent duality" to use Margaret Atwood's famous phrase from the Afterword of *The Journals of Susanna Moodie* – was reinforced by the additional binarisms that established themselves in our political and academic discourse, such as Federal-provincial relations or baseline-hinterland understandings of Canadian cultural and political organization. But after the passing of Scott and Ross's era, these dialectics underwent significant changes. What seemed a potentially stable Federal biculturalism devolved into separate cultures vying for control of their destinies. A reassessment of the place of First Nations peoples led to the view that there were three, rather than two, founding peoples. And, as a result of multiculturalism becoming official policy, what was left of the old biculturalism has been displaced by new and more multiple ways of seeing Canada's cultural composition. What Ross affirmed as Canada's "bifocal" vision (23) no longer adequately describes Canada's cultural makeup.

The effects of these changes may not have been as transformative as this description makes them sound. The addition of First Nations peoples as a third founding group, where once there were two, might seem to have brought into existence a tripartite nation, just as multiculturalism as policy and fact might appear to have fractured any sense of a whole. But as conceptual frameworks, these developments had a tendency to reconstitute binaries by continuing to construct oppositions between dominant and minority cultures. Moreover, as has often been observed, multiculturalism functioned as a support system for a newer kind of doubled cultural identity: the form of "hyphenation" – which encourages individuals to see their identity simultaneously in terms of place of origin and of place of residency.

In Canada, we already had one kind of hyphenation – that of *French Canadians* and *English Canadians* – long before the "hyphen" became associated with multiculturalism. That prior hyphen suggested two founding peoples living separately in a bifurcated nation-state and (no matter what the actual case was) denied the possibility of their having arrived as later immigrants. Although the binary nature of Canada became more complicated with the addition of "Native Canadian" identity, having a hyphenated identity remained consistent with being a member of Canada's "founding peoples." Moreover, despite there now being three founding groups, a dualism continued to define Canada – one that could constitute itself either as Quebec and "the Rest of Canada" or as Native/non Native.

The Canadian celebration of "the mosaic" as a model for culture (an idea that evolved over the course of the twentieth century), and the official multiculturalism that emerged from and reified this model, redefined the nature of the Canadian hyphen. Instead of hyphenated distinctions among the founding peoples, a new form of double-identity groups emerged in which a "multicultural" society was made up of many non "founding" groups. These newly recognized groups named themselves in a way that did not make them a comfortable subset within a national whole but seemed to place them halfway outside of nation. Status defined by a history of immigration rather than as a member of a "founding" peoples became an alternative.

While the hyphenated hybridity produced by Canadian multiculturalism may have moved Canadian culture and literature in the direction of that freeing discursive Third Space that Bhabha envisioned, in which "signs can be appropriated, translated, rehistoricized and read anew" (37), the real change in the Canadian sign often seemed the substitution of "*other*" for "*two*" in the famous phrase about Canada's "two solitudes." That is, we assume a mainstream against which "other solitudes" – a minority collectively struggling against a dominant culture – define themselves, and our official attempts to legislate more complexity into Canadian culture[3] collapse back into the Us-Them dialectic these policies sought to escape.

If state-instituted and culturally-sanctioned multiculturalism has been unable to escape our older dualism, it is a well-intentioned failure that reflects on the way official policy can never truly be adequate to the ongoing flux of individual self-identity and lived experience. *Policy* has an unfortunate tendency to make more solid what it seeks to correct. This sense that such doubleness continues to be with and define us now shows up not so much in those who seek to define some total view of the Canadian nation but instead is a frequent feature in the work of many of the Canadian writers who are understood as part of our new and increasingly "multicultural" literature. This doubleness is, for example, dramatized and continually wrestled with in the work of Dionne Brand.[4]

The fact that official policy must, by simplifying issues, construct or reconstruct binaries[5] is why every culture needs literature: it is the literature of a culture that can balance *law* with *lore*; that is, literature provides us with narratives created outside the boundaries of bureaucracy in order to articulate complexity and raise exceptions. Such lore is necessary because it reminds us of the complexity, nuance, ambiguity, and richness that law, by necessity, treats reductively. In place of "founding nations" and state-sanctioned multiculturalism, the literature of our culture offers us other ways of seeing. Indeed, as Teresa Zackodnik has argued, although Dionne Brand has been concerned with the doubleness that is one consequence of immigrant life, she "voices her dialogic subjectivity in nation language [i.e. the language that has evolved in the Caribbean] *and* in standard English" – and because "nation language is itself polyphonic, . . . the synthesis of nation language and standard English that she achieves in her speakerly poetry exceeds hybridization" (206-07).

Zackodnik's suggestion that Brand *exceeds* hybridity is a crucial one. Models built on binary configuration ignore the way there is always a surplus. It is this unresolved reminder that interests me when I read contemporary Canadian writing.

ii. *Lee, Ondaatje, Wah*

Of the many literary works we might turn to at this point, I would like to look at three from English Canada – SKY Lee's *Disappearing Moon Café*, Michael Ondaatje's *In the Skin of a Lion*, and Fred Wah's *Diamond Grill* – for the way they suggest that binary systems, even those invoking "hybridity," are inadequate to the complex narratives that describes the history of colonization and immigration and the personal histories of its citizens that form Canada. These narratives portray experiences that go beyond *hybridity* into what I propose calling *polybridity* – a neologism I offer as a way of describing inheritance from more sources than two and also as a way of suggest that the complexities of *inheritance* must be understood as not just in terms of the gene pool but also as describing influences and cultural mixing.

SKY Lee's *Disappearing Moon Café* is a useful place to begin because it dramatizes the dangers that arise when a subculture remains isolated and turns in on itself. The Vancouver Chinese community that the novel portrays from the end of the nineteenth century through the late 1980s desires to maintain absolute divisions between itself and the "white ghost" culture of the city's majority. While this strategy may protect the community against the city's racism, it also produces a silence that not only stops communication with the non Chinese community but also inhibits the group internally. In the course of the novel, the Chinese community does eventually find a public voice and a way of opening up discursive space within the heterogeneous society – but that very development highlights the failures of isolationism as seen in destructiveness it produces in the primary family, the Wongs, who continue to be ruled by a limiting tradition and a restrictive silence. Beginning with Wong Gwei Chang's rejection of his Chinese-First Nation wife, Kelora Chin – and of their son – because of his belief that Kelora is a savage and his fear that being with her is turning him into one, the Wong family repeatedly makes choices based on unnecessary binaries: they act as if one must choose between being civilized or not; as if one must choose between being Chinese or not; as if one must choose between acting like their ideal of the overseas Chinese or behaving like an impure Canadian-born Chinese; as if one must choose – if a man – between having a "real" wife (that is, a woman raised in China) or marrying a corrupting outsider (whether she is of Chinese descent or not); as if one must choose – if a woman – between being tormented for bearing no children or for having children by someone other than your husband; and as if one must choose – if a young woman – between being a slave to one's mother-in-law or disgracing oneself by finding a career. Yet all the members of the family really feel that they either have no actual choice at all or that the limited choices they can make can only take place silently and in secret.

What Lee shows her readers is that the opposed pairs from which these choices must be made are illusory and distort the dynamics of complex situations. In making his decision to leave Kelora, Gwei Chang loses connection to his first-born son, Wong Ting An, and becomes trapped in a loveless marriage. Since his son later shows himself capable of crossing the line that has closed off the Chinese community and held it apart from the dominant culture, Gwei Chang has also lost the opportunity to become a part of the land to which he has come and in which he at first seemed able to make himself home. The Wongs desire to hold themselves apart from both "white" and Native societies so restricts individual choice that the results are incest, hatred, and death. The principal storyteller in the novel, Woo Kae Ying, a Wong granddaughter, eventually realizes that neither the unity of the community that constrains her nor the escape into some alternative world of the Other is as simple as she had hoped: "I am so very disappointed," she tells us: "I've been brought up to believe in kinship . . . I thought that by applying attention to all the important events such as the births and deaths, the intricate complexities of a family with chinese roots could be massaged into a suant, digestible unit. Like a herbal pill – thought I could swallow it and my mind would become enlightened" (19). Instead, she adds: "nobody has told me the whole messy truth about anything!" (20). It is this adjective "messy" that the novel contrasts with that which Kae *had* "respectfully remembered," that is, a simplified and often false family history of purity. As Tanis MacDonald has observed of *Disappearing Moon Café*, *contamination* is an force in the text, proving simultaneously corrupting and freeing. The Wong narrative that Kae tells over the course of *Disappearing Moon Café* is her acknowledgement of an inevitable loss of purity within the closed community. Wong blood turns out not to have been solely Chinese, and Kae becomes the first person in the family to affirm aspects of the family that others have viewed as polluting. By doing so, she restructures the stories of her family, moving them from silent, tragic narratives (179) to stories the young Wong women can voice and make meaningful.

Kae realizes that the family hasn't died because the male line did, and that its continuance depends on her ability to find a satisfactory *mixture*. As Wei Ming Dariotis has observed of this novel, "resolution of the conflict between insider and outsider" comes as a result of the "recognition of the Other as kin" (192).[6] The promise of a more open future is confirmed in Lee's narrative when it concludes not with a disappearing moon but a new one – and with a new story – in which Gwei Chang, having died, returns to Kelora and finally moves into the world in which he feared to live.

Reading Lee's novel alongside Michael Ondaatje's *In the Skin of a Lion* emphasizes the way identity in Canada resides neither within some unitary construction of nation nor in the binary nature of the doubled immigrant experience but in the complex mixture that now arises when individuals from many groups come together. The way these groups create a new *cosmopolitan* existence as they build a city and, by implication, a country suggests that no one is simply "Canadian." And identifying with ancestral cultures, even those of the "founding" cultural groups, is not sufficient to produce stable identity in this changing world. Patrick Lewis, a native-born Anglo Canadian, is so dislocated by moving from the country to the city and the new urban and immigrant culture he comes to has so much impact on him that he becomes more an "immigrant" than those who have come to Canada from Europe. The narrative follows Patrick's journey from the isolated world of Canadian childhood, in which he lived in a place so remote that it didn't appear on any map, to his immersion in a community of immigrant workers who, early in the twentieth century, are literally building and in more intangible ways forming what will become modern Toronto:

> On Saturday afternoons the dye washers and cutters, men from the killing beds, the sausage makers, the electrocuters – all of them from this abattoir and tannery on Cypress Street – were free. After bathing under pipes they walked up Bathurst Street to Queen, the thirty or so of them knowing little more than each other's false names or true countries. *Hey Italy! . . . Hey Canada!* A wave to Patrick. (135)

Literally and figuratively an orphan, a man without inheritance, Patrick Lewis finds he must assemble a new culture in this new cosmopolitan world:

> He lived – in his job and during these evening walks – in a silence, with noise and conversation all around him. To be understood, his reactions had to exaggerate themselves. The family idiot. A stroke victim. "Paderick," the shopkeepers would call him as he handed them money and a list of foods Hana [his lover] had written out in Macedonian, accepting whatever they gave him. He felt himself expand into an innocent. Every true thing he learned about character he learned at this time in his life . . . He was always comfortable in someone else's landscape, enjoyed being taught the customs of a place. Patrick wanted the city Hana had constructed for herself – the place she brought together and held as if on the delicate thread of her curiosity . . . Hoo's Trading Company where Alice bought herbs for fever, gaslit diners whose aquarium windows leaned against the

> street. They watched the water-nymph follies at Sunnyside Park, watched Italian gymnast at the Elm Street gym, heard the chanting of English lessons to large groups at Central Neighbourhood House – one pure English voice claiming My name is Ernest and then a barrage of male voices claiming their names were Ernest. (138)

Trying to find his own name and place in this new cultural mix, Patrick feels that his "own life was no longer a single story but part of a mural, which was a falling together of accomplices. Patrick saw a wondrous night web – all of these fragments of a human order, something ungoverned by the family he was born into or the headlines of the day . . . – the detritus and chaos of the age was realigned" (145). Arranging "detritus" into a web and mural is an evocative metaphor, but Patrick does more than absorb and reshape the rich environment of which he is a member: like Kae, he breaks the silence that keeps the workers' contributions to the building of the city invisible. He gives others the ability to tell their own stories – as can be seen when, by asking Nicholas Temelcoff about his remarkable rescue of a falling nun, Patrick opens his friend up to the world:

> Nicholas is aware of himself standing there within the pleasure of recall. It is something new to him. This is what history means. He came to this country like a torch on fire and he swallowed air as he walked forward and he gave out light. Energy poured through him. That was all he had time for in those years. Language, customs, family, salaries. Patrick's gift, that arrow into the past, shows him the wealth in himself, how he has been sewn into history. Now he will begin to tell stories. He is a tentative man, even with his family. That night in bed shyly he tells his wife the story of the nun. (149)

In learning how to tell his own story, Nicholas becomes more than an immigrant and more than a hyphenated Canadian. His link to Patrick and the falling nun connects him to other cultures: to an actress of uncertain national origins who is fluent in several languages; to a Finnish labour organizer; to an Italian who escapes prison by painting himself blue. *In the Skin of a Lion* shows how *Canadians* such as Temelcoff – the workers and the immigrants who helped construct Canada's cities, must tell their stories or have them told. When, at the end of the novel, Patrick says to his stepdaughter, Hana, "I'll tell you the whole story" (244), he also takes on the role of storyteller. This final step, when Patrick can tell someone about the cultures he has absorbed, returns us to the first page of the novel, which we recall was "a story a young girl gathers in a car during the early hours of the morning," and we can now recognize Patrick as the man Hana "listens to . . . as he picks up and brings together various corners of the story, attempting to carry it all in his arms" (1).

Thus while *Disappearing Moon Café* suggests that a minority culture cannot keep itself pure, *In the Skin of a Lion* shows how the members of the older cultures also need to gather together new stories, traditions, and inherited identities. Patrick's future is neither as a member of some founding peoples nor as a hyphenated Canadian. Instead, he has entered the modern world in which, as Ondaatje's epigraph from John Berger reminds us, "Never again will a single story be told as though it were the only one."

Where Ondaatje's novel traces the individual finding his place in a newly configured polybrid social order and Lee's book shows us the individual coming to a new understanding of the complexities of family relationships, Fred Wah's *Diamond Grill* – part autobiographical (or biotextual) narrative, part self-reflexive meditation – focuses on the individual as he records the dynamics that take place *within* himself as a person whose own heritage and experience of being Canadian is inherently multiple. This sequence of prose pieces suggests that our understanding of a mosaic or multicultural Canada made up of separate subgroups is inadequate – challenged by the existence of multicultural *individuals*. Wah's autobiographical account is the story of a man who is himself a polybrid – born in Canada to a Swedish mother and to a half-Chinese father, a father who, though born in Canada, was raised in China.

Inheritance and influence were not initially issues with which Wah concerned himself. Growing up in several small western towns surrounded by many distinct immigrant communities, he did not see himself as different from those around him because he did not make racial distinctions until he went to school. There, others formulated categories for him. Children call him "Chink" and his teacher insisted that his racial origin had to defined in a distinct way:

> When I was in elementary school we had to fill out a form at the

> beginning of each year. The first couple of years I was really confused. The problem was the blank after Racial Origin. I thought, well, this is Canada, I'll put down Canadian. But the teacher said no Freddy, you're Chinese, your racial origin is Chinese, that's what your father is. Canadian isn't a racial identity. That's turned out to be true. But I'm not really Chinese either. Nor were some of the other kids in my class *real* Italian, Doukhobor, or British. (53)

Now that he has grown old enough to understand the way such identity formation worked, Wah rejects this reduction by emphasizing the recurrent complexity that characterized his experience. Although he could usually "pass for white," Wah was encouraged by his society to live a hyphenated existence, which he now seeks to redefine, without rejecting his heritage. He suggests that in his experience of not being reducible to a hybrid he was not alone: "Quite a soup. Heinz 57 Varieties. There's a whole bunch of us who've grown up as resident aliens, living in the hyphen" (53). Living *in* the hyphen seems Wah's alternative to living a hyphenated identity,[7] and because Wah rejects the bifurcated identity assigned him, he has decided to think about what being *Canadian* means. Writing that "The only people who call themselves Canadian live in Ontario and have national sea-to-shining-sea twenty-twenty CPR vision," he seeks to redefine "Canadian" – to take over this term for people like him:

> If you're pure anything you can't be Canadian. We'll save that name for all the mixed bloods in this country and when the cities have Heritage Days and ethnic festivals there'll be a group that I can identify with, the Canadians. When the government gives out money for cultural centres we'll get ours too. These real Canadians could gain a legitimate marginalized position. The French Canadians would have to be Québécois, the Mennonites Mennonite, Brits Brit. And if you're a Scot from Hamilton or a Jew from Winnipeg, then be that; I don't care.
>
> But stop telling me what I'm not, what I can't join, what I can't feel or understand. And don't whine to me about maintaining your ethnic ties to the old country, don't explain the concept of time in terms of a place called Greenwich, don't complain about not being able to find Tootsie Rolls or authentic Mexican food north of the

49th. (53-54)

It is in Wah's redefinition of the "real" and in his rejection of the "authentic" that we particularly see the way polybridization challenges conventional constructions of racial identity. Describing a family photograph, he tells us:

> I'm just a baby, maybe six months (.5%) old. One of my aunts is holding me on her knee. Sitting on the ground in front of us are her two daughters, 50% Scottish. Another aunt, the one who grew up in China with my father, sits on the step with her first two children around her. They are 75% Chinese. There is another little 75% girl cousin, the daughter of another 50% aunt who married a 100% full-blooded Chinaman (full-blooded, from China even). At the back of the black-and-white photograph is my oldest boy cousin; he's 25% Chinese. His mother married a Scot from North Battleford and his sisters married Italians from Trail. So there, spread out on the stoop of a house in Swift Current, Saskatchewan, we have our own little western Canadian multicultural stock exchange.
>
> We all grew up together, in Swift Current, Calgary, Trail, Nelson and Vancouver (27% of John A's nation) and only get together now every three years (33%) for a family reunion, to which between 70% and 80% of us show up. Out of fifteen cousins only one (6.6%) married a 100% pure Chinese.
>
> The return on these racialized investments has produced colourful dividends and yielded an annual growth rate that now parallels blue-chip stocks like Kodak and Fuji . . . (83)

Wah's ironic quantification of race and his free-market metaphor is a response to the universalizing tendencies of both an older dominant order and of multiculturalism. This mixed heritage isolates Wah from the Chinese immigrants that he knew in his childhood: not only his acquaintance with his European as well as his Chinese extended family but also the modernity of his father's diner, and the music he heard on the jukebox there, along with the games he played and the cars he first drove have shaped him into the *Canadian* he claims to be. Yet he in some sense is also isolated from all those in Canada whose backgrounds differ from his.

To explain how he and thus all of us remain held apart, Wah focuses on language. Growing up in Canada with English as his first language, his experience differs from that of immigrant Chinese, but their use of language has shaped his own and made it distinct. Although Wah emphasizes the dangers for the immigrant of becoming "languageless" and understands the frustration and anger that arise when one cannot speak the dominant language with authority, he has also learned the vital and mutating way of speaking that did serve the immigrants he knew, as they created an English mixed with Chinese and terms from other languages. For example, of the way the women who immigrated managed the social as well as linguistic difficulties of expression, he writes:

> Yet the oceans of women migrant-tongued words in a double-bind of bossy love and wary double-talk ... pious pages partial pronouns translated letters shore-to-shore Pacific jetsam pretending love forgotten history braided gender half-breed loneliness naïve voices degraded miscourse racist myths talking gods fact and fiction remembered faces different brothers sisters misery tucked margins whisper zero crisscross noisy mothers absent fathers high muckamuck husbands competing wives bilingual I's their unheard sighs, their yet still-floating lives. (6-7)

Wah suggests that a significant part of his identity resides in these experiences of language, and passages such as this one suggest that his linguistic experiences became a source of his own poetry and creative power. Yet if identity resides in language that makes it not only unstable and impure but not really *authentic* either. Of his father's difficulties with English and how he meets these with by turning his mistakes into jokes, he writes: "So he fakes it, and I guess I pick up on that sense of faking it from him, that English can be faked. But I quickly learn that when you fake language you see, as well, how everything else is a fake" (66).

One word in the language Wah's family spoke, *muckamuck*, shows up – in this form or variants – from the very first page of *Diamond Grill* ("You mucka high!"). Wah originally associates the word with his Chinese grandfather: "Whenever I hear grampa talk like that, high muckamuck, sitkum dollah, I think he's sliding Chinese words into English words just to have fun" (68). What he later discovers is that "he's using Chinook jargon, the pidgin vocabulary of colonial interaction, the code-switching talkee-talkee of the contact zone"[8]:

> He has fun alright, but I now realize he also enjoys mouthing the dissonance of encounters, the resonance of clashing tongues, his own membership in the diasporic and nomadic intersections that have occurred in northwest North America over the past one hundred and fifty years. . . . The term grampa uses most is high muckamuck (from hyu muckamuck, originally among First Nations meaning plenty to each and then transformed, through the contact zone, into big shot, big-time operator). . . . Though my grandfather seems to say the phrase with a kind of humorous and testy tone, my father translates high muckamuck into a term of class derision. (68-69).

Language, like cultures and individuals, flourish by being enriched, not contained. Coming to live in English Canada, immigrants learned to speak English but not the same English that was spoken prior to their arrival. A polyglot language arises out of origins and experiences and reflects a polybrid nation. For Wah, the menu in his father's Diamond Grill expresses his understanding of the world. It is "your typical improvised imitation of Empire cuisine" that has "mutated" into an "authentic mixed grill" (2).

iii. others

The mixed grill of language, of identity, and of tradition – like the "falling together of accomplices" in *In the Skin of a Lion* and the way it can lead to the "detritus and chaos of the age" being realigned – are what these writers offer us. They are Canadian in all the ways we now understand that word, yet, as Ondaatje observes: "Our influences today come from all over the world. The recent novels from Africa and Australia influence us as much as books from Ontario" (Hutcheon, 202). Tomson Highway, a Native, gay playwright, enculturated in North America and Europe, similarly emphasizes the way his work reflects the meeting and intermixing of cultures:

> I think that white culture in Canada is very much changing and transforming as a result of living with native culture; likewise Cree culture, native culture ... I can't help but be influenced by the fact

> that I've seen *Superman* or Joan Collins or *Archie* comic books or for that matter, that I've heard the works of Beethoven. They are all irreparably, irretrievably, a part of my imagination now. I have absolutely no intention or any way of rejecting them. I'll use them to create something that is from my imagination. . . . [I use the] myths and music which I know – everything from Cree mythology to Teutonic myth to Las Vegas to Saskatchewan pow-wow . . . (354-55)

This contemporary sense of *mix* is different from the *internationalism* important to writers in the first half of the twentieth century. As writers, Lee, Wah, and Ondaatje have been affected by a wide range of cultural influences, yet their Canadian *readers* continue to hear the specifics concerns about character and ways of handling situations and larger ethical issues as a part of – as responsible to and influential on – of contemporary Canadian writing and to assign meaning within a Canadian context.

Understanding the role of ethnic identity is important to our encultured and grounded understandings of the texts we read and study, but even for those authors who do not emphasize their mixed heritage to the degree that Wah does, Canadian writers demand of us a sense of their complexity. We are reminded of that need, for example, when George Elliott Clarke observes how "Tussling with our own double consciousness, African-Canadians question whether the 'Canadian' half of the epithet 'African-Canadian' is merely a convenience referring to our geographic residency or whether it hints at an identity. Is it possible to think of the hyphen as an ampersand, or is it really a double-edged minus sign? . . . the African-Canadian consciousness is not simply dualistic. We are divided severally . . . African-Canadians possess, then, not merely a double consciousness but also a poly consciousness" (17).[9] Clarke's conclusion is that he wants to find a way to construct "not a model, but a modal 'blackness'" (43).

Those early twentieth century writers who wanted to be identified with "international modernism" rejected tradition and nation to embrace what they saw as unifying – an international style characterized by innovation and a new set of concerns that were more universal than local. In contrast, contemporary Canadian writers inherit and embrace an increasingly complex culture in which they see dissonance as the rule. Intensely aware of one another yet eschewing a shared aesthetic, Canada's writers most often come together in accepting the impure mixtures of (in Wah's words) "the mix, the breed, the half-breed, metis, quarter-breed, trace-of-a-breed true demi-semi-ethnic polluted rootless living technicolour snarl . . . [of] just being Canadian" (*Diamond Grill* 53). Whatever word we use to describe it, something like "polybridity" is becoming the best way to describe both the culture of individual Canadians and of Canada itself.

NOTES

1. Inevitably some of the debate is over what hybridity means exactly and what its theoretical implications are. See Smadar Lavie's discussion of hybridity, which contrasts Bhabha's theory with what she describes as its polar opposite, Gloria Anzaldua's. Lavie argues that (among other things) Bhabha's model produces hybrids characterized by "a fragmented Otherness" that nevertheless "can be mended together . . . so that they can be narrated in a Cartesian linear manner," while for Anzaldua, because "the hybrid … is a Self that fractures into multiple subjectivities," no "Cartesian linear narration" is possible (68). Though, as will be apparent, I have reservations about hybridity, I am more sympathetic to Anzaldua's vision.

2. Kamboureli also warns, however, that the diasporic critic should also be careful of not turning the concept of hybridity into an idealizing metanarrative.

3. That is, the "Announcement of Implementation of Policy of Multiculturalism within Bilingual Framework" in the House of Commons on 8 October 1971, as well as of the Canadian Multiculturalism Act of 1988.

4. For a useful discussion of one aspect of Brand's treatment of the "cultural hybridity" that results from holding two national identities in mind, see Jason Wiens, "'Language Seemed to Split in Two': "National Ambivalences and Dionne Brand's 'No Language Is Neutral.'"

5. There have been many discussions of the limitations of multiculturism as official policy, including at least three book-length works: of these Richard Day's *Multiculturalism and The History of Canadian Diversity* (2000) is the most theoretically informed.

6. Dariotis develops this notion of a "kin-aesthetic," one that goes beyond the conventional notions of kinship to permit the "recognition of the Other as kin," thereby establishing "the complex interrelations of individual, familial, and national identities" (177).

7. Wah's theory of *hyphenization* is complex and worth more attention than I can give it here. In addition to the comments he makes in *Diamond Grill* about the role of the hyphen, see his "Half-Bred Poetics." See Julie McGonegal's essay expanding on Wah's ideas, "Hyphenating the Hybrid 'I': (Re)Visions of Racial

Mixedness in Fred Wah's *Diamond Grill*," which is a valuable supplement to my remarks. Though I am less confident of the general value of hyphenization than she is, her separation of hyphenization from hybridity (see, for example, her conclusion, 191) is informative.

8. In a footnote, Wah calls attention to Mary Louise Pratt's *Imperial Eyes: Travel Writing and Transculturation* (1992) as his source for the terms "code-switching" and "contact zone."

9. Further to this, Clarke adds, in a footnote: "Paul Gilroy admits that British blackness, like its American cousin, depends upon a bifurcation of identity: Striving to be both European and black requires some specific forms of double consciousness" (1). To be African Canadian, however, is to allow for an almost continuous splintering of identity (47). For more on the issues of race and mixture in a literary context, see the collection edited by Jonathan Brennan, *Mixed Race Literature* (2002). In the introduction, Brennan argues that "a reliance on traditional theories of racial formation . . . overlooks cultural transformations and complex structures of identity formation and representation in favor of perpetuating imprecise and reductive racial categorizations of literary traditions, thus overlooking much of the literary and political significance of mixed race texts (48).

WORKS CITED

Atwood, Margaret. *The Journals of Susanna Moodie*. Toronto: Oxford University Press, 1970.

Brennan, Jonathan. *Mixed Race Literature*. Stanford: Stanford University Press, 2002.

Clarke, George Elliott. "Contesting a Model Blackness: An Essay on African-Canadian African-Americanism, or the Structures of African-Canadianité." *Essays in Canadian Writing* 63 (Spring 1998): 1-55.

Dariotis, Wei Ming. "Developing a Kin-Aesthetic: Multiraciality and Kinship in Asian and Native North American Literature." *Brennan*, 177-99.

Day, Richard. *Multiculturalism and The History of Canadian Diversity* Toronto: University of Toronto Press, 2000.

Hutcheon, Linda. Interview with Michael Ondaatje. Hutcheon and Richmond. 196-202.

Hutcheon, Linda, and Marion Richmond, ed. *Other Solitudes: Canadian Multicultural Fictions*. Toronto: Oxford University Press, 1990.

Kamboureli, Smaro. *Scandalous Bodies: Diasporic Literature in English Canada*. Don Mills, ON: Oxford University Press, 1999.

Keefer, Janice Kulyk. "'Coming Across Bones': Historiographic Ethnofiction," *Siemerling* 84-104.

Lavie, Smadar. "Blowups in the Borderzones: Third World Israeli Authors' Gropings for Home." *Displacement, Diaspora, and Geographies of Identity*. Durham: Duke University Press, 1996. 55-96.

Lee, SKY. *Disappearing Moon Café*. Vancouver: Douglas & McIntyre, 1990.

McGonegal, Julie. "Hyphenating the Hybrid 'I': (Re)Visions of Racial Mixedness in Fred Wah's *Diamond Grill*." *Essays on Canadian Writing* 75 (Winter 2002): 177-195.

MacDonald, Tanis. "'Dead girl-bag': the Janet Smith case as contaminant in Sky Lee's *Disappearing Moon Café*." *Studies in Canadian Literature* 27.1 (2002): 32-46.

Ondaatje, Michael. *In the Skin of a Lion*. 1987. Toronto: Vintage, 1996.

Ross, Malcolm. "Our Sense of Identity." 1954. *The Impossible Sum of Our Traditions: Reflections on Canadian Literature*, Toronto: McClelland & Stewart, 1986. 21-26.

Scott, F.R. "French-Canada and Canadian Federalism." *Evolving Canadian Federalism*. Commonwealth Studies Center. Durham: Duke University Press, 1958. 54-91.

Siemerling. Winfried, ed. *Writing Ethnicity: Cross-Cultural Consciousness in Canadian and Québécois Literature*. Toronto: ECW Press, 1996.

Valgardson. W.D. Interview with Judith Miller in *Other Solitudes: Canadian Multicultural Fictions*. Ed. Linda Hutcheon and Marion Richmond. Toronto: Oxford University Press, 1990.

Wah, Fred. *Diamond Grill*. Edmonton: NeWest Press, 1996.

———. "Half-Breed Poetics." *Faking It: Poetics and Hybridity, Critical Writing 1984-1999*. Edmonton: NeWest, 2000. 71-96.

Wiens, Jason. "'Language Seemed to Split in Two': "National Ambivalences and Dionne Brand's 'No Language Is Neutral.'" *Essays in Canadian Writing* 70 (Spring 2000): 81-102.

Wilson, Ann. "The First and Founding Nations Respond: Thomson Highway, Interview." *Other Solitudes: Canadian Multicultural Fictions*. Ed. Linda Hutcheon and Marion Richmond. Toronto: Oxford University Press, 1990. 350-55.

Zackodnik, Teresa. "'I Am Blackening in My Way': Identity and Place in Dionne Brand's *No Language Is Neutral*." *Siemerling* 194-211.

Diana Brydon
& Jessica Schagerl

Empire Girls and Global Girls: A Dialogue on Spaces of Community in the Twentieth Century[1]

In "Imperial Feelings: Youth Culture, Citizenship, and Globalization," Sunaira Maira advocates the adoption of the frame of "youthscape" to bring globalization and youth culture studies into dialogue. By attaching Arjun Appadurai's notion of *scape* (which designates global cultural flows) to the notion of *youth* as a specific category of identity production, Maira theorizes the "political and social uses of youth" as a site "embedded within national and global forces" (210). Her work helps us to think about the Canadian girl as she has been mobilized figuratively within the Canadian imagination since the beginning of the twentieth century. Recent high profile cases, such as the Reena Virk murder, have focussed public attention on the girl in ways that prompt us to position her within the broader social spaces of her construction.[2] We situate this paper within the overlapping frames established by critical globalization and diaspora studies, youth studies, feminist critique and contemporary Canadian literary studies to compare two relatively neglected Canadian literary texts from different eras. These texts are helpful to us in suggesting the ways in which a focus on the girl may open up other ways of understanding community. We read E. Maud Graham's *A Canadian Girl in South Africa* (1905) and Larissa Lai's *Saltfish Girl* (2002) for their narratives of the gendered and racialized *scapes* afforded different kinds of Canadian girls at the beginning and end of the twentieth century. These texts, Graham's an autobiographical travel narrative and Lai's a futuristic fiction, invite readers to consider Canadian views of the responsibilities of the girl as they shift from those developed in a newly formed national community within empire to those expected within an increasingly inequitable postnational community. We share Lai's interest in the ways that "ideas flow through various communities at various moments, and how their use and weight changes depending on who is using them, where and when" (Morris & Lai 25). Furthermore, as we read them, these texts confirm Anita Harris's assertion that "young women have taken on a special role in the production of the late modern order and its values" (6), whether the narratives associated with them present a "can-do" or an "at-risk" girl (10). In the readings that follow, we question the narratives that depend on such separations.

While this paper stresses gendered access to national and global communities, our purpose is to raise the following questions: what is new about globalization in contemporary times? What is the value of studying earlier manifestations of global interactions under empire for contemporary analysis? How were gendered Canadian identities produced under Empire and how are they produced within contemporary globality? How are these national identities further inflected by generational, racialized and class differences? How do texts such as these imagine community, identity and belonging for their times? In historicizing identity, community and the interface between them, particularly as exemplified in literary texts, we hope to demonstrate the value of postcolonial and globalization theories for understanding textual constructions of identity within and beyond the nation-state. Each text negotiates in different ways the assumption that a global subject moves beyond nationalism. We do not subscribe to the notion that nation-states have lost their power to control global flows (of capital, people or discourses). Rather, our interest lies in how global circulations of power were understood in 1905 and are being renegotiated in the early twenty-first century.

Girls have gained a certain measure of prominence in our thinking about these questions so that we also wonder what writing that is centrally concerned with gender and generations, two areas that (together with sexualities) are underaddressed in globalization theory, may tell us about possibilities for imagining social identities and communities. The liminality of the girl, somewhere between child and adult, neither a woman nor a lady, makes this term a productive focus for investigations of category construction. Early twentieth and early twenty-first century literature on the girl indicate a profound anxiety about social change

(Harris). According to Engin Isin, late twentieth-century studies of disorder, such as those on anorexia, often "constitute young girls as objects of government." While his interest lies in how such discourse "on teenage girls is targeted at those who govern them" (228), within part of a larger pattern of what he terms "neuropolitics" in the subject formation of the contemporary North American citizen, our interest lies more in the assumptions about order and identity that such discourses imply. The field of girl studies was born "out of the commonplace disregard for issues of gender within youth studies and age within women's studies" (Harris *All About Girls* xviii). The challenge for critics today is to read across these individually differentiated categories so as to understand how they are imbricated within each other. As Sherene Razack argues in *Looking White People in the Eye*, "Analytical tools that consist of looking at how systems of oppression interlock differ in emphasis from those that stress intersectionality. Interlocking systems need one another, and in tracing the complex ways in which they help to secure one another, we learn how women are produced into positions that exist symbiotically but hierarchically" (13). Following her lead, our focus falls, then, on the function of interlocking systems in the construction of the girl. If notions of "girls" and "girlhood" are more often taken-for-granted and seen as givens of social life, then we wish to challenge such assumptions.

In Graham's text, the designation of "girl" indicates her access to employment and mobility. Graham's subject-identity, as the author and autobiographical subject of her text, remains secured through the privileges of race and class fostered by empire although her gender precludes active citizenship. "Girl" is destabilized in Lai's text through its juxtaposition with the preceding words "salt fish." With Lai, conceptualizing a politics of identity means confronting the limits of the social order under neo-liberal globalization. Lai indicates that in *Salt Fish Girl*, she "wanted to create a myth of origins for girls that travel, girls who come from many places at once" ("Future Asians" 173). By placing these texts together, we are asking: what has happened to identity in the interim between these two texts? Nationality, location, whiteness as a norm – each is accepted in Graham's text and problematized in Lai's. We might conclude that whereas empire serves to stabilize Graham's identity as a daughter of empire, secure in herself wherever she travels, globalization disrupts the identities presented in Lai's text, whether she is looking backward to an ancient past in China or forward to a future in what was once British

Columbia.

What is at stake in placing these identities in dialogue? In accepting Stuart Hall's premise that "identities are the names we give to the different ways we are positioned by, and position ourselves within the narratives of the past" (Hall 212), we recognize that our own identities, as junior and senior scholar, are also implicated in the exchange that we develop in this paper. Our awareness that 'dialogue' has "been heavily freighted with positive, even utopian images of equality, reciprocity, and deep satisfaction" (Kaplan 64), is also conditioned by recognition that our dialogue, and the dialogue we set up between these two texts, must also "address questions of access and footing," noting what is required to enter "the cultural conversation," and what might make the attempt worthwhile (Kaplan 65). These are questions that contemporary community studies are negotiating through reconsiderations of the social contract, the rights and responsibilities of citizens, and the grounds on which community and transcommunality may be built. Trans-communality, as theorized by John Brown Childs, "emphasizes a constant process of negotiational construction of organization among diverse participants, rather than an imposed monolithic system" (11).[3] It is a helpful concept for rethinking community beyond the kind of automatic valorization so prevalent in its usage without discarding the values of trust and reciprocity with which it has often been unthinkingly invested yet which have so often been betrayed in the actual experiences of girls and women.

I. The Global Spaces and Literary Worlds of E. Maud Graham

Reading through the lenses of postcolonial cultural studies and globalization studies, we are able to problematize the apparent stability of the identities and communities formed under imperial relations and question the complicities that they offer. On a conceptual level, globalization has intensified the process of contestation that helps us imagine interconnections and that marks constructs such as "community," "nation," and "empire" that are also often left uninvestigated. The "complex connectivity" (Tomlinson 13) that is a hallmark of globalization studies offers a way for researchers to move past disciplinary identifications and productively combine approaches in order to understand the overlapping relations that constitute women's personal and collective involvement in global processes. Yet, we would argue that understanding contemporary globalization involves understanding the interconnections and interactions generated by imperialism; these interconnections, as David Held notes, involve "a *stretching* of social, political and economic activities across frontiers such that events, decisions and activities in one region of the world can come to have significance for individuals and communities in distant regions of the globe" (15). In particular, many critics draw attention to the globalized world at the cusp of the twentieth century, noting that today's global integration, while perhaps noteworthy for its speed and technological and computerized infrastructure, is not so different from the integration of one hundred years ago (see Harvey, Hirst and Thompson). With its invocation of gender and empire, *A Canadian Girl in South Africa* is particularly well suited as a space to reflect the imbrication of large-scale, globalizing processes such as British imperialism and the formations of community that attend it. *A Canadian Girl in South Africa* provides a point of contact to examine the violence of colonial history in Canada and Southern Africa at a particular stage of industrial capitalism associated with commodity exchange and colonial exploitation. Shaped by the structures and conflicts of her local society as well as responding creatively to its pressures, Graham exemplifies the movement of colonial women across the empire both in person and in imagination.

Born in Owen Sound, Ontario in 1876, Ellen Maud Graham attended the University of Toronto from 1892-1896.[4] At the time of her application to teach in the Southern African colonies, Graham was teaching in Quebec City.[5] After a one year assignment turned into an almost two year spate of travelling from camp to camp, Graham sailed back to Canada via Halifax, and from there returned to her parents' home in Owen Sound. Graham was in the Southern African colonies for twenty-five months, beginning 1 June 1902 (*ACGSA* [iii], 39*)*; on her return to Canada in July 1904, she must have immediately begun writing the narrative, which is completed by November 1st, 1905 (when she dates her acknowledgements). The publication of *A Canadian Girl in South Africa* does not appear to have drawn much attention in Canada – not even in Owen Sound, Ontario where her family resided and she had a close kinship network – though it did mean that Graham became the lone Canadian woman to publish a book-length narrative of her time spent teaching in the camps of the Southern African colonies.[6] Graham's story owed its print existence in no small measure to white (imperialist) Canadians' appetite for narratives about imperial responsibilities, the more so if these included justifications for overseas militarized imperial expansion.

Brought to press in late fall 1905, sixteen months after Graham returned from the Southern African colonies, *A Canadian Girl in South Africa* told of her extraordinary time in Canada's "sister colony across the sea" (Graham 192). Written to record the programme that sent female Canadian teachers to work in the "'Refugee' or 'Concentration' camps" (Graham 12) set up by the British during the South African War, *A Canadian Girl in South Africa* reports on the travel via London to the British colonies in southern Africa, the conditions of the camps, and the quotidian life of the teachers while employed by the colonial government. The programme to send teachers to the colonies was conceived of as a social investment, a period of nurturing "British" spirit by those women friendly to the aims of British control in Southern Africa. The "Teachers for South Africa" programme, as it was commonly known, was centrally administered by imperial administrators in London and represents an attempt to reassert a British presence in the region that had dwindled over the course of the South African war. The camp schools were formed on the impetus of Edmund Beale Sargant, the education secretary and subsequently the Director of Education of the Transvaal and Orange River Colony, who worked closely with Sir Alfred Milner, the High Commissioner of South Africa. After seeing that Boer children were being taught in the concentration camps, Sargant formed his own school (at Norval's Pont, a central location in Graham's narrative) and subsequently extended the scheme to all of the camps. As would later be the case in Canada and Australia, Education Departments were contacted and the process of advertisement, application, shortlisting, interviewing, and selection was undertaken. One hundred English and Scottish teachers formed the first groups sent to the Southern African colonies. As E. Maud Graham puts it in her cursory history of the initiative in the opening pages of her book: "In due time, contingents of teachers sailed from New Zealand, Australia and Canada" (12-13). Gaining access to the book's contradictions and interventions in imperialist debates is made difficult because the programme to send forty Canadian teachers to the Southern African colonies has not been fully studied by Canadian historians. Perhaps this is one reason why the book has received little if any attention from literary scholars, even though its genre (a mix of travelogue, personal memoir, and ethnography) and themes (education at the end of empire and the gendered performance of imperialism, among many) are certainly relevant to both postcolonial and Canadian studies, and to scholars focusing on the gendering of travel writing.

The text opens with the comments of a "stalwart Rugby man" claiming, with no hint of irony, "I wish I were a girl. You girls have the best of everything nowadays" (11). The comments point to the many contradictions and paradoxes surrounding white women's involvement in imperial projects. This privileged involvement ". . . allowed . . . transnational women travellers opportunities for self-expression and group-identification which would have been comparatively far more limited, even unacceptable, in the metropolis" (Boehmer and Moore-Gilbert 15). For Graham, travelling to the Southern African colonies was a way to test possibilities of financial and personal independence, education, career, and sexual freedom. In the words of one of the other women who took part in the programme, it was "a great opportunity" and allowed her to "[laugh] at all her mother's fears and [declare] to friends who envied and those who prophesied evil things that she was more lucky than plucky in being able to go" (Randal 411).

As a Canadian "girl" abroad, travelling with the support and protection of the imperial British government, Graham was in a position to depict, both in written and photographic form, the ways the identity of a young white colonial woman could be shaped by the transnational movements of imperialism. "[T]he prefix 'trans' [in 'transnational']," as Graham Huggan explains, "is less indicative of a movement *across* preconstituted national boundaries than of an attempt to conceptualize *beyond* the idea of the national boundary itself and the corresponding ideology of the nation-state it has historically legitimised and maintained" (Huggan 2002: 252-53, his italics). "Girl" therefore names an imaginary category of identity, here tied to the transnational movement of white women as a result of imperial globalizing processes. Notwithstanding these areas of limited and competing autonomies, the "worldiness" of these women needs to be place within the broader discourses of racialized and gendered imperialism, and the overlapping networks linking capitalism and modernity, political and economic relations, and unarticulated racial hierarchies.

Although Ruth Mayer has written a chapter with a title similar to ours, her interest in contrasting "colonial ladies" and "global girls," as two different images of "white femininity on foreign ground" (134), depicted through popular culture of the last twenty years and linked through a fashion system, is quite different from ours. Our purpose in examining these texts is less to study what Mayer terms, in her subtitle, "colonial images in the times of globalization," than to consider the options available to young Canadian women for constructing their selfhood in relation to the nation and the international circuits in which it operated at the beginning and the end of the twentieth century. Our interest, then, is less in the survival of colonial images into global cultural circuits than it is in the restructuring of identities within colonial and global institutional structures, the various ways in which girls gained a "sense of belonging in an insecure world" (Delanty 2003:192).

Graham's ongoing negotiation of self-identity took place in the context of an imperially-sanctioned, even policed, form of identity production that marks one of the limits of white female identity formation at the turn of the twentieth century. *A Canadian Girl in South Africa* not only documents the ideology of benevolence, what Gayatri Spivak calls "the imperial project cathected as civil-society-through-social-mission" (*Critique* 116); but also emphasizes how a gendered rhetoric of social responsibility within the British empire produced and capitalized on specific understandings about the role of dominions' women in maintaining a "healthy" and "unified" empire for the good of society. Because of the threat of "tropicalization" (Henderson 170) as a result of her movement to the Southern African colonies, Graham's newfound "free" identity was from the start linked to mechanisms of control and an anxiety about just how "free" she might be. As a "girl," Graham was seen to need both protection and indulgence. Her status as a "Canadian Girl in South Africa" was further dependent upon passing a medical exam and meeting cleanliness "standards," which served to regulate the purity of the white female body. Cynthia Enloe's useful discussion of the "gender-policing concept, respectability," helps to situate the story of this Canadian girl within larger global contexts (76).

Graham is centrally concerned with the production of identities through difference, a guiding feature of much imperialist thinking. Now able to take advantage of greater personal freedom – that most attractive feature of the European Enlightenment – Graham's text reveals that the narration of white colonial identity must be articulated in concert with the formation of the concentration camp and ethnological myths used to justify domination, in other words through the "economy of exception"

(Diken 87). The borders and limits of identity and community are made manifest in Graham's text with the barbed wires marking the edges of the camp, indicating the sense of endangered privilege and laying the foundation of fears and threat that in the later twenty-first century would come to be labelled "domopolitics," in William Walter's terminology, or, in a wider context, "neuropolitics," in Isin's. The barbed wires protecting the camps from the threat of the black indigenous populations, who are kept at a remove from the space of the camp, seem to underscore Zygmunt Bauman's claim that "[b]elonging would have lost its lustre and seductive power together with its integrating/disciplining function had it not been consistently selective and constantly given flesh and reinvigorated by the threat and practice of exclusion" (Bauman 2004:22). Even if they can take advantage of other forms of gendered citizenship, such as working for the imperial government in teaching that manufactures "consent to colonial domination" (Slemon, *passim*), Graham's "Canadian Girls in South Africa" are denied the political rights of citizenship. The context, then, provides an interesting example of how multiple and even conflicting aspects of identities under globality compete to help shape norms, later taken up in the ongoing negotiations around nationhood, and how the sustained reinflection of privileges was based on denying others access to these privileges. The fear of encroaching difference highlights the social configurations of race and identity, pointing to what Miranda Joseph calls the "conservative, disciplining and exclusionary effectivity of the invocation of community" (xviii-xix).

2. The Local and Transnational Spaces of Larissa Lai's Saltfish Girl

Joseph's argument "against community" charges the "transnational geographies of race" (McCullough 227), which are brought to the fore in Lai's *SaltFish Girl*. Lai's title notes a shift in focus from the national signifier of Graham's identity to the body of the girl herself, shifting identity anxiety away from Canada's place within the waning British empire toward fears about porous borders: between past and present, China and Canada, and especially human, animal and machine.

Lai's text interweaves stories drawn from myth and folk tales to explore options for identity and agency available to her three central characters, Nu Wa, Miranda and Evie, each of them a "saltfish girl" who is also an evolving form of new woman. Nu Wa functions as an original mother and an exemplar of the mermaid into woman motif. She speaks the opening words of the text from the Bank of the Yellow River, pre-Shang dynasty, to narrate an originary bifurcation from her lonely singularity ("In the beginning there was just me" [1]) into her invention of women and men and later into her account of her love affair with someone she names only "the Salt Fish Girl," whom she betrays to enter the City of Hope on the Island of Mist and Forgetfulness. Her story, while it has attracted significantly less critical attention than that involving Miranda and Evie in the future, provides parallels to it, and especially, through the shifting time-space dimensions of this island, a warning against historical forgetfulness.

Lai's Miranda has a name that recalls Prospero's daughter, innocent in wonder, from the standard literary point of view, and complicit in Empire from the perspective of postcolonial critique. Lai, however, shows how each of these views captures only part of the story. Her Miranda is best understood as acting out of a complicit innocence, which Brydon has argued characterizes many Canadian "Mirandas," but which is further complicated in Lai's narrative through this Miranda's family's racial and class status. This Miranda's saltfish smell connects her to the monstrous Caliban and her parents' occupations to those of the servants, rather than the masters, of the state. Their tenuous claim to the protections of the bourgeoisie is first weakened by Miranda's saltfish smell and later destroyed when she loses her father his job as tax-collector and they must leave the fragile security of the protected zones for a hand to mouth existence running a small family shop in the Unregulated Zone. Evie is self-named for the Biblical mother of mankind but her behaviour links her more closely to the powerful dissident, Lilith, who in biblical apocrophya is Adam's rejected first wife. Each of these characters crosses the boundaries that delimit social spaces and mark a designated community role within which they are expected to function.

Lai mixes the mythic with realism to achieve similar boundary-challenging effects, staging within her story an argument between Miranda's parents on the value of mythic stories to show what is at stake in her narrative strategy. Miranda's mother claims myths as "part of our collective unconscious" while her father rejects them as "socially destructive stereotypes" (34). The novel holds both views as true while seeking a route beyond their assumptions, not beyond in the sense of transcendence or surpassing, but beyond in the sense of registering their impact while refusing to accept their scripts. Lai's is a futuristic story that understands the ways in which the past survives into the present even as she offers hope that the colonial past can be forced to lessen, perhaps even to surrender, its grip. In *Saltfish Girl*, she imagines a future in which Canada no longer exists as a colonial nation-state, its generating myths of national innocence conclusively shattered. While Lai's Miranda, like Shakespeare's original, is something of a blank slate, she is definitely not an innocent. Her picaresque adventures enable Lai to compose what is ultimately, in the generic sense, a comic script, even though the story is one of persistently destructive and fully integrated racisms, sexisms and classisms. With David Scott, Lai recognizes the possibility that "[t]he colonial past may never let go" (Scott 220) while refusing to give up the vision of a more just community.

Nu Wa and Miranda narrate alternating sections of the text but Evie, a literalization of Donna Haraway's cyborg, drives the story toward the possibility of a different future. Haraway argues that the cyborg is "the illegitimate child of patriarchy, science and capitalism" (154), and that cyborg identity is "a potent subjectivity synthesized from the fusion of outsider identities" (174). As Evie puts it, she is "a patented new fucking life-form" (158) who rebels against this heritage and the destiny that it dictates for her. One of at least a hundred thousand of identical cloned female workers, part human, part fish, each named a numbered version of Sonia, Evie suspects that she has been created out of the Diverse Genome Project, which "focused on the peoples of the so-called Third World, Aboriginal peoples, and peoples in danger of extinction" (160). Here the racism that fueled the imperialist project is shown to survive through the present into the future within the supposedly neutral realm of scientific investigation and technological invention.

As an early model, Evie was adopted by her creator, a Dr. Rudy Flowers, to fill the role of dutiful daughter but rejects his simulacrum of the nuclear family (in which another clone serves as the mother figure) to find her own way in the world. Miranda, too, is part cyborg, born when her aged mother is impregnated by a wild strain of genetically modified durian, gone out of control in the Unregulated Zone. Their cyborg identities operate partly in the manner identified by Joe Moran in his study of *Interdisciplinarity*, forcing readers "to rethink the whole notion of identity, producing a kind of disassembled and reassembled, postmodern collective and personal self" (Moran 164). But unlike postmodern identities, these characters carry strong memories of their past that function at both visceral and mental levels. Even when they do not consciously remember their ancestral or familial pasts, they remain haunted, as does the text, by echoes and whiffs of what has been left behind yet stubbornly remains, inscribed within their very bodies.

In *Saltfish Girl*, alternative identities are forged in the collectives created by escaped Sonias and through the affinity for one another felt by those who share the saltfish smell and its accompanying "dreaming" or "drowning disease" (100), a reminder that the nightmare of history cannot be escaped. These women, who can self-impregnate through the durian, may be able to escape the curse of the red shoes, a major motif within the novel that demonstrates the ways in which colonial oppressions may mutate into the economics of globalization. For Peter Hitchcock, "the shoe is *the* emblem of the fetishism that links the commodity to desire" ("Fetishism" 113, emphasis in the original). In mobilizing the story of the red shoes, which Rosemary Sullivan identifies as central to Margaret Atwood's oeuvre, in her investigation of how the "aura of the shoe" (Hitchcock "Chronotope" 119) operates within contemporary capitalism, Lai demonstrates, in a fashion parallel to Hitchcock's, just how compacted this fetish has become. The European folk tale of the red shoes acts to forbid the girl's agency and punish her desire. Reworked by Lai by into a "Song for Clara Cruise," the song makes Miranda's mother, a nightclub singer, famous and becomes her bequest to her daughter. As in the classic tale, the song tells the story of a girl who is punished for her unauthorized desire: "The pretty shoes of Clara Cruise/They danced her till her heart did break . . . Shoes danced the bones till they were dust/A drifting heed to those who lust/For things that glitter in the dark . . . " (92). Miranda sells her mother's heritage, the rights to this song, to an advertising firm employed by the global giant Pallas, clearly modeled on Nike. (The double references to classic Greek myth reinforce this connection.) Given the nature of this birthright, perhaps it is best that Miranda unthinkingly sells it, despite her promise to her father not to do so. The question for us is whether or not the sale can free Miranda from the identity that is pre-scripted for girls by the red shoes and what the cost to her of making such a sale might be. In selling the rights to the song, she follows her desire in a way that links her to the girl who first desires and then dies through the agency of the shoes. While *Saltfish Girl* denies the specific moralism of the folktale, the novel also recognizes that there is always a choice to be made and a price to be paid for choices, even for those decisions made without apparent forethought for their consequences.

If the red shoes represent the forbidden power of self-determined desire, then the questions asked by the shoe soles circulated surreptitiously by the Sonias and stamped on the pavements they tread, present a counter message: "What does it mean to be human? How old is history? The shoemakers have no elves" (237).[7] The pointed political critique of the economics of shoes, where profits are built on the slave labour of the undocumented Sonias, is merged with an understanding of the political effort it takes to gender and then cheapen labour (see Enloe 60; also Hitchcock).

Miranda's lengthy dream of shoes concludes with "Dorothy's red shoes, click, click, send me back to China, twelve dancing princesses who waft nightly out their windows and dance until their soles are worn skin-thin" (226-7).[8] In contemplating her narrow escape from foot-binding, only a hundred and fifty years before her time, Miranda's thoughts move to the future and the durian-seeded child stirring in her womb. This child, a baby girl born at the novel's end, brings only a qualified hope: "Everything will be all right, I thought, until the next time" (269). They have just discovered that for the first time, male workers are being cloned too, in the image of Dr. Flowers. Traditional gender and race-based oppressions may be losing ground, but oppression, and the urge to control the messiness of life, once associated with notions of the female, nature and the racialized Other, remain to remind readers of the dangers of community when theorized as a space to be stabilized and protected.

At the end of the novel, Miranda thinks: "A stinking toilet at the end of the story? Why not? This is a story about stink, after all, a story about rot, about how life grows out of the most fetid-smelling places . . . " (268). In a similar vein, Hiromi Goto's "Stinky Girl," suggests that "smell hinges the past to the clutter of present memory" (41). While linked in both stories to an irrational fear of the body and the bodily, associated with women and white racial fears, with the production of the abject and the psychoanalysis of race, smell is reclaimed by Lai and Goto from its status as a denigrated sense and reclaimed for valuing the ways in which girls may live through their senses and within their bodies, reimagining the ways in which they inhabit social space and relate to their communities.

Saltfish Girl explores the implications of Henry Giroux's insight into the place of youth today. Giroux argues: "Youth within the economic, political, and cultural geography of neoliberal capitalism occupy a degraded borderland in which the spectacle of commodification exists side by side with the imposing threat of the prison-industrial complex and the elimination of basic civil liberties" (Giroux 144). By gendering, racializing and nationalizing Giroux's vaguely universalist category of youth, and by finding potential within the "degraded borderland" for hope, Lai provides a more particularized and persuasive analysis of the choices that Canadians face at the beginning of the twenty-first century. It is instructive to compare this novel to Margaret Atwood's far more popular *Oryx and Crake*. Whereas Atwood's global ethic as presented in this text cannot imagine identity in terms beyond what has been prescribed by the twentieth-century realist novel, and provides no space for female subjectivity because of its reliance on its flawed male narrator, Lai, like Haraway, ventures to imagine further metamorphoses of the Chinese girl into what Hiromi Goto calls "hopeful monsters."

3. Theorizing Transcommunal Spaces

In the texts compared here, Graham and Lai grapple with the challenges of their times through a focus on girls in global contexts. For us to invoke the global at this particular historical moment, in 2005, is to signal what Meyda Yegenoglu calls the "new trend" of "thinking locality on structural interaction with globality" (15). In this paper's analysis of spaces of community in two twentieth century Canadian texts, we have sought to confirm a relationship to the past instead of foreclosing the past in the moment of the "new"' Graham's text preceded the creation of Canadian citizenship and Lai's fiction imagines a time when citizenship, while still exclusionary, has lost its power to protect. The hundred years between them suggests how recent, and how fragile, citizenship as a foundational institution of national community and a guarantor of identity may be, while reminding readers that it has always been sexualized and racialized. Graham's investment in empire provides an early model of one type of cosmopolitan community – one that has proven its bankruptcy in the failure of peacekeeping missions, as documented in Sherene Razack's *Dark Threats and White Knights*. Graham's text usefully reminds readers of Canada's complicity in the policing of colonialism globally and locally (with reservations for Indigenous peoples here as the equivalent of camps for so-called "others" in other places and with the construction of white Canadian racial superiority to those apparently requiring that Canadians take up the "White Man's Burden" at home and abroad). Jennifer Welsh's prescription that Canada is well suited to assume the role of "model citizen for the twenty-first century" (187), as our Canadian way of becoming "at home in the world" (her book's title), will also fail unless Canadians can move beyond such colonial views.

How then are we to imagine spaces of community in the twentieth century? These texts may help readers see their choices and understand how they are historically conditioned but the lessons are mainly cautionary. While Lai imagines forms of solidarity across differences, those most apparently successful in generating trust if not in generating social justice, are those based on the absolute sameness of the cloned Sonias, a disturbing thought. In contrast, the friendship (and eventual sexual relationship) between Miranda and Evie remains too tenuous to be seen as a potential ground on which to form a new community – yet this may be precisely Lai's point. Communities work best when formed through alliances in specific times of struggle. They are not to be fetishized as a value in themselves. In *Saltfish Girl*, Lai's focus falls on the singularity of the girl, not to stress individualism but to note the importance of the particular in a world where almost everything, including personhood, has been commodified. In contrast to Graham's use of global others to consolidate her sense of self, Lai's text proliferates metamorphoses. Yet what links these two texts from different ends of the century in troubling ways is the continuity of regulated zones that assign and police identities to govern populations in ways that limit their choices. In retrospect, we see a damaging complicity with empire in Graham's benevolence, and the dystopic strain in *Saltfish Girl* is strong despite its refusal of tragedy. Each text shows identities formed through exchange and struggle, within conditions of limited possibility, where autonomy, the ability to make choices about how to govern oneself, remains an ideal worth striving for. In rejecting the allocation of separate spaces to the "can-do" versus the "at-risk" girl – for Graham, as much as Miranda, is clearly both – these texts show instead the ways in which these identifications are mutually dependent within theorized forms of community that deny the girl full personhood. Perhaps any notions of transcommunal solidarities must begin in such modest ways, if the "degraded borderlands" assigned to today's youth are to afford the kinds of renewal hoped for in transcommunal imaginaries.

NOTES

1. This paper arises out of our interdisciplinary collaboration on the Communities volume within the SSHRC-funded Major Collaborative Research Initiatives team addressing "Globalization and Autonomy." We are grateful to SSHRC for this support, for funding Jessica Schagerl's doctoral research and Diana Brydon's ongoing research into "the ends of postcolonialism." Jessica also thanks the Faculty of Arts, The University of Western Ontario, for research funding in the form of the Mary Routledge Fellowship, that enabled her to conduct research into Graham's personal history. We are grateful to Angela Esterhammer and the Theory group of the International Comparative Literature Association for an invitation to present an earlier version of this paper to their workshop in May 2005. We have benefited greatly from their comments and collegiality.

2. See Tess Chakkalakal, "Reckless Eyeballing: Being Reena in Canada," for an article that contextualizes, within the logic of how racism works in Canada, accounts of the murder of Reena Virk on Nov. 14. 1997 after she has been beaten by eight teens, mostly girls, in a swarming. While Chakkalal focuses on the racialized elements of what she argues should properly be described as a "Canadian lynching" (165), her article also addresses the ways in which the social construction of the girl interlocks with racialized constructions of identity.

3. Childs notes that "From a transcommunal perspective, we can view the Haudenosaunee as a significant example of a complex form of interaction that accepts and celebrates autonomy of distinct groups while also emphasizing cooperation and affiliation among those same participants (49).

4. Bryn Mawr College Archives, Graduate School Student Records, RG 5K.

5. Canadian address for "List of School Teachers sailing from St. John, New Brunswick, on the 18 April, 1902, by S.S. *Lake Ontario* for Service in the refugee camps in South Africa," RG 6, Secretary of State, Series A-1, vol. 103, file 345, National Archives of Canada. See also "Teachers for South Africa" *The Globe*, Wednesday, 2 April 1902, p. 1.

6. This is a point worth drawing attention to, but not lingering over. Newspaper articles were frequently contributed by the women chosen to teach in the camps, and at least one other extended narrative, Florence Randal's "A Year in a Boer School" written for *The Canadian Magazine,* was published before the appearance of Graham's narrative.

7. The notion that the labour that produced the shoe "speaks" from the soles connects Lai's insights here to the epigraph from Amitava Kumar with which Hitchcock prefaces his chapter, "Fetishism (Of Shoes)": "The Indonesian worker

only exists in the sole of my shoe" (109).

8. The mixing of folktale with Hollywood images from the classic film *The Wizard of Oz*, further evokes the linkages made here between ambivalence about the spaces that constitute home and societal fears about travelling or "dancing" girls.

WORKS CITED

Atwood, Margaret. *Oryx and Crake*. Toronto: McClelland & Stewart, 2003.

Bauman, Zygmunt. *Identity: Conversations with Benedetto Vecchi*. Cambridge and Malden, MA: Polity Press, 2004.

Boehmer, Elleke and Bart Moore-Gilbert. "Introduction to Special Issue: Postcolonial Studies and Transnational Resistance." *Interventions*. 4. 1. (2002): 7-21.

Brydon, Diana. "Sister Letters: Miranda's *Tempest* in Canada." *Cross-Cultural Performances*, ed. Marianne Novy. Urbana & Chicago: University of Illinois Press, 1993. 165-84.

———. "Tempest Plainsong: Retuning Caliban's Curse." *Transforming Shakespeare: Contemporary Women's Re-Visions in Literature and Performance*, ed. Marianne Novy. New York: St. Martin's Press, 1999. 199-216.

Chakkalakal, Tess. "Reckless Eyeballing: Being Reena in Canada," in Walcott, ed. *Rude*. 159-67

Childs, John Brown. *Transcommunality: From the Politics of Conversion to the Ethics of Respect*. Philadelphia: Temple University Press, 2003.

Delanty, Gerard. *Community*. New York and London: Routledge, 2003.

Diken, Bülent. "From Refugee Camps to Gated Communities: Biopolitics and the End of the City." *Citizenship Studies*. 8.1. (March 2004): 83-106.

Enloe, Cynthia. *The Curious Feminist: Searching for Women in a New Age of Empire*. Berkeley: University of California Press, 2004.

Graham, E. Maud. *A Canadian Girl in South Africa*. Toronto: William Briggs, 1905.

Giroux, Henry A. "Youth, Higher Education, and the Crisis of Public Time: Educated Hope and the Possibility of a Democratic Future," *Social Identities* 9.2. 2003. 141-168.

Graham, E. Maud. *A Canadian Girl in South Africa*. Toronto: William Briggs, 1905.

Goto, Hiromi. "Stinky Girl." *Hopeful Monsters*. Vancouver: Arsenal Pulp, 2004.

Haraway, Donna. *Simians, Cyborgs and Women: The Reinvention of Nature*. New York and London: Routledge, 1991.

Harris, Anita, ed. *All About the Girl: Culture, Power and Identity*. New York: Routledge, 2004.

Harris, Anita. *Future Girl: Young Women in the Twenty-first Century*. New York: Routledge, 2004.

Henderson, Jennifer. *Settler Feminism and Race-Making in Canada.* Toronto: University of Toronto Press, 2003.

Hitchcock, Peter. "Chronotope of the Shoe (Two)." *Imaginary States: Studies in Cultural Transnationalism.* Urbana & Chicago: University of Illinois Press, 2003. 118-52.

———. "Fetishism (Of Shoes)." *Oscillate Wildly: Space, Body, and Spirit of Millennial Materialism.* Minneapolis: University of Minnesota Press, 1999. 109-42.

Huggan, Graham. "Postcolonial Studies and the Anxiety of Interdisciplinarity." *Postcolonial Studies.* 5. 3. (2002): 245-275.

Joseph, Miranda. *Against the Romance of Community.* Minneapolis and London: University of Minnesota Press, 2002..

Kaplan, Carla. "'Talk to Me': Talk Ethics and Erotics." *Talk Talk Talk: The Cultural Life of Everyday Conversation.* London and New York: Routledge, 2001:63-75.

Lai, Larissa. "Future Asians: Migrant Speculations, Repressed History & Cyborg Hope." *West Coast Line* 44. 38.2 (2004): 168-175.

———. *Salt Fish Girl.* Toronto: Thomas Allen, 2002.

McCullough, Kate. *Regions of Identity: The Construction of America in Women's Fiction, 1885-1914.* Stanford, CA: Stanford University Press, 1999.

Mayer, Ruth. "Colonial Ladies, Global Girls." *Artificial Africas: Colonial Images in Times of Globalization.* Dartmouth: University Press of New England, 2002.

Moran, Joe. *Interdisciplinarity.* London: Routledge, 2002.

Morris, Robyn. "'Sites of Articulation' – an interview with Larissa Lai." *West Coast Line* 44. 38.2 (2004): 21-30.

Randal, Florence Hamilton. "A Year in a Boer School." *The Canadian Magazine.* Vol. XXII, no. 5 (March 1904): 411-417.

Razack, Sherene H. *Dark Threats and White Knights: The Somalia Affair, Peacekeeping, and the New Imperialism.* Toronto: University of Toronto Press, 2004.

———. *Looking White People in the Eye: Gender, Race and Culture in Courtrooms and Classrooms.* Toronto: University of Toronto Press, 1998.

Slemon, Stephen. "Teaching at the End of Empire." *College Literature,* 20.1 (February 1993): 152-161.

Spivak, Gayatri Chakraborty. *A Critique of Postcolonial Reason: Toward a History of the Vanishing Present.* Cambridge: Harvard University Press, 1999.

Scott, David. *Conscripts of Modernity: The Tragedy of Colonial Enlightenment.* Durham: Duke University Press, 2004.

Tomlinson, John. *Globalization and Culture*. Chicago: University of Chicago Press, 1999.

Walcott, Rinaldo, ed. *Rude*. Toronto: Insomniac, 2000.

Walters, William. "Secure Borders, Safe Haven, Domopolitics." *Citizenship Studies*. 8.3 (September 2004): 237-260.

Welsh, Jennifer. *At Home in the World: Canada's Global Vision for the 21st Century*. Toronto: HarperCollins, 2004.

George Elliott Clarke

Towards a Pedagogy of African Canadian Literature

For Dr. Althea Prince (1945-)[1]

Personal

Although I cannot disprove its disreputable but formidable rival's claims to preeminence, teaching might just be the "world's oldest profession." Strangely, however, many of its Ph.D.'d practitioners, who direct thousands of minds over the course of decades-long careers, are casually placed in charge of unsuspecting classrooms without even a single course in pedagogy to their names. It is a curious employment, this role of being a professor, where one must strive to educate, but without any of the training that a kindergarten teacher is expected to have.

I am a good example of this irony: I, too, lack expertise in the area of pedagogy. When I helmed my first class as an Adjunct Assistant Professor, at Queen's University, in the Spring of 1994, purporting to offer guidance in Modern English Literature, I asked a senior professor to vet my syllabus to ensure that it reasonably represented the entirety of poetry, drama, fiction, and nonfiction in American, British, and Canadian literature between 1900 and 1994. Charitably, he did so, but I still ended up with a syllabus that surprised a few of my students with its unstinting emphasis on queer identity, feminism, antiracism, and antiimperialism, despite, perhaps, our strenuous efforts to avoid controversy. Something there is in literature, in the stories we tell, that insists on provocation. Thus, teaching literature can change everything by changing minds.

Given the radical potential inherent in the task, teaching literature is an enterprise fraught, necessarily, with ideological pitfalls. Undoubtedly, Socrates understood this precept, and he paid with his life for his questioning of poetics and for his dissident views on governance, although he was not a writer and he sought no political office. He taught that the ideal Republic should banish poets (Book III), but in the actual polity in which he lived, it was the teacher who was expelled – martyred (*Phaedo*). Even now, in bourgeois-democratic, multicultural society and liberal-progressive culture, to teach, say, Marxism, or the efficacy of terrorism, or sex education, is to welcome threats, censorship, and, occasionally, expulsion – from school, or from society itself, through jailing or exile.

Colouring Between the Lines

The teaching of racial minority literatures should not, ideally, involve such risks. Applying supposedly universalist paradigms, we can say, "They are like us and we are like them," even if the us-and-them paradigm executes a benign violence. Better yet, we can say, "Like us; they bleed; and they want the same things we want: prosperous, healthy, pain-free lives, plus peace, love, and happiness." In practice, though, as literature keeps telling us, the principles of reception and interpretation – of understanding – are not that easy. South Asian Canadian scholar Arun Mukherjee advises that "'Western norms' and 'Western' values" constitute a "'Western' narcissism, this fake universalism which is really Euro American ethnocentrism talking about itself in the vocabulary of 'the human condition' at the same time that it denies the humanity of others" (14). States South Asian Canadian scholar Chelva Kanaganayakam, Mukherjee's "frustration with the constraints of the classroom arises from the normative position of Eurocentrism that masquerades as a form of universalism" (729). Mukherjee insists, "the dominant discourse in North America dehistoricizes and depoliticizes everything so that non-white, non-male, working-class ways of apprehending reality seldom get a hearing" (6). She provides the example of "such classics as Jane Austen's *Pride and Prejudice* (1813) where large dinners are eaten in feudal homes with not a servant in sight as though the dinner had cooked and served itself!" (13) She also recognizes that when a racial minority complains about the depiction of its exemplars in a text, their concerns are dismissed:

> Let the black parents scream about racism in [Samuel Clemens's]

> *The Adventures of Huckleberry Finn* (1884). We will continue to teach it as a classic. And we will continue to exclude texts that the blacks themselves have written. And, yes, we will talk about the spectre of censorship when we hear such talk.[2] (6)

The repression of a discourse of *race* within our – Canadian – literature and criticism (our classrooms) reflects our anxiety about our own racism, i.e., the preservation of Euro Caucasian privilege and power.

Indeed, the Canadian alarm about *race* and racism (a worry inspired, not because the social category and the social practice exist, but because they flourish *here*, in The Great White North), poses particular problems for the teaching of any racial minority literature. This point applies particularly to that literature I choose to term "African-Canadian."[3] Our national imaginary luxuriates in the tales of the Underground Railroad – fugitive African American slaves seeking shelter in truly free, truly welcoming Upper Canada – and in the beautiful baritone of the Rev. Dr. Martin Luther King Jr. sermonizing across the air of our very own CBC (which he did in 1967).[4] We tune out, however, our own practice of slavery, and racial violence (see "The Charivari" incident in Susanna Moodie's *Roughing It in the Bush* [1852]), and the resultant slave cemeteries, in Upper Canada. But we also choose to forget our very own Canadian, anti-black segregation, polite but forceful, conducted in sundry locales across the Dominion, casually inhibiting the careers and inconveniencing the lives of thousands of African Canadians – or Coloureds, or Negroes – as we were then known. The price of our ignorance is, we teach *To Kill a Mockingbird* (1960) – a patriotic, Yankee, race relations tract – instead of *Any Known Blood* (1997), by Lawrence Hill (1957-), which treats us to the spectacle of the Ku Klux Klan at play in Oakville, Ontario, or instead of Joy Kogawa's *Obasan* (1981), which reminds us of the unbearable fact of our dispossession and imprisonment of Japanese Canadians during the Anti-Fascist War. Yet, to teach ourselves about African Canadian literature is to gain entrée to the real history of this country, not the feel-good nostrums of the beer commercials and the televised heritage moments, which, as is glaringly obvious, studiously avoid labour strife, racial *contretemps* (including anti-Semitism), and Aboriginal vs. Crown contestation.[5] To peer at African Canadian literature is to come face-to-face with an analysis of confederate imperialism, voiced by the marginal blacks of African America and the migrant blacks of the Caribbean and the exiled blacks of Africa. Hear Afro Ontarian writer Carol Talbot (b. 1950s): "I am a voice crying in the wilderness, on the fringe of the diaspora" (–). To encounter African Canadian literature is to lose one's comfortable innocence regarding the experience of *race* in this country. New Zealand scholar Mark Williams tells us "Race relations were . . . crucial to colonial New Zealand's sense of superiority" *vis-à-vis* Australia (749). Who could deny that we use the discourse of race to trumpet our moral superiority *tête-à-tête* with the United States? This unreal discourse renders us incapable of hearing the dissent of African Canadians from our adulation of our untainted, 'European' nobility. Most troublingly, given our fervent need to nation-build, to construct a society distinct from Britain, France, and the United States, we must whitewash our history. There is nothing new here. Williams reports "Both Australia and New Zealand since the 1970s have sought independently to fashion 'postcolonial' identities for themselves, yet in both cases the sources of new identity lie in a shared and embarrassing colonial past" (751). African Canadian literature poses this challenge to Canada: Can you accept responsibility for your own past injustices – *Stop talking about the United States!* – and seek not to perpetuate them now or perpetrate them ever again?

Black Letters, White Alphabets

Such urgent, even intemperate questions, Kanaganayakam tells us, "have been asked before and those who ask them often suggest answers hoping that the issues would be put to rest, only to realize later that their views get transformed to join the repertoire of questions" (725). In his germane article, "Pedagogy and Postcolonial Literature; or, Do We Need a Centre for Postcolonial Studies?", Kanaganayakam warns that the ideas and approaches "we use to teach postcolonial literature . . . often [mean] we become accomplices in subjecting postcolonial studies to a form of colonization" (732). To strengthen this charge, Kanaganayakam quotes Dipresh Chakrabarty's argument that "concepts such as citizenship, the state, civil society, public sphere, human rights, equality before the law, the individual, distinctions between public and private, the idea of the subject, democracy, popular sovereignty, social justice, scientific rationality, and so on all bear the burden of European thought and history" (qtd. in Kanaganayakam 732). Wise is Kanaganayakam's caution regarding our ability to teach minority, marginal, or postcolonial literature outside of supposedly European concepts. Yet, we must also account for the powerful ways in which Empire-disseminated ideas (usually practiced with *much* hypocrisy) were mediated by African, Asian, and Aboriginal counter-arguments. For instance, the American constitution evolved first to permit African slavery and then to forbid it.[6] Practically every idea identified by Chakrabarty as "European" in origin was modified and indigenized *via* struggles between settlers and natives, masters and slaves. In brief, the Enlightenment shone on everyone. Its illumination allowed "uncivilized" Africans and "savages" to see the deep cracks within and vast bloodstains upon the marble edifice of European civilization. Moreover, all the splendor of Rome, the majesty of Paris, the glory of London, and the magnificence of Madrid were founded on the gold looted from the Americas *via* the sweat and blood of African and Amerindian slaves, and, later, the coerced, migratory labour of South Asians and Chinese. When Jean-Jacques Rousseau wrote, in *Du contrat social* (1762), "Man is born free, but everywhere he is in chains," an African, toiling in Montreal or Mississippi or Martinique, could have answered, "No, monsieur, you are free; I am in chains." Slavery and imperialism constitute the Original Sins of modernity. Thus, Paul Gilroy posits, in *The Black Atlantic: Modernity and Double Consciousness* (1993), that the migrations of black intellectuals, during slavery and afterward, and their subsequent theorizations, produce "a Counterculture of Modernity" (1).

Both Kanaganayakam and Chakrabarty must leave room, then, for the ways in which the marginalized speak back to their "downpressors," and challenge, thereby, modern discourses of liberal humanism to produce humane behaviour, not excuse inhumanity. African diasporic discourses attempt, usually, to answer Macchiavelli with Martin Luther King – if not Malcolm X. For instance, in his *Foundations of an African Ethic* (2000, 2001), Bénézet Bujo asserts that "communitarianism in its critique of the 'unfettered self' or of 'atomism' against liberalism is entirely in keeping with African ethics, which rejects the idea that being a human person and acting responsibly is merely the result of having assented to rational principles, or arguing and thinking rationally" (4). "For Black Africa," Bujo goes on to state, "it is not the Cartesian *cogito ergo sum* ('I think, therefore I am') but an existential *cognatus sum, ergo sumus* ('I am known, therefore we are') that is decisive" (4). In other words, the colonized and enslaved *Others* (of Europe's imperium) retained alternative belief systems – philosophies and faiths – that checked the Occident's violence-prone and money-hungry liberalism. Europe imposed modernity, via cannon and gun, but the subjugated made haste to force reform upon it. The concepts that Chakrabarty deems *European* were actually tested, disputed, refined, and even improved in the very realms that Europeans thought uncouth.

In teaching African Canadian literature then, for instance, one may note the rhetoric of liberty employed by the master class, but applaud the ways in which African Canadian slaves and free people worked to undermine the political economy of slavery via a counter-discourse foregrounding the hypocrisy and cruelty of the masters. See the African American *cum* African Nova Scotian writer David George (c.1743-1810), who, in his memoir (1793), recognizes the irony of having had a vicious master whose "name was Chapel – a very bad man to the Negroes" (32). In the first sentence of Robin W. Winks's *The Blacks in Canada: A History* (1971), we encounter again the voice of the archetypal black that wittily talks back to white authority. In this case, a black youth answers an apostle (or an apologist) of *white* Christianity:

> "You say that by baptism I shall be like you: I am black and you are white, I must have my skin taken off then in order to be like you." Thus in 1632 did "*un petit nègre*" rebuke the Jesuit missionary Paul le Jeune for claiming that all men were one when united in Christianity. (1)

The Neanderthal practices of European modernism elicited, from its coloured victims, responsive discourses that had the effect of truly modernizing modernity. Part of the power of the revolutionary poetry collection, *She Tries Her Tongue, Her Silence Softly Breaks* (1989), which employs Greek myth to poeticize the reunification of archetypal African Caribbean mothers and daughters, derives from the opening essay, "The Absence of Writing or How I Almost Became a Spy," by Tobago Canadian author M. NourbeSe Philip (1947-). Here she offers further proof that the violence of European conquest liberalism, in this case, visited upon African linguistics, met with an opposing indigeneity:

> The havoc that the African wreaked upon the English language is, in fact, the metaphorical equivalent of the havoc that coming to the New World represented for the African… Language of the people. Language for the people. Language by the people, honed and fashioned through a particular history of empire and savagery. (18)

In the end, "The linguistic rape and subsequent forced marriage between African and English tongues has resulted in a language capable of great rhythms and musicality; one that is and is not English . . . " (23). The libertine aggression of slavery and colonialism was countered by the verbal inventiveness of its subjects, who, despite their disempowered status, altered the imposed European tongues, driving them toward a condition of music, but *black* music.

Kanaganayakam notices that because "postcolonial studies is a fallout from Empire and that English departments tend to be custodians of postcolonial literature, there are commonalities across the globe and these departments function in similar ways to inscribe certain forms of knowledge" (730). Given the duplication of models of inquiry from English department to English department, as well as the replication of syllabi and theoretical approaches, Kanaganayakam wonders whether practitioners of postcolonial studies "may be guilty of recolonizing the field" (728). His concern is a galvanizing one. But there may be no useful response other than to demand repeatedly that those who teach the literatures of the once-dispossessed and the twice-exiled anchor their pedagogy in historical and sociopolitical analysis. As Ato Quayson states in his 2004 article, "Symbolization Compulsion: Testing a Psychoanalytical Category on Postcolonial African Literature," our duty is "to interrogate a social domain into view" (759). Mukherjee admonishes teachers: "What is needed is explication, not erasure and assimilation" (66). The texts of sub-alterns must be explained, set in their own original contexts of political disputation and social discord, not whitewashed – reduced to blandishments – by a wishy-washy universalism. Describing so-called Commonwealth novelists, Mukherjee reminds us they have had to build "structures which . . . allow them to capture the spider-web of relationships which constitute community life in the developing countries" (25).

These writers – and African Canadian ones are no exception – tend to imbue their texts with the realism of lived experience (no matter how much "magic" they may also invoke).

In an elegant article, "Whose Story Is It, Anyway? An Interdisciplinary Approach to Post-modernism, Narrative, and Therapy" (2001), Euro Canadian scholars Herb Wyile and David Paré, announce "postmodernism's embrace of multiplicity and contingency opens texts to alternate interpretations that may be beneficial to clients and readers alike; and, furthermore, that this emancipatory potential may be problematized but certainly not rendered invalid by postmodernism's emphasis on relativism and indeterminacy" (154). Their positive embrace of postmodernism apparently ignores, however, Mukherjee's concern that, in literary criticism, "an upper-middle-class, usually male and white, point of view is presented with the authority of the universal" (6). She also wonders, "whether it is possible to read texts by non-white writers, both male and female, in the framework of aesthetic theories developed in Euro-America" (13). Of course, postmodernism is yet one more aesthetic protocol of Euro American provenance. However, as Wylie and Paré suggest, postmodernism feeds "a resistance to established, dominant narratives and emphasise[s] the importance of the social construction of subjectivity . . . as the basis for a resistance to those metanarratives" (170). Their most useful assertion, though, is the simple note that "experience is multi-storied" (164). Coupled with Mukherjee's wish that we "encourage and reward students for reading and researching writers of their own ethnic background" (xv), so that they begin to question the curriculum and interrogate "the enveloping cloud of racism in which we live as a society" (13), it means one is both *en vogue* – and justified – in teaching African Canadian literature.

Certainly, the teaching of postcolonial texts, or of minority literatures, should be as uncomfortable and as discomfiting as the realities that forced them into being. Why should the teaching of a slave narrative make anyone feel good? When Marie-Josèphe Angélique, a slave woman in colonial Montreal, relates her life story, telling of how she was forcibly bred for the sake of profits for her master, and when we read of her torture and execution for arson in Montreal in 1734, we ought to feel disturbed.[7] But we should read her story alongside the satirical sketches of the pro-slavery, British North American (Nova Scotian) intellectual, Thomas

Chandler Haliburton, who bids his main mouthpiece and most famous character, Sam Slick, to utter this infamous statement: "niggers . . . . those thick skulled, crooked shanked, flat footed, long heeled, wooly headed gentlemen, don't seem fit for much else but slavery" (176). Such sentiments help us to understand why African peoples had to struggle so long and with such difficulty to achieve the abolition of slavery, and to appreciate that Negrophobia and anti-black racism date back to the origins of European modernity.[8] Similarly, when David George relates his experience of Virginian slavery – "the greatest grief I then had was to see them whip my mother, and to hear her, on her knees, begging for mercy" (32), we must connect it, almost genetically, to African Nova Scotian (Africadian) singer-songwriter Faith Nolan (1957-) and her song, "Marie Joseph Angelique" (1986):

She ran away from the home
she could never call her own
to burn Mount Royal down.
She lit her torch of freedom
and set the building on fire.
She said, If I can't be free,
I will burn in the mire.

Slave owners took her to the jail cell
and whipped her body;
then marched her through the town
for the wicked to see;
then they burned her at the town square.
I heard her screams.

My soul is my own
for no man to keep. (120)

It is not difficult to move from Nolan's agonizing song about Angélique to Montreal native Lorena Gale (1958-) and her play, *Angélique* (1999), where one reads, "Then is now. Now is then" (3). Gale bids us consider slavery as an earlier mode of black immigrant (woman) labour exploitation: "Unless otherwise stated, the slaves are working in every scene in which they appear, either in a modern or historical context" (3). In one scene in the play, Angélique's master, François, "*reaches around and removes ANGÉLIQUE's uniform, revealing period undergarments beneath her modern clothing*" (34). Such anachronistic imaginings compel us to address slavery, not as a long-passed spasm of history, but as a living component of contemporary labour (and race) relations. Teachers of such texts must move just as fluidly in history, navigating canal systems of "periods," toing-and-froing, as necessary, to allow for an adequate *explication de texte*.

Civics & The Humanities

Critics may bridle at this impolitic emphasis on the politics of a text. Crucially, Kanaganayakam compels us to "defend . . . the textuality of the text" (736). Although it "may well reflect several aspects of contemporary or historical reality, . . . its primary function is to work within its own status as an artifact" (736-37). Aesthetics are the basis of the Humanities, I agree, but so is civics. Hence, the poetics of a text should be excavated *along with* its politics. In his 2004 essay, "Postcolonialism and Diaspora: A Contribution to the Critique of Nationalist Ideology and Historiography in the Age of Globalization and Neoliberalism," Kanishka Goonewardena pushes for a holistic criticism, asserting, trenchantly, for instance, "those who do not want to talk about global capitalism should be silent about postcolonialism and diaspora" (672).[9] Our central duty, as teachers, is to get the history right, which means utilizing several sources and approaches, from the anthropological and folkloric to analyses of the practices of political economy. Perry Anderson cautions us, sagely, that the major problem in contemporary historiography is "representation omitted rather than misrepresentation committed" (quoted in Goonewardena 678). Thus, we must seek out histories that set forth narratives encompassing race, culture, gender, and class analyses. This must be one of the criteria, as Indian scholar Sumit Sarkar witnesses, "for distinguishing between less and more valid versions of the past" (quoted in Goonewardena 679). While Kanaganayakam holds, properly, that "writers would like their texts to be read and taught as texts rather than as position papers" (735), their plays, poetry, novels, short stories, essays, histories, letters, songs, libretti, journalism, and scientific analyses are wholly embedded within the discourses of their moment, while they also impinge on the discourses of our own.

Perhaps it is the failure to explore the resonant, real-world contexts of texts that reduces their teaching to a rendering of rote interpretations that rout their upheavals. Mukherjee advises, "simply teaching Third World literary texts does not change consciousness" (xii). Euro Canadian literary scholar Diana Brydon believes "postcolonial theories have yet to make a difference beyond the academy" (692). She feels that postcolonialism's "entry into the academy has been additive rather than transformational" (692). Verily, a mere theory of postcoloniality – without a theory of neoimperialism – becomes an abject helpmate of globalization. South Asian Canadian scholar Balachandra Rajan warns, "The global enterprise . . . will emphasize the local, the neighbourhood, the mosaic with its inlaid promise of stability, the solicitous concern of the imperium for exotic detail" (719), a catalogue of interests harmonious with postcolonialism *as usually practiced – or read.* Ironically though, as Rajan spells out, "Postcolonial dispositions of reading may be the best means of critiquing the rapidly compounding rhetoric of globalism" (723). Still, "postcolonial ways of thought must subject themselves to a sharp revisionary turn if they are to comment effectively on an imperialism radically different from its predecessors [because it is deterritorialized]" (723).

Accessing the African Canadian Library

The *entrée* of African Canadian literature into the Canadian academy will provoke and stimulate discussions of the usually unspoken. For instance, if we teach "I Fight Back" (1982), a poem by Jamaican Canadian Lillian Allen (1951-), we will accent the North American capitalist adventurism named in this stanza:

> ITT ALCAN KAISER
> Canadian Imperial Bank of Commerce
> These are priviledged [sic] names in my County [sic]
> But I AM ILLEGAL HERE [in Canada] (15)

In classical, African Diasporic fashion, Allen emphasizes the irony of the welcomed presence of American and Canadian transnational corporations in Jamaica, while her own body, black and female and Caribbean-raised (after the displacement effected by slavery), is not welcome in Canada. Beyond this reading, though, lurks yet another, a deeper analysis, one that should outline Canada's unspoken, unheralded imperialism in the Caribbean. Indeed, in the 1870s, the Anglo Canadian nationalist and British imperialist Canada First movement called for "closer trade relations with the West Indies, with a view to ultimate political connexion" (qtd. in McNaught 157). As a self-governing state in the Empire, one whose Anglophone leaders viewed it as a conduit of British power in North America, some were tempted to move beyond the colonizing of the "North-West Territories" and to venture into the Caribbean. Although Canada could not establish a political dominion within the Caribbean, several of its transnational corporations – Alcan, the Bank of Nova Scotia (Scotia Bank), and the Royal Bank of Canada, to name a few – did "invade" the region.

While Allen's work – like that of Philip's play, *Coups and Calypsos* (2001) – allows us to contemplate aggressive, Canadian commercial and political policies in the Caribbean, we may inspect the writings of the white Anglo Canadian author, William Stairs (1863-92), a Halifax, Nova Scotia native, for a better understanding of Canadian imperialism in Africa. Indeed, Stairs's adventures in Africa in the late Victorian Era included "condoning decapitation and mutilation" (dust jacket flap).[10] If we dare to recall Canada's imperialist ventures, on behalf of or in support of Great Britain (when it was, by hook and by crook, "great"), we might better appreciate why the 1993 Somalia peacekeeping and food distribution mission ended in elite, Canadian soldiers torturing two Somali youths and lynching one. In other words, we will grapple with the ways in which *race* and *racism* have always influenced Canadian foreign policy. In addition, we could follow up our revelations about the Somalia Affair with a reading of a poem, "Sister (Y)Our Manchild at the Close of the Twentieth Century," by Trinidadian Canadian Claire Harris (1937-), treating this grotesque episode.[11]

To consider black immigration to Canada, one may examine a rich assortment of texts from African Canadian literature, including a novel by Trinidadian Canadian Dionne Brand (1953-), *In Another Place, Not Here* (1996). Mauritian Canadian literary scholar Geeta Paray-Clarke, in her class notes titled "Canada, Toronto and Immigrants," lists the various moments in the novel where one of the protagonists, Verlia, and her relatives in Sudbury, Ontario, respond to white Canadian, anti-black racism:

> P.140-142: Verlia's uncle and aunt who live in Sudbury do their best to blend with the whites and be accepted by them. They think that there is no racism, you only have to work hard and you will blend with the others. They want to pretend that they are not seen as being different from others. They do their best not to show theirblackness... P.164: Verlia imagines how the Sudbury uncle and aunt are practising self-deception. P.165: She sees her uncle's life as that of capitulation and dying. (5)

This descriptive summary of significant passages foregrounds the interlocking complex of race and identity – or identification – in urban Canada. African Canadian literature, in general, demands this confrontation with – this accounting of – the *facts* of white supremacy and black resistance in Canada.

Because civic experience is multifaceted and *superficially* ahistorical, the history and currency of African Canadian *cultures* may serve to reveal the operations of oppressive state practices, both domestically and internationally, and foster probing of these institutions of domination. Most importantly, the examination of this literature allows readers to encounter fine and fiery texts that stimulate judgment and judgment calls. As Sartre declares, "negritute [sic] is, in its essence, poetry. Upon this one occasion at least [i.e. the 1948 publication of *Orphé noir*], the most authentic revolutionary program and the purest poetry derive from the same source" (64): the black revolt – against imperialism, against racism, against second-class treatment. I sound Sartre again: "[T]o each epoch its poetry, for each epoch the circumstances of history elect a nation, a race, a class, to seize again the [revolutionary] torch, in creating situations which can express or surpass themselves only through Poetry . . . (65)" Perhaps that moment, that opportunity, filters through – I mean, *also* through – African Canadian writers today.

*

From Prelude to Practice

My conclusion is a practical one: a provisional syllabus for African Canadian literature. To design such an instruction vehicle, I must needs divide the literature into a series of themes or periods or both. However, in the case of African Canadian literature, which possesses both a long history (beginning in 1785) and a relatively small group of contemporary literary texts (the majority dating back to 1964), periodization enacts, in itself, practically a thematization.[12]

My proposed categories are, nevertheless, not so much a product of historical dates, but rather of chief concerns that reflect the different periods in which different groups of African Canadians arrived and settled. My tentative schema employs these "silos":

1. Slavery (in Canada and experienced by proto "Canadians" elsewhere);
2.Settlement (i.e. narratives situated in the historic African Canadian communities);
3. Immigration (mainly since 1955);
4. Homelands (commentaries on originating colonies/nations)
5. Diaspora (meditations on the African Diaspora, via slavery, imperialism, and economic migration);
6. Urban (city-based, pop-culture-influenced contemporary writing);
and two generic categories, *Criticism* (academic writing or *belles-lettres*);
and *Juvenile*.

Naturally, this schema is only tentative, suggestive, selective, and brief.[13]

NOTES

1. Althea Prince is a stellar African Canadian intellectual and writer. Originally from Antigua, she was actively involved in the Canadian Black Arts and Black Empowerment struggles in urban Canada in the 1960s, as well as in the Feminist movement. An author, with a doctorate in sociology, she provides incisive analyses of gender and race as lived experience, in both her fiction and nonfiction. When she was Managing Editor at the Canadian Scholars Press International and the Women's Press, she was instrumental in advancing new

voices, academic and artistic, from marginalized communities.

2. Mukherhee's judgment here is not merely rhetorical. When my Africadian (African Nova Scotian) sister-in-law, Brenda Clarke, protested, with other black parents, the teaching of Harper Lee's *To Kill a Mockingbird* (1960) in the high schools of Digby, Nova Scotia, in 2002, various august authorities lectured her and other Africadians about the literary greatness and effective antiracism of Lee's novel. Some folks even stated that the black community's real problem was its insufficient literacy. These benighted rubes could not understand, it was hinted, how the novel transcends and contradicts the brutish circumstances of redneck racism, even if the word nigger, as a matter of vinegary verisimilitude, if not tastefulness, peppers the white-sugar liberalism of the text. Yet, none of the white-liberal critics of the black parents bothered to analyze the novel for the ways it fails to uphold an antiracism agenda. Indeed, the sociopolitical hamartia of the novel is that it foregrounds good whites as saviours of blacks; it robs the black characters of agency; they must rely on the charity of a white benefactor to palliate their predicament. Moreover, the false consciousness the novel foregrounds is an American one, thus permitting Canadians to continue to revel in our own propaganda that this country did not tolerate slavery or segregation and does not practice racism today. Nevertheless, Harper Lee's novel need not be banned. Rather, its teaching needs to be supplemented with the teaching of writing by African/Negro-heritage authors, especially African Canadian ones, where their characters are agents, not cast as reactionary mutes. Perhaps the unstated issue is, blacks have written nothing worth teaching. Certainly, this presumption was voiced by a visiting professor, who taught Southern American (U.S.) Literature here, at Queen's University, in the summer of 1991. This course was memorable partly because the American professor did not list a single African American author on the syllabus. When I challenged him about this omission, he replied that none were good enough. I did enjoy reading Carson McCullers, William Faulkner, and William Styron. However, their greatness did not excuse the absence of Richard Wright, Jean Toomer, Zora Neale Hurston, Alice Walker, and Ernest J. Gaines.

3. I know that other scholars are gracious enough to deem African Canadian literature as "Black writing in Canada." But this alternative nomenclature robs the literature of both its continental heritage and its historical connection to the clutch of invasive, British/French colonies-turned-provinces we now call Canada.

4. See King's *Conscience for Change: Massey Lectures*, Seventh Series (1967).

5. But that is not to say we will hear a cascade of positives when we begin to allow African Canadian voices to enter our heads and our classrooms. French philosopher Jean-Paul Sartre warned, way back in 1948, in *Orphé noir*, "What would you expect to find, when the muzzle that has silenced the voices of black

men is removed? That they would thunder your praise?" (7). No, no, we have too much to remember, too much to forgive, to unthinkingly lavish paeans and elegies upon a civilization that found it just to seize foreign citizens, imprison and transport them across seas, and extract their labour without pay, and then to sell their offspring into bestial servitude.

6. See Article IV, Section 2, Clause 3, and then Note 11 (regarding its repeal).

7. See Marcel Trudel, *L'Esclavage au Canada français* (1960).

8. Although they may have been ignorant of the sources of their own racism, the two or more young white men, in – excuse the irony – a souped-up black car, who leaned out a window and screeched "NIGGER!" at me while I was walking one night, in July 1993, back to the Queen's University Graduate Residence in Kingston, Ontario, felt presumably some claim of ownership upon me. My reaction, however, was completely unlike my dissertation-writing, doctoral candidate persona: I dropped the two bags of groceries I was carrying and went running down the middle of the street after the speeding car in an attempt to hurl a rock at its back window. I had gone straight from the end of the xx-century back to the Stone Age.

9. I cannot resist noting that the first global industry was slavery. See also my play, Beatrice Chancy (1999), especially p. 25.

10. Fascinatingly, Stairs's diaries, published wholly in 1998, are edited by the then-High Commissioner, for Canada, to the United Kingdom, Hon. Roy MacLaren, whose editorial asides sometimes update the ethnocentric assumptions of Stairs. See my article, "Writing the Pax Canadiana: Terror Abroad, Torture at Home" (2005).

11. See Harris's collection, *Dipped in Shadow* (1996), pp. 51-62. But also see Sherene Razack's brilliant analysis of the Somalia Affair, *Dark Threats & White Knights: The Somalia Affair, Peacekeeping, and the New Imperialism* (2004).

12. For a working history and bibliography of African Canadian literature, see my "Surveys" section in *Odysseys Home: Mapping African-Canadian Literature* (2002), pp. 323-448.

13. The syllabus of African Canadian texts is not included here but is available from the author.

WORKS CITED

Allen, Lillian. "I Fight Back." *Rhythm an' Hardtimes*. Toronto: Domestic Bliss, 1982. 15.

Brand, Dionne. *In Another Place, Not Here*. Toronto: Alfred A. Knopf Canada, 1996.

Brydon, Diana. "Postcolonialism Now: Autonomy, Cosmopolitanism, and Diaspora." *University of Toronto Quarterly*. 73.2 (Spring 2004): 691-706.

Bujo, Bénézet. *Foundations of an African Ethic: Beyond the Universal Claims of Western Morality*. Trans. Brian McNeil. New York: Crossroad Publishing Company, 2001. Trans. of Wider den Universalanspruch westlicher Moral. Freiburg, Germany: Verlag Herder, 2000.

Clarke, George Elliott. *Beatrice Chancy*. Victoria, BC: Polestar Books, 1999.

———. "Surveys." In *Odysseys Home: Mapping African-Canadian Literature*. Toronto: University of Toronto Press, 2002. 323-448.

———. "Writing the Pax Canadiana: Terror Abroad, Torture at Home." In *Building Liberty: Canada and World Peace, 1945-2005*. Eds. Conny Steenman-Marcusse and Aritha van Herk. Groningen, NL: Barkhuis Publishing, 2005. 213-36.

Gale, Lorena. *Angélique*. Toronto: Playwrights Canada Press, 2000.

George, David. "An Account of thr Life of Mr. David George, from Sierra Leone in Africa, given by himself in a Conversation with Brother Rippon in London and Brother Pearce of Birmingham. 1793." *In Fire on the Water: An Anthology of Black Nova Scotian Writing*. Vol. 1. Ed. George Elliott Clarke. Lawrencetown Beach, NS: Pottersfield Press, 1991. 32-39.

Gilroy, Paul. *The Black Atlantic: Modernity and Double Consciousness*. Cambridge, MA: Harvard University Press, 1993.

Haliburton, Thomas Chandler. *The Clockmaker; or, The Sayings and Doings of Sam Slick, of Slickville*. [First Series.] Halifax, NS: Howe, 1836.

Goonewardena, Kanishka. "Postcolonialism and Diaspora: A Contribution to the Critique of Nationalist Ideology and Historiography in the Age of Globalization and Neoliberalism." *University of Toronto Quarterly*. 73.2 (Spring 2004): 657-90.

Harris, Claire. "Sister (Y)Our Manchild at the Close of the Twentieth Century." In *Dipped in Shadow*. Fredericton, NB: Goose Lane, 1996. 51-62.

Hill, Lawrence. *Any Known Blood*. Toronto: HarperCollins, 1997.

Kanaganayakam, Chelva. "Pedagogy and Postcolonial Literature; or, Do We Need a Centre for Postcolonial Studies?" *University of Toronto Quarterly*. 73.2 (Spring 2004): 725-38.

King, Martin Luther. *Conscience for Change: Massey Lectures*, Seventh Series. Toronto: Canadian Broadcasting Corporation, 1967.

Kogawa, Joy. *Obasan*. 1981. rpt. Toronto: Penguin, 1983.

Lee, Harper. *To Kill a Mockingbird*. New York: J.P. Lippincott, 1960.

McNaught, Kenneth. *The Pelican History of Canada*. London: Allen Lane-Penguin Books, 1978.

Moodie, Susanna. "The Charivari." *Roughing It in the Bush; or, Life in Canada*. 1852. Toronto: McClelland & Stewart, 1989. 193-216.

Mukherjee, Arun. *Oppositional Aesthetics: Readings from a Hyphenated Space*. Toronto: TSAR, 1994.

Nolan, Faith. "Marie Joseph Angelique." 1986. *In Fire on the Water: An Anthology of Black Nova Scotian Writing*. Vol. 2. Ed. George Elliott Clarke. Lawrencetown Beach, NS: Pottersfield Press, 1992. 119-20

Paray-Clarke, Geeta. "In Another Place, Not Here: Dionne Brand." Lecture notes. 1-5. TS in the possession of the author.

Philip, M. NourbeSe. *Coups and Calypsos.* Toronto: Mercury Press, 2001.

———. [as Marlene Nourbese Philip] *She Tries Her Tongue, Her Silence Softly Breaks.* Charlottetown, PEI: Ragweed Press, 1989.

Plato. Book III. *The Republic*. In *The Republic and other Works*. Trans. B. Jowett. Garden City, NY: Doubleday-Anchor Press, 1973. 71-107.

———. *Phaedo*. In *The Republic and other Works*. Trans. B. Jowett. Garden City, NY: Doubleday-Anchor Press, 1973. 487-552.

Quayson, Ato. "Symbolization Compulsion: Testing a Psychoanalytical Category on Postcolonial African Literature." *University of Toronto Quarterly*. 73.2 (Spring 2004): 754-72.

Rajan, Balachandra. "Imperialism and the Other End of History." *University of Toronto Quarterly*. 73.2 (Spring 2004): 707-24.

Razack, Sherene H. *Dark Threats & White Knights: The Somalia Affair, Peacekeeping, and the New Imperialism*. Toronto: University of Toronto Press, 2004.

Rousseau, Jean-Jacques. *Du contrat social; ou, Principes du droit politique*. 1762. Paris: M.M. Bousquet, 1766.

Sartre, Jean-Paul. *Black Orpheus*. Trans. S.W. Allen. Paris: Présence Africaine, 1976.Trans. of *Orphé noir*. Paris: Éditions Gallimard, 1948.

Stairs, William. *African Exploits: the Diaries of William Stairs, 1887-1892*. Ed. Roy MacLaren. Montreal & Kingston: McGill-Queen's University Press, 1998.

Talbot, Carol. *Growing Up Black in Canada*. Toronto: Williams-Wallace, 1984, 1989.

Trudel, Marcel. *L'Esclavage au Canada français*. 1960. Montréal: Les Éditions de l'horizon, 1963.

United States Constitution. www.house.gov/Constitution/Constitution.html

Williams, Mark. "On the Discriminations of Postcolonialism in Australia and New Zealand." *University of Toronto Quarterly*. 73.2 (Spring 2004): 739-53.

Winks, Robin W. *The Blacks in Canada: A History*. 1971. Montreal, QC, and Kingston, ON: McGill-Queen's University Press, 1997.

Wyile, Herb, and David Paré. "Whose Story Is It, Anyway? An Interdisciplinary Approach to Post-modernism, Narrative, and Therapy." *Mosaic*. 34.1 (2001): 153-72.

Paulo Lemos Horta

Ondaatje and the Cosmopolitan Desert Explorers: Landscape, Space and Community in The English Patient

The centenary celebrations of the Royal Geographical Society in 1930 afforded a forum for its leaders to reminisce on a time when "the lure of the unknown was everywhere attracting the young and adventurous" and to stress the cosmopolitan scope of the society's mandate to provide fellowship for the geographical explorers who braved "vast blanks on all the maps [that] bore only the fascinating inscription 'Unexplored'."[1] In 1830 the society's original goals had included, in addition to providing maps, instruments, and funds for explorers, the promotion of intellectual exchange between British explorers and members of kindred societies elsewhere in the world. At the centenary forum RGS President Sir Charles Close and others portrayed the society as a British enterprise with a cosmopolitan trajectory and future, for (in the President's words) the subject of geography was "no less wide than the study of the Earth itself, but particularly includes the study of the Earth as the home of man."[2] To explore blank spaces "on all the maps" was to be educated in a cosmopolitan worldview, a notion most boldly stated by the Marquess of Zetland (RGS President from 1922 to 1925) in remarks that praised the society for recognizing through funding, awards and publications the foreign explorers who helped broaden its horizons. The Marquess argued that, if Einstein could affirm that the universe "is finite but without boundaries," geographers could assert the same "of the planet on which we live," not merely in the sense "that we recognize no boundaries capable of arresting the advance of our explorers" but further "in the sense that where our science is concerned we treat the political and linguistic boundaries which separate one nation from another as non-existent."[3] The society's cultivation of fellowship among "geographers of all nations" thus served not only the interests of science but strengthened "the bonds which unite within the common fold of humanity peoples of all races and of all creeds."[4] The Marquess's idealized view of the RGS's cosmopolitan history and purpose will be familiar to readers of Michael Ondaatje's *The English Patient.* In Ondaatje's novel "explorers" "of all nations" gather at the Geographical Society in London in the 1920s and 1930s bound by a cosmopolitan fellowship. Ondaatje's explorers too find that the unmapped desert has "taught" them to "Erase nations!" and to desire to walk upon (in a paraphrase of the Marquess's planet "without boundaries") "an earth that had no maps."[5]

The centenary celebrations also afforded the society's past presidents the chance to reclaim the centrality of adventure to the fellowship of the RGS in an age when, in the words of one of the explorers that would inspire Ondaatje, "the type of adventure pursued by the geographical explorer grow increasingly hard to find" for "mechanical invention has dwarfed the dimensions of the Earth and will soon leave no corner unsurveyed, no obstacle unsurmounted."[6] Past RGS presidents Douglas Freshfield (president from 1914 to 1917) and Sir Francis Younghusband (from 1919 to 1922) lamented the loss of adventure as a common basis for fellowship and cautioned against acquiescing to the more humble technical goals of modern geographical science. Freshfield reminisced on "the legendary mid-Victorian years" when then president Sir Roderick Murchison advised him that "in reading [to the society] you can leave out the geography; print it afterwards: give us the adventure."[7] Likewise Younghusband recalled his first address to the society in 1888, when after feeling a "guilty inadequacy" for importuning "a scientific body" with impressions of "the beauty of the desert nights and evenings," he was relieved to find that the RGS was "composed of human beings" who "enjoyed a spice of adventure."[8] Younghusband lamented however that the society he inherited as president three decades later viewed expeditions such as the proposed ascent of Mount Everest as "sensational" and "therefore unsuitable for a scientific Society."[9] It was the aim of his presidency to stimulate anew a "spirit of adventure" and "an interest in natural beauty," for he believed that while "travellers should be measurers certainly," if "they have something of the artist in them they should not suppress it when addressing this society."[10] The nostalgic voices of Freshfield and Younghusband ring familiar in the lament of Ondaatje's narrator in *The English Patient* that in the 1930s the increasingly "modest" concern of the RGS with the "hard currency" of facts about the "earth's surface" and its "interesting geographical problems" had relegated to "the far side of the issues being discussed" consideration of the "human" experience and "behaviour" of the explorers.[11]

Ondaatje's affinity for the reaffirmation of the explorers' "spirit of adventure" and "interest in natural beauty" is reflected in his expression of gratitude in *The English Patient* toward the RGS "for allowing me to read archival material and to glean from their *Geographical Journals* the world of explorers and their journeys – often beautifully recorded by their writers."[12] Ondaatje's acknowledgment imparts perhaps more than he intended to, and more than previous scholars have cared to investigate, for a comparison of the novel and its sources demonstrates that he has literally scraped together "the world of explorers and their journeys" through substantial and – with a single exception[13] – unacknowledged citation and close paraphrase from the accounts in the *Geographical Journal.* Moreover, as his telling choice of words indicates, Ondaatje gleans from the explorers not merely descriptions of routes and landscapes and what he slyly terms "information" but "the *world* of explorers and their journeys" in the full sense of a worldview in which the exploration of blank spaces on maps is the basis for the forging of a cosmopolitan fellowship. For Ondaatje to describe, in his acknowledgments and his fiction, the world of the RGS of the 1930s in terms of lyrical accounts of exploration and fellowship entails siding with Freshfield and Younghusband against modern professional geographers who deemed such accounts unscientific and unworthy of a regular section at the program of the international geographical society. His novel's insistence on the cosmopolitanism of the exploration of the unmapped desert echoes the Marquess's idealistic account of the RGS and contradicts a historical record characterized by the belated colonial scramble for uncharted and therefore unclaimed territory in accordance with the international legal principle of *res nullius* invoked by Italy in occupying Libya. It sides with the RGS presidents who viewed exploration as an education in a cosmopolitan fellowship and sensibility, against the recorded view of many of their colleagues that expeditions could be gauged only in terms of their service to the cause of science or empire.

The precise contours of the cosmopolitanism of blank spaces advocated in *The English Patient*, as well as its aesthetic and political implications, come into focus when the novel's invocation of the world of the explorers and their journeys is juxtaposed with the source material. This exercise affords an opportunity to test against the evidence of Ondaatje's handling of his sources the hypotheses of a rich body of scholarship that has sought to theorize, and more recently to historically contextualize, the novel's internationalist credo. The governing assumption derived from the theoretical musings on the text by postcolonial thinkers such as Bruce Robbins is that its internationalism possesses impeccably multicultural and antiimperialist credentials and concomitantly a progressive politics.[14] This line of inquiry often claims that the novel's treatment of history is postmodern but Ondaatje's allegedly postmodern and postcolonial historiographic concerns have yet to be demonstrated, or refuted for that matter, with substantial reference to his treatment of his acknowledged sources. Scholars too readily assume that the trademark features of the novel's cosmopolitanism – the lyrical and philosophical musings on desert exploration, Almasy's reflections on Herodotus, the laments on the future of exploration and the RGS – are original to Ondaatje. In turn the governing assumption of the promising historicist line of inquiry developed by Totosy is that the cosmopolitanism of the historical Almasy, and by extension of Ondaatje, is not reactionary.[15] The uncovering of treasure troves of source material on the historical Almasy at the RGS, the Foreign Office and in Hungarian archives, however, has once more not been matched by a demonstration of the degree of Ondaatje's debt and engagement with this material. The rich theoretical and historical contextualization of Ondaatje's cosmopolitanism to date enables the present study: the theory provides questions to ask of Ondaatje's handling of his sources, and the wealth of newly discovered and translated sources on Almasy allow a more precise determination of the extent and manner to which Ondaatje is indebted to the accounts of exploration in the *Geographical Journal*.

The quest for the lost oasis of Zerzura perfectly serves Ondaatje's idealized portrait of exploration in *The English Patient* since, for the explorers who contributors to the *Geographical Journal*, Zerzura was more than a place, it symbolized the love of exploration itself. The "halo of romance" surrounding the oasis[16] represented the only source of agreement among explorers who argued over the derivation of Zerzura ("the olive oasis",

"oasis of the blacks" or "oasis of the small birds"), its surmised place in Herodotus's *Histories*, *The Book of Hidden Pearls* and the writings of the nineteenth-century explorer I. G. Wilkinson, its geographical location (in Egypt, in Libya proper, or in the Northern Sudan?), and even whether it could or ought to be found.[17] The Zerzura explorers acknowledged that scant geographical knowledge would be gained by their enterprise and that only the Zerzura legend and that of the vanquishing of Cambyses' Persian army of 50,000 by a sandstorm leant "a romantic interest" to the South Libyan desert. The odds of locating either the army's remains or the Oasis were so small that "no one who did not love exploration for its own sake would ever trouble his head about them."[18] The historical Almasy linked the two legends by speculating that Cambyses' army would not have attempted to cross the Libyan desert had it not known of the Zerzura oases which would have made the crossing feasible.[19] While Almasy claimed to have solved the related mysteries by identifying the third and final Wadi of the Zerzura Oasis as the Wadi Hussein in 1935, members of his own and rival expeditions preferred to conceive of Zerzura as metonymic of the last blank space on the map that would always remain to be explored. Ralph Bagnold, founder of the Zerzura Dinner Club at the RGS, proclaimed that Zerzura would always remain elusive, "still to be discovered," for though with the passing of time it might "become smaller, more delicate and specialized," only with the elimination of "all difficulties of travel" would "Zerzura begin to decay."[20] Zerzura in this view equals the allure of the unknown. In a comparably philosophical vein Richard Bermann, chronicler of the expedition led by Almasy and Penderel (Madox), would express the hope that "the beautiful old legend will never quite be cleared up by a mere discovery."[21]

Seekers of Zerzura nonetheless differed fundamentally on whether to explore by camel or by motorcar and consequently on whether they sought the romance of pre-modern desert tribe cultures or that other romance of conquering the desert through the modern instruments and technology of exploration. In contrast with the historical Almasy's innovative use of the motorcar and airplane in desert exploration, Ondaatje's Almasy is cast in the mold of the traditionalists among the Zerzura explorers who pursued adventure and natural beauty rather than strictly the advancement of modern geography. Bill Kennedy Shaw, a member of the Zerzura Club, captured the oasis' appeal for the adventurous explorer when he acknowledged: "A psychologist would say, perhaps, that to take pleasure in deserts is a form of escapism, a surrender to the same impulses which made hermits of the early Christians, a refusal to face the unpleasant realities of modern life. He may be right."[22] It is under this rubric that Ondaatje presents the gathering at the RGS of his fictionalized Zerzura explorers, who clutching their "old maps" and handwritten notebooks get lost in the local London trains and "are not too comfortable with the etiquette of taxis, the quick, flat wit of bus conductors."[23] Ondaatje likens his "sunburned, exhausted" romancers of Zerzura to "Conrad's sailors,"[24] a comparison that deftly links Ralph Bagnold's description of his tired men emerging from the desert and the nostalgia for adventure of both Conrad's sea novels and his nonfiction.[25] Indeed the novel's introductory comparison of the Zerzura explorers in the twenties and thirties to the "river seekers" of the nineteenth century, flattering to the former in terms of scientific and cultural import, capitalizes both on the nostalgia of the RGS presidents Freshfield and Younghusband who believed the exploration of the Nile to be the society's golden age and on Conrad's account of his first childhood memories of explorers filling in the blanks of his map of Africa: "Regions unknown! My imagination could depict to itself there worthy, adventurous and devoted men, nibbling at the edges, attacking from north and south and east and west, conquering a bit of truth there and sometimes swallowed up by the mystery their hearts were so persistently set on unveiling."[26]

Ondaatje's apprehension of the romance of desert exploration and the fellowship it affords as an escape from the modern is borne out by the first journey of the fictional Almasy in *The English Patient* in search of Zerzura, a seven-day camel ride from Jaghbub to El Taj modeled not on an excursion of the historical Almasy (who neither explored this route nor used camels) but on the journey of Egyptian explorer A.M. Hassanein Bey of his journey from Jaghbub through Kufra to Darfur.[27] In Ondaatje's reimagined chronology of Almasy's quest for the lost oasis of Zerzura, it is during these fictional first excursions into the desert by camel between 1930 and 1932 (rather than the excursions by motorcar that Ondaatje pushes back to 1933 and later) that the explorers' encounter with the Bedouin teaches them how to become "nationless." Crisscrossing the desert at the same pace as the Bedouin, observing the "rivers of desert tribes, the most beautiful humans I've met," Almasy and the Zerzura explorers learn from the Bedouin "that the desert could not be claimed or owned" and hence acquire an indifference to the boundaries of modern nation-states.[28] The Bedouin caravan Almasy joins during a camel excursion, like caravans of times past that leave "nothing behind," teaches him and the other explorers how to "remove the clothing of our countries" and "disappear into landscape" and how "to slip across borders, not to belong to anyone, to any nation."[29] The journey borrowed from Hassanein Bey's experience thus provides the fictional Almasy with the pivotal initiation into the Bedouin-inspired cosmopolitanism that he will draw upon in educating Katherine, Kip, Hana and Caravaggio in the sensibility of the "international bastard." It forms the novel's foundational narrative of loss of nation, and it is echoed in the idealized use of the term "nomad" to denote other post-national characters at the Villa San Girolamo outside Florence.

In its romance of open spaces Hassanein Bey's cosmopolitanism resembles other contemporary accounts of the quest for lost oases in the Libyan Desert in the *Geographical Journal*, but it differs from these in its cultural sensitivity and political motivation. Fellows of the RGS would find familiar the desire to brave "a vast tract of unexplored desert [beyond Kufra] where no stranger from the outside world had yet penetrated," and the confession that "vague rumours of 'lost oases' that even the people of Kufra know only by hearsay and tradition" leant the expedition an "additional attractiveness."[30] This echoes the RGS's praise of the adventure of open spaces, and it is not surprising that the society awarded Hassanein Bey its Gold Medal for his quest for the Libyan desert's lost oases and his correction of the position of the Kufra oases.[31] Less familiar to the society's fellows was the Egyptian explorer's insistence that "any story of the Libyan desert would be incomplete without some consideration of the [religious order of the] Senussi" as "the most important influence in the region"[32] and his privileging of such knowledge as integral to the success of desert exploration. Hassanein Bey's expedition from Jaghbub through Kufra to Darfur in 1923 was inspired by a previous expedition to Kufra in 1916 to persuade Sayed Idris to exert his influence as head of the Senussi to prevent Badawi raids across Egypt's western frontier, and Bey's account of the 1923 expedition makes a strong case for the preservation of the autonomy of the Senussi, who acted as a moderating force for peace among the region's tribes. Hassanein Bey's account of his expedition thus reflects a distinct discourse of fellowship in which he acknowledges the crucial contribution of the "friendship" and "kind solicitude" of the Senussi leader.[33] An old friend of the Egyptian explorer's father, the Grand Senussi provided Hassanein Bey with the tracks which Hassanein Bey's caravan followed from the Siwa oasis to Jaghbub and with letters of recommendation that guaranteed him safe passage and hospitality in Jaghbub, Jalo and Kufra.[34] Hassanein Bey's discourse of exploration is singularly cosmopolitan in that it effectively argues that the "blank" spaces on Eastern maps possess rich histories of their own and social relations which the Western educated geographer must possess a familial intimacy to navigate:

> 1930. Our first journey, moving south from Jaghbub into the desert among the preserve of Zwaya and Majabra's tribes. A seven-day journey to El Taj. Madox and Bermann, four others. Some camels a horse and a dog. As we left they told us the old joke. "To start a journey in a sandstorm is good luck."

The opening lines of the novel's description of Almasy's 1930 journey from Jaghbub to El Taj, each closely paraphrased from Hassanein Bey's account of his 1923 journey, make evident the ways in which Ondaaatje transfers the experience of the fellowship that Hassanein Bey enjoys with his companions and Senussi guides and hosts to Almasy and his fellow Zerzura explorers. In place of Bey and his four named Egyptian and Libyan companions,[35] Ondaatje inserts Almasy, Madox, Bermann and four unnamed Arabs, though the mention of camels and "a horse and a dog" remains.[36] While Bey explains that the Badawi traditional saying, "to start a journey in sandstorm is good luck," simply makes a virtue of necessity,[37] Almasy, Penderel and Madox share a laugh at the phrase as an old explorers' joke. In this fashion Ondaatje further attributes to the explorers the playful banter that characterized Bey's camaraderie with the men of his caravan. The emphasis in Bey's account is on the necessity of keeping up the good spirits of the caravan, something which he felt could only be achieved through respect for Bedouin and Badawi customs, in particular ceremonies of hospitality and mealtime. If these are observed, Bey suggests, the men will march well and in good humour. Notably Bey also includes in his account jokes made at his expense as an important part of the comradeship necessary for a successful expedition. In contrast the humour of Almasy and the Zerzura explorers reinforces the fellowship between each other to the exclusion of the men in their service. In light of its original context the explorers' joke in the novel comes effectively at the expense of Badawi tradition. Elements of Bey's cosmopolitanism are appropriated but tweaked by Ondaatje to suit the de-politicized worldview articulated by his fictional Almasy, who proclaims *"deserts of Libya"* the "loveliest phrase I know" if one only "remove[s] politics."[38]

In contrast to the novel, Bey's account of his expedition reveals the importance of understanding the history and politics of this desert region in order to even begin the quest for the lost oasis. Before venturing to the "unexplored desert," Bey journeys west to Jalo and south to Jaghbub and Kufra following the sphere of influence of the Senussi, who he notes have located their schools strategically in order to bring peace between warring tribes.[39] Bey explains the tribal rivalries which have led the Egyptian government to bar its borders to the Zwaya, and he hopes that the Grand Senussi's efforts to establish peace in this region will continue through the renewal of the 1917 agreement with the Italian government which recognized the Grand Senussi's right to administer the affairs of this area. In *The English Patient* Ondaatje removes the intricacies and obstacles of geography and culture for his Cairo-based Zerzura explorers, who strangely set out from Jaghbub on the Libyan side of the border and impossibly reach Taj several hundred kilometers south (rather than the nearby Jalo) in seven days by camel (a journey which took Bey several weeks).[40] Most pertinently he strips the Hassanein Bey-inspired cosmopolitanism he attributes to the fictional Almasy of its political concerns with the Italian occupation of Libya, tribal rivalries and the self-determination of the Senussi. Ondaatje's selective use of the source material allows his "rivers of desert tribes" and Zerzura explorers to flow with ease across tribal, national and colonial boundaries even though Bey's account indicates they could not. In the universe of the novel it is this boundless mobility that allows the explorer to learn from the Bedouin how to forsake the pull of ethnic, linguistic and national belonging.

While Bey's familiarity with the religious order of the Senussi earned him safe passage and hospitality among the Badawi, Ondaatje's Zerzura explorers enjoy unexplained good fortune and a luxurious welcome among the Badawi on the route from Jaghbub to El Taj. Ondaatje attributes a preternatural and reciprocal affinity between the Zerzura explorers and the Bedouin by investing this bond with elements from Bey's interactions with the Bedouin of his caravan and his Senussi hosts. Most strikingly he transposes the welcoming feast offered by the Senussi to Bey inside the private quarters of the Senussi chief's labyrinthine house into the feast the Badawi of El Taj offer the Zerzura explorers in a town square in *The English Patient*:

> There was set before me a feast fit for the gods… lamb, rice, vegetables, delicious bread, rich Badawi cakes, sweet vinegar, sour milk, followed by coffee, milk with almond pulp beaten in it, and finally the ceremonial three glasses of tea, flavoured with amber, rose-water, and mint.[41]

> In the central square of El Taj we sat and ate lamb, rice, *badawi* cakes, and drank milk with almond pulp beaten into it. All this after the long wait for three ceremonial glasses of tea flavoured with amber and mint.[42]

Bey stressed the cultural specificity of this welcoming feast which was made possible only by the Senussi's introduction into the Kufra oasis of the cultivation of mint and roses "from which they make rose-water and mint essence, so essential in their ceremonies of hospitality."[43] Ondaatje in contrast exports not only Bey's private feast to the town's central square but extrapolates "an alley of clocks" and "street of barometers" for his Zerzura explorers to wander through from Bey's description of the Senussi chief's collection of clocks and barometers in his most luxurious room.[44] In effect he borrows from the familial bond of Bey and the Senussi to affirm the mutual public fascination of the Badawi of Taj and the Zerzura seekers. And yet the easy camaraderie Ondaatje spies between Bedouin and explorer runs counter to Bey's account of the Bedouins' suspicion that the explorer's map-making could be a prelude to conquest.[45]

If in his first desert expedition by camel, formative of his cosmopolitanism, Almasy is imbued with Bey's familial kinship with the Bedouin and the Senussi, in his last desert journey by foot from the Cave of Swimmers to Taj the Hungarian explorer exhibits the uncanny ability to navigate without instruments that Bey attributed to his Senussi guide in 1923:

> When the caravan is all but ready, I have a few words with the guide about the direction of our day's march. He draws a line on the sand and says there lies our way. I take a bearing of the line by my compass . . . On the whole the precaution proves unnecessary, however, for Senussi Bu Hassan goes as straight to his mark as a homing pigeon. Only in the middle of the day he sometimes wobbles a bit… He travels by his shadow, as he explains, "when the sun is high and the shadow lies between my feet" . . . There is one other hour of the day when the guide's task is a perplexing one. In the twilight hour between the setting of the sun and the appearance of the stars, all directions on the desert's vast disc are the same. . . . Once I caught the guide in the hour between sun and stars going almost 90? off direction.[46]

> No compass. Only moon and his shadow. He found the old stone marker from the past that located the direction of El Taj, north-northwest. He memorized the angle of his shadow and started walking. Seventy miles away was the souk with the street of clocks . . . There were two periods of time when he could not move. At noon, when the shadow was under him, and at twilight, between sunset and the appearance of the stars. Then everything on the disc of the desert was the same. If he moved, he might err as much as ninety degrees of his course.[47]

In the novel's narrative of the protagonist's education in a cosmopolitan sensibility (his becoming an "international bastard"), this completes the shift in which Almasy is first attributed with a preternatural bond with the Bedouin and then described as possessing the characteristic traits of the Senussi caravan guide. In his desert expeditions by camel, which the novel dates to the early 1930s, the unacknowledged borrowings from Bey provide an aura of historical authenticity to Almasy's progression from admirer of the desert tribes to member of a Bedouin caravan and preacher of their nationless ways. These borrowings underpin the implied contrast between his harmonious bond with the Bedouin and the sexual imperialism of Fenelon-Barnes, who joins a caravan only to tie a small Arab girl to the bed in his tent, and they explain the renewed communion between Almasy and the Bedouin after his plane is shot down over the desert. Bey's portrait of the Bedouin and the Senussi inform the novel's privileging of the nomad as the model for the "international bastard" at San Girolamo, where Almasy (in his guise as the mysterious "English patient") is absolved by Hana and ultimately even by Kip and Caravaggio of his perceived crime of handing over his maps of Libya to the Germans in exchange for a plane that would allow him to retrieve his lover's body from the Cave of Swimmers.

While Ondaatje gleans from Hassanein Bey details of Almasy's fictional desert journeys by camel and foot and elements of his worldview, the notion of cosmopolitanism the fictional Almasy is initiated into by the Bedouin in his camel expeditions is further shaped by an imperial romance constructed on the presumed fellowship between the British and the Bedouin. The romantic notion of an affinity between British officers and the Bedouin as the gentlemen warriors of the desert partook of the broader rhetorical assumption of the fellowship among martial races which informed eighteenth- and nineteenth-century discourses of British imperialism. In this vein the English diplomat Sir Rennell Rodd framed the appeal of Hassanein Bey's writings for the British by speculating "it is possible that the blood of his Bedouin forefathers made intimacy with them easier for him, since the Briton and the Bedouin not infrequently find in one another a certain kinship of instinct which compels their mutual regard."[48] The reviewer in the *Geographical Journal* of the Egyptian's book-length account of his journey would go one step further and praise the unprecedented "blend of East and West in its author": "if ever those 'twain' have met, it is in this travel book, the first written in the English of Balliol by an Arab of cosmopolitan experience and culture, who remains a fervent Moslem and a mystic."[49] For the reviewer Hassanein Bey cannot quite realize the goal of perfect authenticity – "that a Beduin should write of Beduins" – but succeeds in fulfilling the no less formidable aim of the marriage of the Bedouin and British sensibility: "that Hassenein is an Arab, a Moslem, and a mystic proved as essential to his success as that he is a man of prompt action, of Western science, and of cosmopolitan curiosity."[50] In this process the imperial romance of the kinship between the British and the Bedouin familiar from Victorian letters is transmuted into the language of the cosmopolitanism of geographical exploration – here, in the context of Hassanein Bey's quest for the lost oasis of Zerzura. Ondaatje's Almasy resembles the Hassanein Bey of the RGS reviewer in that he not only feels an affinity for the Bedouin but himself blends the best qualities of the European RGS explorer and Bedouin guide. Further, in Ondaatje's novel the presumed martial basis for the fellowship between British and Bedouin is preserved through the explanation of the wounded Almasy's value to the Bedouin caravan in terms of his ability to identify European weapons.[51] This martial fellowship between Almasy and the "gun tribe" that heals him is echoed in the friendship between Almasy and the Sikh sapper Kip as the two bond over knowledge of bomb disposal.[52]

An analysis of Ondaatje's acknowledged source material reveals the extent to which the cosmopolitanism attributed to Almasy and his fellow Zerzura seekers is shaped by romance and nostalgia. In *The English Patient* the romance of the fellowship of open spaces is projected onto the interwar exploration of the South Libyan desert, in the novel a period of boundless mobility in which explorers of all nations spill over borders like "rivers of desert tribes" from which they learn the irrelevance of the borders of modern nation-states.[53] The novel dates the breakdown of the fellowship of desert exploration among the Zerzura seekers to the outbreak of the Second World War, yet Ondaatje's sources make evident that the colonial scramble for South Libya between European powers was already underway in the twenties and early thirties and detail the difficulty of navigating the borders of modern nation states for both Bedouin and explorer. Hassanein Bey's account mentions the Italian occupation of Cyrenaica and Tripoli and describes the Bedouin suspicion of the activity of map-making in the context of the claims on Libya by Italy, France, Germany, Turkey and Britain.[54] The accounts of Penderel and Bermann, the source for the novel's depiction of Almasy's expeditions by motorcar, describe the hospitality Penderel and Almasy enjoyed for days at a time at the Italian missions at Kufra and 'Uweinat and encounters with Italian survey parties "occupied with map-making" and detail how at 'Uweinat Professor Ludovico de Caporiacco of the Italian mission was one of the first witnesses of Almasy's discovery of the Cave of Swimmers.[55] Ondaatje's acknowledged sources make explicit the difficulty of securing passage through the territory of a rival tribe or colonial power and the need for government sanction for each expedition, in contrast to the novel's statement that desert exploration was unofficial and "privately funded."[56]

The form of Ondaatje's borrowings from the accounts of the quest for Zerzura in the *Geographical Journal* and from Hassanein Bey's "Through Kufra to Darfur" suggest the limits of the novel's gestures towards a post-colonial sensibility in the passages that describe the fellowship of open spaces of the desert explorers. In 1989 a note in the *Geographical Journal* explained that the existence of an uninhabited oasis believed to be a candidate for Zerzura "had been known for many decades before it was finally 'discovered' and its position fixed in 1925." It suggested that the shallow well Almasy found a decade later in Wadi Hussein thirty-three kilometres north-east had been made in 1904 by a "Bedai guide, Bidi Awdi," although the well was "not scientifically located until Almasy published his map in 1935."[57] Three years later *The English Patient* appeared to promise a similar ironic revision of Almasy's claims to have discovered Zerzura in a passage that remarks on the tendency of the explorers of the Geographical Society to write of "the first step by a white man across a great river, the first sight (by a white eye) of a mountain that has been there forever."[58] Expectations of a postcolonial interpretation of the quest for Zerzura in the twenties and thirties are heightened in the novel through two passages that recall Bey's claim that no account of venturing into the "unexplored desert" of Libya could be complete without a consideration of the history of its peoples and in particular the Senussi:

> The desert [had been] given a hundred shifting names long before Canterbury existed, long before battles and treaties quilted Europe and the East.[59]

> I was walking not in a place where no one had walked before but in a place where there were sudden, brief populations over the centuries – a fourteenth century army, a Tebu caravan, the Senussi raiders of 1915.[60]

Yet the suggested postcolonial revision of the internationalism of Almasy and his fellow European explorers never fully materializes.

The novel does not sustain the skepticism towards Almasy's claim of discovery expressed in the notes in the *Geographical Journal* from the thirties to the eighties, nor does it share the curiosity about the history and fate of the Bedouin, Tebu and Senussi manifested by contemporary Zerzura explorers and authors such as Hassanein Bey, R.F. Peel, W.J. Harding King, and Pat Clayton.[61] In contrast to the original travelogues of the historical Almasy, the novel does not condescend to name and personalize the Bedouin and Sanusi members and guides of the fictional Almasy's expeditions.[62] All it has to offer is the eroticization of the Bedouin, first as "the most beautiful humans I've met in my life" in the fictional Almasy's recollections of his desert expeditions by camel, and later (when Almasy is reabsorbed into a Bedouin community after he is shot down over the desert) in the form of the sexual communion literally enacted by the offering by the Bedouin to Almasy of the sperm of a young boy the explorer had admired dancing and "arousing himself."[63] This form of "positive stereotyping" appears more in tune with the imagination of the French Orientalist master Gerôme than with a progressive postcolonial politics. This context makes salient the opportunism of Ondaatje's transference of what the contemporary authors of the RGS recognized as Hassanein Bey's singular cosmopolitanism to the fictional Almasy. Bey's own story lacked neither postcolonial significance nor novelistic possibilities: the Oxford-educated Egyptian diplomat and explorer corrected the position of the Kufra Oasis, set in motion the quest for the Zerzura oasis by RGS explorers in the twenties and thirties, and published an account of his RGS Gold Medal-winning expedition heralded in book form as one of the foremost travelogues of the day. In *The English Patient* the "grand old man of the 1923 expedition" only makes an appearance as the host of the party where Katherine seduces Almasy.[64] To what end does Ondaatje appropriate Bey's words, experiences, worldview and skills and those of his Sanusi guide and attribute these to Almasy? The lack of any acknowledgment of these borrowings preempts a redemptive reading along the lines of an intended postmodern irony or play on Almasy's impostures or disguises. Rather the borrowed nature of the elements that constitute Almasy's cosmopolitanism speaks to the superficial and opportunistic engagement with non-Western cultures in the text. Such a trivialization of non-Western knowledge is exemplified by Ondaatje's transformation of the Badawi saying regarding the good fortune of riding out in a sandstorm into an old explorers' joke.

Ondaatje recently described how in his research on the historical Almasy he came across a narrative of cosmopolitanism forged in the culture of desert exploration in the 1930s and lost in the war that followed:

> I went to the Royal Geographic Society and I decided I should find out about this man and who he was and who his associates were I found this wonderful desert culture of the thirties where archeologists, explorers and scientists were working from various countries in the world and then this group eventually scattered all over the world and started fighting each other.[65]

Disappointed at finding little of value on Almasy and convinced that the mystery of his loyalty as a spy would remain unresolved, Ondaatje chose to capture through the character of Almasy the "the general ambience of the desert in the 1930s" and its cosmopolitan ethos.[66] The principal insight into the *The English Patient* shed by an analysis of Ondaatje's sources and his use of them is that while they can be construed to corroborate the doomed romantic fellowship among desert explorers of different nationalities, they also document national loyalties and rivalries. The vision of a "wonderful desert culture" where explorers disregarded their national allegiances until the outbreak of war is present only in the nostalgic sentiments of the RGS presidents of the interwar period. This romantic spirit is difficult to square with the accounts of the Egyptian, British and Austro Hungarian explorers used by Ondaatje, which detail Italian colonialism in Libya, the Bedouin suspicion of map-makers and explorers, and the barriers to the circulation of Bedouin tribes and geographers' expeditions across tribal, national and colonial borders. In this context it becomes evident that Ondaatje, who borrows far more substantially than he acknowledges from the accounts of the RGS explorers, has taken sides in the debates he encountered in the minutes of the society. Ondaatje's novelistic presentation of an interwar Libyan desert of unencumbered mobility for Bedouin and explorer echoes the idealistic conception by past RGS presidents of geographical exploration as inherently cosmopolitan and in particular the Marquess's affirmation that this pursuit recognizes neither physical nor intellectual boundaries. Ondaatje has borrowed selectively from the explorers' account to further the old-fashioned conception of geography as an adventure of blank spaces on maps.

NOTES

1. Hugh Robert Mill, RGS Vice-president, "The Centenary Meeting: Addresses on the History of the Society," *The Geographical Journal,* Vol. 76, No. 6 (Dec., 1930): 458.

2. Sir Charles Close, RGS President, "The Centenary Meeting," 457.

3. The Marquess of Zetland, RGS President (1922-1925), "The Centenary Meeting," 470.

4. The Marquess of Zetland, "The Centenary Meeting," 471.

5. *The English Patient* (Toronto: Vintage, 1993): 139, 261.

6. Orde Wingate, "In Search of Zerzura," *The Geographical Journal*, Vol. 83, No. 4 (April 1934), 281.

7. Douglas Freshfield, "The Centenary Meeting," 462.

8. Sir Francis Younghusband, "The Centenary Meeting," 466.

9. Sir Francis Younghusband, "The Centenary Meeting," 468.

10. Sir Francis Younghusband, "The Centenary Meeting," 468.

11. Michael Ondaatje, *The English Patient*, 134.

12. Michael Ondaatje, *The English Patient*, 304.

13. The exception is the author's acknowledgment of "Hassanein Bey's wonderful account" of desert storms (137, 304), though it should be noted that the three paragraphs preceding the italicized quotation and the three following (136-138) are also closely paraphrased from Bey with no acknowledgment (as discussed below). See Ondaatje (136-138) cf. A. M. Hassanein Bey, "Through Kufra to Darfur," *The Geographical Journal*, Vol. 64, No. 4 (Oct., 1924), 280-281.

14. Most notably Bruce Robbins "The Village of the Liberal Managerial Class," in Vinay Dharwadker, ed. *Cosmopolitan Geographies: New Locations in Literature and Culture* (London: Routledge, 2001).

15. Steven Totosy de Zepetnek, "Michael Ondaatje's *The English Patient*, 'History,' and the Other," *CLCWeb: Comparative Literature and Culture: A WWWeb Journal* 1:4 (1999), http://clcwebjournal.lib. purdue.edu /clcweb99-4/totosy99-2.html> (30 September 2005).

16. The phrase is W.J. Harding King's in "The Lost Oases," *The Geographical Journal*, Vol. 75, No. 1 (Jan., 1930): 61.

17. A useful summary of the debates until 1930 is provided by the editor's introductory note, "The Zerzura Problem" (48) and the three essays that follow it: De Lancey's Forth's "More Journeys in Search of Zerzura" (48-59), E.A. Johnson-Pasha's "Zerzura" (59-61) and W.J. Harding King's "The Lost Oases," *The Geographical Journal*, Vol. 75, No. 1 (Jan., 1930): 61-64.

18. Orde Wingate, "In Search of Zerzura," *The Geographical Journal*, Vol. 83, No. 4 (April 1934), 281-2.

19. Bermann, "Historic Problems of the Libyan Desert," 459.

20. R.A. Bagnold, *Libyan Sands: Travels in a Dead World* (Haag, 1987 [reprint, London, 1935]), 284.

21. Richard Bermann, "Historic Problems of the Libyan Desert," 463.

22. Bill Kennedy Shaw quoted in Saul Kelly's *The Hunt for Zerzura: The Lost Oasis and the Desert War* (London: John Murray, 2002): 65.

23. *The English Patient*, 133.

24. *The English Patient*, 133.

25. See in particular "Geography and Some Explorers," *Last Essays* (London: J.M. Dent & Sons Ltd., 1926), 1-31; and Conrad's preface to Richard Curle's *Into the East: Notes on Burma and Malaya* (London: St. Martin's Press, 1923), ix-xxv.

26. "Geography and Some Explorers," 19-20.

27. A. M. Hassanein Bey, "Through Kufra to Darfur," *The Geographical Journal*, Vol. 64, No. 4 (Oct., 1924), 273-291.

28. *The English Patient*, 138-139.

29. *The English Patient*, 138-139.

30. A.M. Hassanein Bey, "Through Kufra to Darfur," *The Geographical Journal*, Vol. 64, No. 4 (Oct., 1924), 274.

31. Forty miles South/ South-East of its location in previous maps.

32. Hassanein Bey, "Through Kufra to Darfur," 277.

33. Hassanein Bey, "Through Kufra to Darfur," 276.

34. "Through Kufra to Darfur," 276.

35. "I had four men of my own by this time – Abdullahi and Ahmed, Egyptian Nubians whom I had brought from Cairo; Hamad, engaged at Sollum; and Ismail, whom I picked up at Siwa," "Through Kufra to Darfur," 280.

36. Cf. "Through Kufra to Darfur," 283.

37. "Through Kufra to Darfur," 280.

38. *The English Patient*, 257.

39. "Through Kufra to Darfur," 278.

40. "Through Kufra to Darfur," 273-291.

41. "Through Kufra to Darfur," 288.

42. *The English Patient*, 138.

43. "Through Kufra to Darfur," 289.

44. "On the walls hung the well-remembered collection of clocks, barome-

ters, and thermometers," "Through Kufra to Darfur," 288. Cf. *The English Patient*, 137, 249.

45. "In the taking of my observations I had to be cautious, for the Badawi are suspicious of anything so elaborately scientific-looking as a theodolite. They were sure to say that I was making a map with a view to coming back and conquering their land." "Through Kufra to Darfur," 283.

46. "Through Kufra to Darfur," 284-285.

47. *The English Patient*, 249.

48. Sir Rennell Rodd, "Introduction" to A.M. Hassanein Bey's *The Lost Oases* (London: Thornton Butterworth, 1925): viii.

49. D.G.H., Rev. of *The Lost Oases* by A.M. Hassanein Bey, *The Geographical Journal*, Vol. 66, No. 6 (Dec., 1925) 551.

50. D.G.H., Rev. of *The Lost Oases* by A.M. Hassanein Bey, *The Geographical Journal*, Vol. 66, No. 6 (Dec., 1925) 552, 551.

51. *The English Patient*, 257.

52. "Kip, hearing from Caravaggio that the patient knew about guns, had begun to discuss the search for bombs with the Englishman. He had come up to the room and found him a reservoir of information about Allied and enemy weaponry… Soon they were drawing outlines of bombs for each other and talking the theory of each specific circuit." *The English Patient*, 88-89.

53. *The English Patient*, 138.

54. "Through Kufra to Darfur," 279.

55. "Historic Problems of the Libyan Desert," 460, 461.

56. *The English Patient*, 133.

57. Vance Haynes, "Oyo: A 'Lost' Oasis of the Southern Libyan Desert," *Geographical Journal*, Vol. 155, No. 2, July 1989, 189.

58. *The English Patient*, 141.

59. *The English Patient*, 138-139.

60. *The English Patient*, 141.

61. See in addition to the history of the Sanusi in "Through Kufra to Darfur," W.J. Harding King's "The Libyan Desert from Native Information," *The Geographical Journal*, Vol. 42, No. 3 (Sept., 1913), 277-283; R.F. Peel, "The Tibu Peoples and the Libyan Desert," *The Geographical Journal*, Vol. 100, No. 2 (Aug., 1942), 73-87; and Bill Kennedy Shaw's account of Pat Clayton's rescue of Sanusi refugees after the Italian bombardment and invasion of Kufra in the Times, 25 May 1931, quoted in Saul Kelly's *The Hunt for Zerzura: The Lost Oasis and the Desert War* (London: John Murray, 2002): 31-32. It should be noted that the *Geographical Journal*, again anticipating Ondaatje, did not always indulge this curiosity of its contributors, printing a note to Peel's wartime paper on the Tibu: "Owing to paper restrictions it has been necessary to omit the first part of this paper, comprising a summary of the historical evidence, and of references to

native peoples in the records of modern expeditions to the Libyan Desert" (75).

62. As noted by Eugene Sensenig-Dabbous, "Will the Real Almasy Please Stand Up! Transporting Central European Orientalism via *The English Patient*," *Comparative Studies of South Asia, Africa and the Middle East*, 24:2 (2004): 172.

63. *The English Patient* 138, 22.

64. *The English Patient*, 236.

65. Anthony Minghella and Saul Zaentz, *The English Patient: Miramax Collector's Series*, "About Michael Ondaatje," "About Writing the Novel" (Miramax Home Entertainment, 2005), 4:05-5:00.

66. "About Michael Ondaatje," "About Writing the Novel," ibid.

John Clement Ball

Canadian Crusoes from Sea to Sea: The Oceanic Communities of Douglas Glover's Elle *and Yann Martel's* Life of Pi

In his 1986 lecture "What is a Classic?" the South African writer J.M. Coetzee considers why T.S. Eliot, in *his* 1944 lecture of the same name, chose the *Aeneid* as the "originary classic" of Western civilization (3). Eliot, Coetzee argues, enlisted Virgil's Roman epic to support his view of a unitary Western civilization that, for Eliot, was descended from and still sustained by the Roman Catholic Church – with some prior assistance from its political wing, the Holy Roman Empire. In that context, it is also significant that Eliot's chosen classic should be a tale of seafaring is also. As the Mediterranean was to the Romans, the sea is the space that most Empires have had to master: – to transform from a space space that separates different peoples and protects them from each other – a barrier – a barrier – to a space that links them, a conduit that enables a powerful few to access and rule vast numbers of others on distant continents. The earth's oceans, – which can be seen as one big ocean, – connect its people, and there is perhaps no greater symbol of the world's oneness (or its people's restlessness) than its oceans.[1]

Coetzee's essay, written the same year his novel *Foe* was published, goes on to meditate on the meaning of "classic" and ends with a rallying cry to fellow scholars. "The classic," he writes, "defines itself by surviving. Therefore the interrogation of the classic, no matter how hostile, is part of the history of the classic, inevitable and even to be welcomed." Indeed, he says, criticism is "duty-bound to interrogate the classic: . . . rather than being the foe of the classic, criticism . . . may be what the classic uses to define itself and ensure its survival" (16). In this essay, the point of origin of my own critical duties is both the conspicuous, punning use of the word "foe" in that last sentence and the essay on *Robinson Crusoe* that follows on the very next page of Coetzee's *Stranger Shores*. Daniel Defoe's oceanic tale of shipwreck, mastery, and survival, which critical consensus has deemed not just the first English novel – an originary classic, if you like – but also a "modern myth" (James 1), has itself survived for three centuries by being regularly interrogated in both imaginative and critical writing. It has been a magnet for postcolonial writers and critics; indeed, Brett McInelly remarks that "some of the more provocative postcolonial analyses of Defoe's novel appear not in criticism but in postcolonial literature such as Derek Wolcott's [*sic*] *Pantomime* and J.M. Coetzee's *Foe*, works that 'write back' to Defoe's 'master narrative of empire'" (1). Those two texts – and the postcolonial critics who engage them or their *Ur*-text directly – highlight the themes of power, authority, and entitlement in Defoe's archetypal narrative, as well as those of race and language – all themes at the heart of postcolonial criticism.

While Canadian writers haven't traditionally been as compelled by Crusoe as, say, their Caribbean counterparts, two very recent Canadian novels respond imaginatively, if less directly than Coetzee and Walcott, to *Robinson Crusoe*. A century and a half after Catherine Parr Traill wrote *Canadian Crusoes* (1851), Douglas Glover's *Elle* (2003) and Yann Martel's *Life of Pi* (2001) adapt *Crusoe*'s main elements in ways that not only address the aforementioned postcolonial themes but also offer fresh perspectives on Canada's history and contemporary communal relations. John Thieme has described Robinson Crusoe's enduring appeal as, in part, the attraction of "playing the role of Adam . . . in Eden, creating the world all over again, a reading that has particular resonance with regard to the New World milieu of the text" (55). Published at the beginning of the new millennium, and set respectively at the beginning of Canada's history as Europe's "New World" and in the early years of our contemporary era of official multiculturalism, *Elle* and *Life of Pi* are new enough that they have not yet been critically analyzed within the so-called Robinsonade tradition, apart from references in reviews. As these award-winning[2] Canadian novels creatively revisit Crusoe's originary narrative, and the ever-popular shipwreck and sea-deliverance genres more generally, they invite scrutiny through three overlapping lenses: first, of Canada's re-visioning of itself in recent decades as a nation of many cultures, including those of its aboriginal peoples and its non-European immigrants; second, of postcolonial theory's increased emphasis, beginning in the 1990s, on the mutuality and reciprocity (as opposed to the unilateral hierarchy) of colonialism's power relations and transformative effects; and third, of the ocean as a relational, conjoining space associated, among its manifold historical and cultural significations, with transformation and fluid identities.

The motto on Canada's coat of arms is "a mari usque ad mare": from sea to sea, though nowadays our politicians favour the more terrestrial and inclusive "from coast to coast to coast." Either way, Canada is represented as a nation that begins and ends at the oceans that link it to the rest of the world. Doing so may rather conveniently elide that other, southern extent of the nation's territory, but those five Latin words, in what they choose to name and not name, also privilege the framing seas over the implied but nonetheless unsignified land. Traditionally, when literary critics ask how distinctively Canadian preoccupations, attitudes, and anxieties infuse and unite our collective literary endeavours, they have found the answer in our attitudes to our terrestrial spaces and our ways of inhabiting them – physically, psychologically, imaginatively. Glover's and Martel's seafaring narratives place the ocean as a literal and symbolic space at the centre of their visions of Canada and Canadian community. *Elle*, like *Robinson Crusoe*, spans the Atlantic, while *Life of Pi* traverses the Pacific; all three books begin and end on land but, like the *Aeneid*, are defined by the ocean. As these two recent novels rewrite and relocate Defoe's classic from sea to sea, the oceanic nature of their unique imaginations makes them important specimens not just for the scattered cottage industry of Crusoe-watchers, but for postcolonial criticism and Canadian self-understanding as well.

"Like Odysseus embarked for Ithaca," Coetzee writes, "Robinson Crusoe with his parrot and umbrella has become a figure in the collective consciousness of the West, transcending the book which – in its multitude of editions, translations, imitations, and adaptations . . . – celebrates his adventures. Having once pretended to belong to history, he finds himself in the sphere of myth" (17). But if, in Pierre Macherey's words, Defoe's novel "initiates . . . the theme of the man on an island" (240), Crusoe is not just a modern point of origin but an ancient archetype whose progenitors stretch back for millennia. Tales of sea voyages and disasters feature in Western culture's oldest stories – from Noah and Jonah to Odysseus and Aeneas – but Defoe's text inaugurated a vogue for narratives of seafaring, shipwreck, island survival, and deliverance in the eighteenth century that has never disappeared: in the current short century alone, witness not just novels like *Life of Pi* and *Elle* but a film like *Castaway* and, on television, the *Survivor* series. The widely assorted texts influenced by *Crusoe* selectively, and with varied seriousness and success, address a variety of themes found in the original: isolation and self-discovery; sin and redemption; providence and faith; survival as a test of human ingenuity and skill; mastery of the self and of an alien environment and peoples. Such narratives often have the appeal of a controlled experiment: put this person (or small group) into this isolated situation under these extraordinary conditions and see what happens. In some cases, such as *Crusoe* and *Life of Pi*, the experiment purports to show humanity at its best, rising admirably to the challenge; in others, such as *Lord of the Flies* (1954), *The Island of Dr. Moreau* (1896), or the fourth book of *Gulliver's Travels* (1726) (to name one from each of the previous three centuries), the result is a pessimistic view of human degeneracy.

The drama of colonial intervention, however much it may have brought out the best and the worst in its actors, never took place under the controlled conditions of a theatre or laboratory. But part of the appeal of Crusoe's novel has always been its audacious and optimistic distillation of colonial relations – messy, violent, and unpredictable as they are – into the story of a single man achieving peaceful dominion over a single island and, until quite late, a single male other. From an experiment God has imposed as punishment for Crusoe's "original sin" – usurping control over his life – Crusoe's castaway existence gradually becomes an experiment that he, having embraced God and improved himself in other ways, can control, in part *because* he is so long outside the sphere of human society. In his confident mastery of the island and of Friday, the ideally acquiescent and grateful subject, Crusoe becomes, as James Joyce once described him, "the true prototype of the British colonist, as Friday . . . is the symbol of the subject races" (356). Later, Edward Said would call Defoe's novel the prototype of the realistic English novel and, not coincidentally, its protagonist "the founder of a new world" (70). An attribution of origins and beginnings seems unavoidable in discussing *Crusoe*, and McInelly's article goes beyond Said to argue that Defoe's book "indicates ways in which British colonial history made the genre of the novel possible" (2). The enlarged sense of self that Crusoe's singular salvation and long isolation instills in him gives him the self-assurance to rule others when they arrive, McInelly says; this expanded, confident self represents "precisely the mindset" that "an expanding empire . . . would require" (5). He argues that the realistic novel is also made possible by that sense of self-importance, premised as it is on the notion that the ordinary individual's daily activities, thoughts, and feelings are, like Crusoe's, worth reading about in detail.

Thus *Robinson Crusoe* heralded both the novel and an incipient empire that didn't yet fully exist at the time; in McInelly's words, *Crusoe* "stands as an allegory or figure of colonialism, not an exhibit of it" (3). Indeed, it only *as* an allegory that Defoe's novel can purport to represent colonial rule at all; relations in real colonial contact zones were (and are) never so simple and straightforward. Some territories may be as hospitable and adaptable to the colonizers' needs, and individual others will prove as pleasingly obedient and receptive to having a master, a name, a language, and a religion unilaterally imposed on them as Friday does, but the immensely varied lands and communities of people Empire invaded manifestly did not. Defoe's presumptive fantasy of English supremacy confidently claimed and gratefully accepted is so baldly steeped in racial and cultural superiority that it demands a postcolonial response. And if that response isn't an outright condemnation – as when Biodun Jeyifo calls it the "classic 'megatext' of Eurocentrism" (114) – Defoe's novel may become the source-text for playful reimaginings of its archetypal figures that speak to the postcolonial condition. Precisely because they are so schematically and allegorically opposed, Crusoe and Friday cry out to be corrected or at least complicated. In texts like Walcott's *Pantomime* (1980) or Sam Selvon's *Moses Ascending* (1975), they become contemporary figures whose old racial identities and hierarchical relations are rendered topsy-turvy in a spirit of playful, irreverent comedy and satire. In Coetzee's *Foe* (1986) they are deconstructed in a metafictional meditation on power as a function of race, gender, class, language, and authorship. In Walcott's essay "The Figure of Crusoe" and his various poems on inspired by Defoe, Crusoe becomes a complex, multifaceted figure for the shipwrecked artist on the New World island faced with the challenge of making things – names, a local language, a literature, a culture – from the dislocations, losses, and absences of the past. His creative responsibility is determined and defined by the ocean as the space where West Indian history happened. As Walcott's poetic persona, Crusoe represents the various groups whose oceanic and terrestrial experiences contributed to that brutal history and to the new culture that must be built out of it and, in a sense, in spite of it.

This vision of the ocean as a space of historical and inherited relations is not unlike that of Paul Gilroy in *The Black Atlantic*, for whom the Atlantic, site of the middle passage and of postimperial migration and resettlement, is *the* space of black history. Encouraging his readers to view the Atlantic as "one single, complex unit of analysis in their discussions of the modern world and [to] use it to produce an explicitly transnational and intercultural perspective" (15), Gilroy chooses for his symbol of a collaborative cultural history the ships that crisscrossed the ocean. As "the mobile elements that stood for the shifting spaces in between the fixed places they connected" (16), the ships become figures also for the unstable, transient, mutable identities that have resulted. Similarly, scholars in the growing field of Atlantic history are apt to see the early modern Atlantic world as the first ever "hemispheric 'community,'" whose constituent societies affected each other to such an extent that they became "fundamentally different from what they would have been without participation in the new transatlantic network" (D. Eltis qtd. in Bailyn 59). Ian Baucom also goes beyond black history and identity to see the Atlantic more generally as the site of what he calls a "circumambient modernity"; careful study of its "complex network of historical and cultural traffic" promises a "rerouting of fixed categories of knowledge" (4, 5). The ocean, like Walcott and his ocean-crossing Crusoe figure, therefore takes us beyond fixed identities and relationships; as a physical space of transportation and transformation, the sea constantly mixes and combines its own elements and those on the shores it washes. And it invites us to think of the mutual, fluid connections between and within separate spaces and peoples. Glover's version of Crusoe in *Elle* is a postcolonial exemplar of this sense of the oceanic.

Elle is a Governor General's Award-winning historical novel based loosely on the story of a young French woman named Marguerite who was marooned on an island in the Gulf of St. Lawrence by her uncle, Sieur de Roberval, during Jacques Cartier's third voyage to Canada in 1542. She survived over two years before her rescue and return to Europe. If, as Coetzee claims, "The disobedience that Crusoe claims as his original sin is . . . a precondition of the interest in his story" (20), then it is apt that Glover's unnamed heroine (referred to hereafter as "Elle") opens her narrative with a lively description of a rather seasick sexual encounter with her lover Richard – for which sinful disobedience her stern Calvinist uncle punishes her. (As the nineteenth-century historian Francis Parkman rather primly notes in his account of Marguerite's abandonment, Richard's "love was too well requited" (227). Unlike Crusoe's, Elle's punishment is inflicted by human rather than divine authority, and her story departs from his in other significant ways while constantly reminding us of it. As she heads into banishment along with Richard and her nurse, Bastienne, Elle remarks that her uncle "has decided to endow me with a fief, a duchy, . . . a colonial outpost in the new land of Canada, wherein I may purify my soul of its noxious vagrancy" (27). Then, echoing Crusoe's designation of himself as "King" and "Lord of the whole Island" (Defoe 116), she calls her new home "my little island kingdom" (Glover 35), making sure, as she gets off the boat, that she is "the first French woman to set foot in this world, … the first colonist in Canada" (37). It is hard to say if she is being naïvely Eurocentric or slyly ironic here; Glover's playful use of anachronisms – do we think of her as alluding to Defoe's novel or anticipating it? – makes Elle seem to be both of her time and of ours. However we read these statements of possessive entitlement to the island on which she's about to be stranded, her journey in the novel will take her to a wholly different, even contemporary re-visioning of her place in the New World.

She begins quite conventionally, again echoing Crusoe and, perhaps, Walcott. After achieving landfall, she calls Richard "a new Adam" and herself "the new Eve – expelled from the garden (the General's ship, miniature of my civilization) into the world beyond (read wilderness) for my sin" (39, 40). There is a whole Canadian literary and critical tradition behind that statement: as W.H. New explains it, at times of first contact "binary paradigm[s]" such as "garden vs wilderness, heavenly vs. hellish" sustained perceived hierarchies "by constructing limits to social and intellectual options, as though these limits were given or 'natural' or axiomatic" (*Land* 22). They may be natural to the young Frenchwoman initially, but they will not remain so for long. At that same moment of arrival Elle emphasizes the newly arrived threesome's absolute silence, as if, she says, "the ship's departure has robbed us of the power of speech" (39). Richard may be an Adam but he is, in her words, "dumb and useless" – not the namer of things his biblical namesake is – and Bastienne, normally "a font of malicious gossip, salacious tales, erotic arcana" and the like, is similarly bereft of words (39). But this silence, this absence of language, however temporary, is symbolically important at this moment of transition from one world to the other. The Old World's association with "civilization" has just five pages earlier been undercut by Elle's ironic description of the ship's men, "Civilization's vanguard," as "mostly one-eyed, impoverished, limping, lousy, raggedy, snaggle-toothed dregs, led by a captious and judgemental social climber" (35). In that context, leaving civilization doesn't sound so bad, and greeting the new with silence may at least allow something more promising to begin taking its place. Robert Kroetsch and others have articulated the importance of silence – and what Kroetsch calls un-naming – to a New World aesthetic (e.g., see "Unhiding" 17). It is interesting that Elle, the only nameless character of the three, is the one who survives. Richard and Bastienne do not last long, perhaps because, rather than letting the new be heard in that silence, they try to impose too much of the Old World – witness Richard's obsessive and futile building of tennis courts or Bastienne's lack of "imagination other than the fantastical erotic variety," which means, Elle laments, that the nurse "cannot even find solace in seeing herself, as I do, as part of some tragic drama" (55).

The characters do go on to speak (though dialogue is sparse), but this temporary silence or failure of language anticipates other undoings in the realm of religion and identity. As a teenager back in France, Elle recalls, "I loved God and myself and despised Protestants and heretics" (31) – echoing both Crusoe's egocentrism and, albeit ironically, his born-again Protestantism. But on arrival on the island she immediately perceives it as "a place where the old definitions, words themselves, no longer apply" – as "a place without God" that makes her (unlike Crusoe's newly expansive self) feel "suddenly tiny on the edge of this vast, unknown and inscrutable continent" (38). After a week, with her body shrinking from starvation, both her sense of self and of God are defined by absence and loss: "I am no longer beautiful, or French, or related to anyone, or learned," she says, followed by "On the eighth day, it occurs to me that there may be no God at all" (45). This dismantling of the self and its support structures in the wilderness, reminiscent of Margaret Atwood's unnamed heroine in *Surfacing* (1972), combines with the deaths of her companions to make Elle much more receptive than Defoe's hero when, one page after a dream involving cannibalism, she discovers footprints in the snow. In contrast to Crusoe's terror at the footprint he finds, she is excited by this discovery; she feels "suddenly not dead. It's almost as good as having a social life" (61). So open to otherness is she that when she encounters a polar bear she speaks to it, though it doesn't reply, leading her to say, like a precocious postcolonialist, "This is the trouble when two worlds collide: It is difficult to discern the identity of the other" (69). The bear opens its mouth not to speak but to eat her; instead, as it opens its jaws, it collapses dead on top of her. By the time the human other who made the footprints arrives, an aboriginal hunter named Itslk, the starving Elle has eaten the bear's heart and crawled inside its guts for warmth, where she dreams of herself as a bear.

That climbing inside the bear, that rebirth through a merging with and into the other, is the defining image of the novel. In her relations with Itslk and then other indigenous peoples, she will undergo a sea-change in perception; as she gains weight and a new society, the remainder of her stay on the island, and later on the mainland, will be defined by a new kind of knowing associated with indigenous valuing of dreaming, and with transformation into a new kind of hybrid bear-woman. Where Crusoe establishes mastery and hierarchy over the indigenous other, imposing an Old World name, racial order, and religious doctrine onto the New, Elle claims she has "entered [Itslk's] dream world and established a colony there" (98) – inside the other's modes of perception. Whereas the asexual Crusoe comes to a kind of sexless love for Friday that never threatens the unequal terms of their relationship, the lusty, bawdy Elle writes that "Founding a colony in the New World is like the act of love. You make camp in the heart of the other. Nothing is the way you expected it. You have to learn another language. . . . You are not the same as you were before you fell in love. When it's over, you leave part of yourself behind" (108). There is a sense of humility and reciprocity – a recognition of give and take, of mutual gains and losses – in this view of colonization that is unlike anything in *Robinson Crusoe*. It is also unlike anything Jacques Cartier or Sieur de Roberval brought to their first encounters. Cartier's commission for his third voyage depicted the New World as "possessed by savage peoples living without the knowledge of God and without the use of reason" (*Voyages* 135); and de Roberval's commission as first Governor of Canada was to bring those lands "into our [French] possession, through friendly means or amicable arrangements, if possible, and [if not] through force of arms, violence, and all other hostile means" (*Voyages* 146).

As Elle surrenders a major part of her consciousness to local peoples' ways of knowing and being, their basis in dreams creates in her something like the feeling of unbounded limitlessness that Freud called the "oceanic" feeling. She describes her new self's "sudden fluidity" as "one effect of entering a New World" (137); "I am the herald of the new," she announces later (141), "infected with otherness" (157), "a citizen of neither the New World nor the Old" (165). It is the privilege of Glover's twenty-first-century consciousness and penchant for anachronism that he can make her both respond in this way and then, in describing her experience of hybridity, anticipate the postcolonial discourses a contemporary intellectual might use to describe it. As Herb Wyile notes in his review of *Elle*, the novel "portrays contact as a transaction much more complicated than a simple, unilateral imposition of colonial power" (133): this, he writes, is "contact as a mutual infection, a reciprocal destabilization of New World and Old World cosmologies" (132). The fluid identity Elle adopts and the mutuality of her cross-cultural relationships can be symbolized by the ocean that separates and joins those two worlds, which she crosses to get from one to the other, and on which her island "colony" is de facto located – she may be in the St. Lawrence, the "Great River of Canada," she says, but "I cannot see the other side of its huge mouth. It looks and acts like the sea or ocean" (35).[3] As she absorbs elements of the colonized into herself, she embraces indigenous ways of seeing in a way few Europeans did; as New writes, "For most European observers, indigenous mythologies represented a primitive past rather than an alternative future" (*Land* 71).[4] Through the lens of a contemporary consciousness, Elle provides a glimpse of how New World history might have been different if its actors had, like she, opened themselves to that influence and recognized its transforming presence. Such recognition eluded Crusoe and his author in their time, and it eluded Cartier and de Roberval in theirs. In our conflicted, imbalanced relations with Native peoples in Canada today, and in our larger struggles with what Charles Taylor calls "the politics of recognition" that underlie multiculturalism, Canadians are still contending with the tragic fallout of that failure to recognize the dignity and worth of others.

Elle writes after her return to France, "We change ourselves by plunging into the thick of things (a wife, a lover, a New World). We change ourselves or die" (194). Pi Patel, the Indian boy who drifts across the

Pacific in a lifeboat with a hungry Bengal Tiger named Richard Parker, learns that same lesson in *Life of Pi*. Pi's tale of shipwreck, starvation, and survival is also a narrative of transformation; faced with a life-threatening other, he has to change the identities and control the instincts of both himself and the tiger to prevent them both from dying. The heart of the novel is his fascinating, detailed account of how he managed it. Coetzee describes Defoe's similar feat in *Robinson Crusoe* as follows: "For page after page – for the first time in the history of fiction – we see a minute, ordered description of how things are done. It is a matter of pure writerly attentiveness, pure submission to the exigencies of a world which, through being submitted to a state so close to spiritual absorption, becomes transfigured, real" (20). Those words could describe *Life of Pi* as well: despite its debts to predecessors such as *Crusoe*, Yann Martel's book has an absorbing freshness of conception that makes it read like the first of its kind, as well as a sufficiently compelling illusion of reality (despite its extraordinary premise and metafictional play) to suggest that, even if it does not accomplish what its jacket copy and one of its characters promise – make readers believe in God, it may well renew their faith in the power of fiction. Discussions of the novel in several major reviews and in two recent articles in *Studies in Canadian Literature* (see Cole, Stratton) wrestle with the conundrum of belief in God versus faith in storytelling, which is prominently raised in the novel's final pages; more than any other, this issue has dominated serious commentary on the book. As the following reading circles around that same question, it will endeavour to show how the stated ambition of Pi's story to transform its readers – and its transformation of Defoe's novel – may also imply faith in a newly transformed Canada.

When *Life of Pi* was published, reviewers were more eager than reviewers of *Elle* would be to locate its origins in *Robinson Crusoe*, although its plot has less in common and its allusions are relatively few. Charlotte Innes's long review of *Pi* in *Nation* is titled "Robinson Crusoe, Move Over," and Linda Morra's in *Canadian Literature*, entitled "Re-Visioning Crusoe," spends most of its time comparing the two books. Even the religious journal *First Things* puts Defoe's novel at the top of its list of Yann Martel's influences (see Boyagoda 69). If on one level this simply reminds us of *Crusoe*'s iconic status, it is still somewhat surprising, since it would be hard to find a text among the dozens of supposed *Crusoe* rewrites that takes fewer details from the original than *Life of Pi*. While it shares the controlled-experiment shipwreck scenario, the attentiveness to practical details of solitary survival, and the earnest religiosity of Defoe's book – and while the twentieth-century Pi can make direct reference to that book in a way sixteenth-century Elle cannot (Pi's mother wants him to read *Crusoe* to correct his perverse adherence to three religions) – the primary setting of a boat and a makeshift raft in the middle of the Pacific, and the substitution of an animal for a human significant other, alter the colonial theme and the spiritual one significantly.

Simply put, a lifeboat cannot be a colony. Any territorial or interpersonal power claims exist purely temporarily, in the present, since there is no place on which to establish and project longer-term entitlement and rights. The ocean is a space, not a place, and the lifeboat a place only for as long as it takes to reach a better one: dry land. The heart of Pi's story takes place at sea and is defined by the ocean's literal and symbolic dimensions to a degree Crusoe's and Elle's and other island-bound tales cannot be. Pi cannot for a minute think of himself as a colonizer or king. He sometimes describes the sea in the language of landscape and territory – as "a city" (194), "a great wall" (343), or as "imitat[ing] every land feature – every hill, every valley, every plain" (122) – just as he sometimes anthropomorphizes the tiger. But such identities are temporary, a function of the sea's metamorphic fluidity, just as Richard Parker, despite his name, is more tigerish than human; Pi's ocean is more typically defined by "flatness and infinity" (177). Moreover, as Pi defines his position, "To be a castaway is to be a point perpetually at the centre of a circle. However much things may appear to change . . . the geometry never changes. Your gaze is always a radius. The circumference is ever great" (239). Pi's depiction of the sea as abstract, geometric emptiness – undefined space – associates it with recent significations of the Pacific in what Christopher Connery calls "Pacific Rim discourse." Because, Connery says, "A rim encircles, . . . its interior, in rimspeak, is the void that gives substance to what surrounds it" while remaining "subordinate to the Rim's . . . terrestriality" (288). Land is privileged over what lies in between. But while recognizing the sea's notorious blankness and resistance to signification, Connery slyly asks whether it is really "the [interstitial] void beyond and outside of the terrestrial real" or whether the sea could be "the real beneath the floating discontinuousness of land" (290).

Pi's journey from India to Canada via the Philippines and Mexico on Japanese vessels inscribes a wobbly diameter across that circle, along which the ocean becomes the defining space – the real – of Pi's personal and narrative achievement much more than do any of the discontinuous lands it links. The ocean's very unreadability and unboundedness, along with its power to capriciously destroy or facilitate human ambition, have caused multiple significations to cling to it like barnacles over millennia of cultural history. Ancient associations with sin and hubris, disorder and catastrophe, suffering and deliverance, death and rebirth – ably historicized in books such as W.H. Auden's *The Enchafèd Flood* and Alain Corbin's *The Lure of the Sea* – still affect how we see the sea. They inform all kinds of shipwreck and castaway stories, including Defoe's and Martel's. In *The Sea Voyage Narrative*, Robert Foulke writes that for seafarers, living at the interface of "the unstable ocean that mirrors an equally mutable sky . . . always holds out the possibility of extraordinary experience" (7). What the extraordinary experience narrated in *Life of Pi* most significantly draws our attention to beyond the time-honoured associations listed above is the way the sea's mutable nature symbolizes and necessitates transformation in the individual who would make it his temporary home. In *Post-Colonial Transformation*, Bill Ashcroft draws on Husserl's phenomenology to advance the concept of horizon – that which lies beyond the constraints of "epistemological, cultural, and spatial boundaries" (16) – as a metaphor for possibilities that will take us beyond the ingrained notions of difference that inform human relations and habitation:

> It is in horizonality that the true force of transformation becomes realized, for whereas the boundary is about constriction, history, the regulation of imperial space, the horizon is about extension, possibility, fulfillment, the imagining of post-colonial place. The horizon is a way of conceiving home, and with it identity, which escapes the inevitability of the imperial boundary. Horizonality is, possibly, the only way in which the predominance of the boundary in Western thought can be resisted. (183).

On the ocean, of course, horizons appear in all directions and mark the place one is heading to but never quite reaching. If, as New suggests, scholarly views of Canada traditionally "derive from . . . various forms of boundary rhetoric" (*Borderlands* 5), Ashcroft's horizonal thinking, which "transforms boundaries by seeing the possibility – the horizon – beyond them" (182), offers an alternative to such limiting discourses.

As Pi dedicates himself to mutual survival – his own and Richard Parker's – he has to learn to think like a tiger and transform the tiger's ways of thinking as well. His need to assert territorial and psychological dominance – in his words, "to make him understand that I was the top tiger" – may sound classically colonial, but thc inhuman, unreasoning nature of this other demands it. Indeed, to put it in Ashcroft's terms, Pi needs to overcome the boundaries that define and divide different beings, expanding the horizons of both sides of the encounter so they can relate to each other, across species and language barriers, not as two solitudes but as an interdependent community. Pi does this to help them both; there is mutuality here, since if the tiger eats Pi instead of the fish Pi catches, that will be his last meal. Moreover, Pi realizes, he needs the tiger because "if [Richard Parker] died I would be left alone with despair, a foe even more formidable than a tiger. . . . He pushed me to go on living . . . Without Richard Parker, I wouldn't be alive today to tell you my story" (182). The tiger gives him strength to go on and delivers him from despair – that is a role usually reserved for God in such stories. The pious Pi is an enthusiastic believer, and even lists "1 God" at the end of his Crusoe-like list of his possessions, right after "1 Bengal tiger," "1 lifeboat," and "1 ocean" (162). But God is invoked much less often during the long castaway section of the book than in the sections describing his life before and after; it is as if Richard Parker, Pi's necessary obsession at this time, has at least partly displaced God. It is notable too, I think, that when he describes the ocean as a vast empty circle, he also describes the skies above as distressing geometries of circular sun, circular moon, and stars – "the Sea of Tranquility" – all of which make him feel trapped, afraid, angry, mad, hopeless, and apathetic (239). There is no sign of God in those abstract, forbidding heavens.

Martel's circle motif has a terrestrial dimension as well. The Canadian city Pi's family were moving to before the shipwreck was Winnipeg, which is more or less at the physical middle of North America. In other words, if the continent were a huge circle, Winnipeg would be its centre – more or less equidistant and very far from the three seas that border Canada's coast-to-coast-to-coast land mass. Other than being dreaded by Pi for its "gale-force winds and minus-two-hundred-degree winters" (98), Winnipeg has no presence in the novel – as a destination it is usurped by the lifeboat at the centre of the Pacific Rim's circle. But the first time Pi uses the circle image, it is to express an epiphany of harmonious unity he once felt between the land, sea, and sky while standing on the coast back in India. This moment made him feel like he was "in heaven," "an immortal," and therefore, he says, "like the centre of a small circle coinciding with the centre of a larger one" (67, 68). In the next paragraph he says that the only other time he "felt God come so close to me" was years later, on a snowy winter day in Canada when "All nature was blanketed in white" – in other words, when it was as blank and seemingly unbounded as the ocean. These are the only significant references to Canada in Pi's first-person narrative, but these various overlapping circles and land-cum-seascapes implicitly associate Canada with in-betweenness (or in-the-middle-ness), undefinedness or boundedness (which can also mean potential for transformation), aesthetic harmony (or unification of disparate elements), and closeness to God. It is tempting to read an oblique thumbs-up to the young, multiculturally transformed middle power that is Canada today in all of this. We do see Pi through another narrator's eyes two decades later happily settled in a suburb of Toronto (a different Canadian centre), with his family and a "temple"-like house full of Hindu, Islamic, and Christian icons (49). Can one read this "pacific" novel as an allegory of immigrant transformation in peace-loving, multicultural, multifaith Canada – into what Ashcroft would call a newly "horizonal" Canada that leaves behind old boundaries of human difference, including those whom colonial discourse deemed closer to animals than humans? Such a reading may seem forced and perhaps naïvely utopian, but it is tempting.

Martel's reworking of *Robinson Crusoe*'s Protestant tale of conversion and deliverance inverts the original – Crusoe discovers faith in God on the island and more or less forgets about it at home. Pi's piety is reversed – he brings God fully on board, just as he initially helps Richard Parker get afloat – but while he doesn't entirely lose sight of God, his field of vision, in all that cosmic and oceanic unboundedness, shifts to the here and now of practical survival, enabling Richard Parker to step into God's role as deliverer. In Pi's last words before announcing his safe arrival in Mexico, he writes that after more than 200 days at sea, "It was natural that, bereft and desperate as I was, in the throes of unremitting suffering, I should turn to God" (315). So is that what saves him? If this renewal of a half-buried faith, this *deus ex machina*, is the novel's bid to make us believe in God, as some reviewers suggest, it is a bit facile and perfunctory. But Martel's emphasis is rather different; the debate at the end of the novel between Pi and the skeptical Japanese transport officials over which version of his story is true – which shifts into a debate about which one is "the better story" – in the end convinces them that the tale with the tiger is the better story – the one we want more to believe in – than the second, Godless, brutally human one he offers as an alternative. If we, like the Japanese officials by the end, choose the long account with animals over the short one with people, what are we believing in? God? Tigers? The human capacity to survive an extraordinary situation by adapting – by transforming? Perhaps, but are we not also believing in the power of fiction – which is always about change, otherwise there is no story to tell, but which is also by definition evaluated not by its truth but by how its imaginative representation of human change "betters" our understanding of the world? Better, however, subjective and personal, is a more relevant category than truer or less true, even if one measure of "betterness" is often verisimilitude or realism. The brutal human story may be more realistic in some ways, but that doesn't necessarily make it better. A world with God would be a better world than one without God, Martel seems also to suggest, even if we can't guarantee its truth.

Every Crusoe-influenced text mentioned in this paper, including the original, foregrounds questions of truth, authorship, and representation. Defoe's Preface introduces what we would now call a metafictional problematic when his authorial voice pretends to be an editorial one merely presenting, rather than making up, Crusoe's story. Walcott's Crusoe in all of his guises is linked to writing – with a problematized English language and literary inheritance. Coetzee allows the shipwreck-island narrative only 40 pages before giving over the remaining three-quarters of *Foe* to scenes concerned with the telling of that story and issues of authorial fidelity, responsibility, and power. Glover's *Elle* reverses *Foe*'s proportions, giving three-quarters of the book to the castaway story and the remainder to the heroine's involvements back in France with François Rabelais, who wants to write her story but embellish it; after he dies, she finishes *his* last book and writes her own memoir of her New World experiences, which is the first-person account that constitutes the novel. Martel, for his part, plays other metafictional games besides the Japanese interview segment, including a Defoe-like rendering of himself in an Author's Note that freely blends conventional autobiography and thanks with the story of how he supposedly met Pi Patel and came to present his story in Pi's first-person voice (see v-xi); this Martel-like narrator then intrudes regularly on the first pages of Pi's narrative with accounts of their meetings that sustain the illusion that Pi is a real person, now in his forties, living in Toronto.

All of this seemingly obligatory worrying away at issues of writing and truth in Crusoe rewrites may be a kind of homage to Defoe's original gaming; it may also be an indirect, playful recognition of the audacity and responsibility involved in revisiting this most famous of English classics – this tale of survival which has itself survived by being transformed and refashioned over the centuries for diverse purposes. *Elle* and *Life of Pi*, the most recent specimens, offer the rapidly changing societies, and the mobile and fluid identities of this young century two remarkable stories of youthful transformation in alien environments and with radically different others. At opposite ends of Canada's history so far, their stories are of new Canadians undergoing oceanic, mutual transformations: people who, by overcoming apparently insurmountable physical challenges and mental differences, manage to conjoin rather than divide worlds of difference. As models for Canada's terrestrial community in a new millennium – a Canada to believe in – these oceanic, horizonal tales sound like good places to start.

NOTES

1. This was most recently brought home with the 2004 Asian Tsunami, which united the entire Indian Ocean basin and the far-flung places from which its tourists came in a shared, simultaneous tragedy.

2. *Elle* won the 2003 Governor General's Award for fiction, and *Life of Pi* won the 2002 Man Booker Prize.

3. Elle's reference to the St. Lawrence as a "mouth" sounds like an echo of Northrop Frye's famous description of the early European explorer's experience of arrival in Canada as that of "a tiny Jonah entering an inconceivably large whale": "to enter Canada is to be silently swallowed by an alien continent" (217).

4. Elle's immersion in otherness does, however, bear some relation to the process of "'indigenization,' the impossible necessity of becoming indigenous" (194) that Terry Goldie argues enabled some white Europeans (especially writers) to counterbalance their experience of being an alien other in Canada.

WORKS CITED

Ashcroft, Bill. *Post-Colonial Transformation*. London and New York: Routledge, 2001.

Auden, W.H. *The Enchafèd Flood: or The Romantic Iconography of the Sea*. 1950. New York: Vintage, 1967.

Bailyn, Bernard. *Atlantic History: Concepts and Contours*. Cambridge: Harvard University Press, 2005.

Baucom, Ian. "Introduction: Atlantic Genealogies." *The South Atlantic Quarterly* 100.1 (2001) Spec. issue on Atlantic Genealogies. 1-13.

Boyagoda, Randy. "Faith, Fiction, Flotsam." Rev. of *Life of Pi*, by Yann Martel. *First Things: A Monthly Journal of Religion and Public Life* 133 (May 2003): 69-72.

Coetzee, J.M. "Daniel Defoe, *Robinson Crusoe*." Coetzee, *Stranger Shores: Literary Essays 1986-1999*. New York: Penguin, 2001. 17-22.

———. *Foe*. 1986. London: Penguin, 1987.

———. "What is a Classic?: A Lecture." *Stranger* 1-16.

Cole, Stewart. "Believing in Tigers: Anthropomorphism and Incredulity in Yann Martel's *Life of Pi*." *Studies in Canadian Literature* 29.2 (2004): 22-36.

Connery, Christopher L. "The Oceanic Feeling and the Regional Imaginary." *Global/Local: Cultural Production and the Transnational Imaginary*. Ed. Rob Wilson and Wimal Dissanayake. Durham: Duke University Press, 1996. 284-311.

Corbin, Alain. *The Lure of the Sea: The Discovery of the Seaside 1760-1840*. Trans. Jocelyn Phelps. Harmondsworth: Penguin, 1994.

Defoe, Daniel. *Robinson Crusoe*. 1719. Ed. Michael Shinagel. Norton Critical Edition. New York: Norton, 1975.

Gilroy, Paul. *The Black Atlantic: Modernity and Double Consciousness*. Cambridge: Harvard University Press, 1993.

Goldie, Terry. "Semiotic Control: Native Peoples in Canadian Literature in English." 1990. *Unhomely States: Theorizing English-Canadian Postcolonialism*. Ed. Cynthia Sugars. Peterborough: Broadview, 2004. 191-203.

Foulke, Robert. *The Sea Voyage Narrative*. 1997. New York and London: Routledge, 2002.

Glover, Douglas. *Elle*. Fredericton: Goose Lane, 2003.

Innes, Charlotte. "Robinson Crusoe, Move Over." Rev. of *Life of Pi*, by Yann Martel. *The Nation* 275.6 (19/26 Aug. 2002). 25-29.

James, Louis. "Unwrapping Crusoe: Retrospective and Prospective Views." Spaas and Stimpson, ed. 1-9.

Jeyifo, Biodun. "On Eurocentric Critical Theory: Some Paradigms from the Texts and Sub-Texts of Post-Colonial Writing." *Kunapipi* 11.1 (1989): 107-18.

Joyce, James. "Daniel Defoe." Defoe 354-57.

Kroetsch, Robert. "Unhiding the Hidden." *Robert Kroetsch: Essays*. Ed. Frank Davey and bpNichol. Spec. issue of *Open Letter* 5th ser. 4 (Spring 1983): 17-21.

Macherey, Pierre. *A Theory of Literary Production*. Trans. Geoffrey Wall. London: Routledge & Kegan Paul, 1978.

Martel, Yann. *Life of Pi*. 2001. Toronto: Vintage, 2002.

McInelly, Brett. "Expanding Empires, Expanding Selves: Colonialism, The Novel, and *Robinson Crusoe*." *Studies in the Novel* 35.1 (Spring 2003): 1-21.

Morra, Linda. "Re-Visioning Crusoe." Rev. of *Life of Pi*, by Yann Martel. *Canadian Literature* 177 (Summer 2003): 163-64.

New, W.H. *Borderlands: How We Talk about Canada*. Vancouver: University of British Columbia Press, 1998.

———. *Land Sliding: Imagining Space, Presence, and Power in Canadian Writing*. Toronto: University of Toronto Press, 1997.

Parkman, Francis. *Pioneers of France in the New World: France and England in North America*. Part First. 1865. Toronto: Morang, 1898.

Said, Edward W. *Culture and Imperialism*. New York: Knopf, 1993.

Selvon, Sam. *Moses Ascending*. 1975. London: Heinemann, 1984.

Spaas, Lieve, and Brian Stimpson, ed. *Robinson Crusoe: Myths and Metamorphoses*. Hounsdmills: Macmillan; New York: St. Martin's, 1996.

Stratton, Florence. "'Hollow at the core': Deconstructing Yann Martel's *Life of Pi*." *Studies in Canadian Literature* 29.2 (2004): 5-21.

Taylor, Charles. *Multiculturalism and "The Politics of Recognition."* Ed. Amy Gutmann. Princeton: Princeton University Press, 1992.

Thieme, John. *Postcolonial Con-texts: Writing Back to the Canon*. London and New York: Continuum, 2001.

The Voyages of Jacques Cartier. Introd. Ramsay Cook. Toronto: University of Toronto Press, 1993.

Walcott, Derek. "The Figure of Crusoe." 1965. *Critical Perspectives on Derek Walcott*. Ed. Robert D. Hamner. Washington: Three Continents, 1993. 33-40.

———. *Pantomime*. In *Remembrance & Pantomime: Two Plays*. By Walcott. New York: Farrar, Straus and Giroux, 1980. 89-170.

Wyile, Herb. "Lost in Transit." Rev. of *Elle*, by Douglas Glover. *Canadian Literature* 184 (Spring 2005): 132-33.

Christopher Levenson

Concepts of Community in Five North American and South Asian Poems

Living in a rigidly stratified and insular society, the great Victorian poets did not have to worry about community. If as happened occasionally, for instance in the case of James ("B.V.") Thomson's *The City of Dreadful Night*, their view of the city was dystopic, there could at least be agreement about the existence of factories, slums, dockyards, etc, even though most of them, unlike the major novelists, refused to look at them directly in their poetry. After the First World War, more specifically after the publication of Eliot's *The Waste Land* in 1922, the assumption of a coherent, agreed-upon community could no longer be sustained and it has been a primary task of the modern long poem to attempt to reassemble, to rebuild, our sense as readers of what it means to be a member of a community.

Not of course that the terms "city" and "community" are interchangeable. Small towns and villages, as fiction writers from Alice Munro to R. K. Narayan, have shown, nurture their own forms of community, but whereas in large cities most people will seek out,, or establish, networks of friends with similar social, political, religious or sexual orientations, the smaller the physical area, the less diverse these options tend to be. This is especially true of artists in all media, whose literally ex-centric take on the local norms will often cause them to feel like outsiders or indeed force them to leave in search of greater tolerance, even if it is merely the negative tolerance of being ignored and left alone.

As town planners and urbanists such as Lewis Mumford, and Jane Jacobs, along with the more visionary architects such as Canada's Moshe Safdie, have long realized, the idea of community is nothing if not personalized, that is, conceived in terms of interactions between individuals, families and smaller groupings. Although we may harbour what the Germans term *Lokalpatriotismus* for a city the size of Toronto, London or Bombay, what we really cherish as citizens are neighbourhoods, places where we know and are known, above all where we feel accepted.

What I want to do in the following essay, then, is to look at a few examples from North American poetry – William Carlos Williams's *Paterson* (1963), Dennis Lee's *Civil Elegies* (1972) and Daphne Marlatt's *Steveston* (1979) – and then juxtapose them with two examples drawn from English-language poetry from India, Rukmini Bhaya Nair's *Ayodhya Cantos* (1999) and Arun Kolatkar's *Kala Ghoda Poems* (2004), in order to see whether the North American concept of community is even relevant to Indian conditions and, if so, to what extent it overlaps.

In twentieth-century English language poetry, as the audience conditions that gave us the long narrative poems of the Victorian period such as Tennyson's *Idylls of the King* came to seem impossibly artificial, a new kind of "synthetic" long poem exemplified by *The Waste Land,* took their place. This new version of the long poem, as an alternative among other things to the disconnected outbursts of an increasingly alienated Romantic lyric "I," was to prove particularly appropriate for works that sought by methods of accretion and juxtaposition to convey a sense of the city and a sense of what community and neighbourhood might still represent as a counterpoise to the homogenizing influences of mass-marketing and mass communications.

Community presupposes a sense of context, of recognized particulars and of historical and geographical background. This in turn implies not just reference but documentation, especially when a long poem is set in an earlier period: for, without the common knowledge of myth or legend that Tennyson could rely on, and without the often prosaic flexibility of the blank verse medium that Wordsworth uses to such good effect in *The Prelude*, the contemporary poet is obliged to provide the literal contexts for his or her re-creations or imaginings not through footnotes, which would immediately proclaim the work to be "academic," but through the wholesale insertion of prose passages. Thus we find in, say, Michael Ondaatje's *The Collected Works of Billy the Kid* (1970) or in Paulette Jiles's *The Jesse James Poems* (1988), passages of narrative prose, newspaper clippings, court transcripts, posters, advertisements, membership lists and similarly "unpoetic" raw material forming part of the patchwork quilt that is the poem. But at least in these two cases as also with, say, Kim

Morrissey's *Batoche*, the poets can count on some degree of recognition for their protagonists or settings. This is much less the case with Don Gutteridge's series of book length poems focused on the Lambton County area of South Western Ontario; with Florence McNeil's *Barkerville* (1984) (a British Columbian ghost town) or with countless other books of Canadian poetry over the past thirty years that deal with the histories of individual families complete with family trees and photo album snapshots. Indeed, without great thematic control and other organizing strategies, the Canadian long poem seems at times to aspire to Henry James's; description of the novel as a "great baggy monster"!

Which brings us to the ur-long poem, Williams's *Paterson,* published in five parts from 1946 to 1963. Even if, as M.L. Rosenthal and Sally M. Gall have claimed in *The Modern Poetic Sequence: the genius of Modern Poetry,* the poem is as much concerned with such linked issues as "sexual interaction and the artistic imagination," the poem has a continuing importance for many subsequent poets as an example of how to incorporate, in the sense of taking into the body of the work, disparate elements of the urban community, in a poem without the clear narrative structures that would have been demanded in earlier literary traditions. These elements are disparate in several ways: there is no one narrator but instead a collage of (sometimes unidentified) voices, some public, others very private, such as the letters addressed to the poet himself by a woman poet and by the youthful Allen Ginsberg; there is no one tone, but instead an intermingling of clippings from newspapers, paragraphs from guide books and other archival material, fragments of overheard conversations, and lyric outbursts, running the whole gamut from the most colloquial to the most official and formal; past and present overlap and interfuse and the only constant is the setting, the town of Paterson, New Jersey. What we get ultimately is a portrait of a city through its history and its topography certainly, with the Passaic River and the Falls taking on symbolic roles, but also through a cross-section of its citizens, both en masse, as mobs and as spectators, and individually.

When we turn to Dennis Lee's *Civil Elegies* we find not just a difference of scale – Lee's sequence is after all only twenty four pages long compared to two hundred and seventy eight pages for *Paterson* – but also a difference of emphasis. Lee's civic landscape is much more overtly political. Toronto, the setting of his poem, represents not just itself but Canada as a whole, so that citizenship takes on a national as well as a purely civic significance and is indeed defined, at least in part, as is often the case in Canadian politics and literature, in terms of difference from, and opposition to, tendencies that are seen as emanating from the United States. As George Grant points out, "Along with many others [Lee] saw that Canada was part of an empire which was trying to impose its will by ferocious means right around the other side of the globe. He saw with many others that Canada was complicit in the acts of that empire . . . He saw with some others that the technological multiversity was not outside that complicity but central to it. This was true not only in the obviously technological parts of the university but had taken hold in the very way that the liberal arts were practised." So, although he shares with Williams a concern with the search for an adequate language "to speak what we are," in Lee's case the need to articulate a specifically Canadian sense of being, of identity, is complicated, as it was not for Williams, by his awareness of whose interests control that language through advertising, political rhetoric and commerce. He is aware too of the lives wasted in the exploitation of raw materials and their legacy in the "cities dying of concrete."

At times, as in the Fifth Elegy, his castigations of Canada as "a nation of losers and quislings," his reproach of complicity due to "a nation"s failure of nerve," his statement that "fear of life"[is] "the mark of Canada" and his inveighing against Canadian complicity in the US use of napalm in the Vietnam, war, however much as readers we agree with the points made, verge on rhetoric, but such passages do not seriously unbalance the poem as a whole, mainly because they can be felt to be a legitimate part of an overriding total reaction to certain aspects of the modern malaise and the countervailing desire "to be made whole," "some saner version of integrity." In any case, whereas Williams assembles a collage of evidence that stops and starts and amalgamates the prosaic and the lyrical, Lee's focus is much more on creating a viable verse form supple enough to accommodate within itself a wide range of tones from the formal, academic or bureaucratic through to the colloquial and slangy. His language and his verse movement is in constant flux. After all, the poem is not meant to be a call to action, but rather to *in*action, observation, "letting be." Nor is it narrowly political for its own sake: the political is merely an aspect of a much larger issue.

And he is at least as concerned as Williams with man's, the citizen's, place in the natural world. Indeed, with his stress on cadence, his long, flowing often dactylic lines, and the greater frequency of lyrical passages, he reminds one at times of Rilke in the *Duino Elegies*.

At a length of forty pages, Daphne Marlatt's *Steveston* differs from *Civil Elegies* not just in length but also in scale. Marlatt focuses on, indeed for the length of the poem inhabits the eponymous fishing and fish-canning community south of Vancouver, which at that time, 1913, was inhabited mainly by Japanese and Chinese but, today, with the decline of the industry on which it depended, is mainly a tourist site.

In terms of its form on the page there is little in *Steveston* that resembles the traditional lyric, even to the extent that this is found in Lee and Williams: the various sections, vignettes drawn from the everyday life of the fishing community and arranged like a sequence of grainy sepia photographs, make up a work that can be classified as prose poems. But then those who are familiar with the writing of such Canadian poets as Roo Borson and Susan Glickman will know that this term does not in any way preclude the lyrical. Indeed, one of the attractions of Marlatt's text is precisely the way she is able to organize her material by the use of recurrent phrases, leit motivs, repeated sounds, etc. As we can see here from the beginning of one such section, "Low Tide. A beached vessel:"

> small grey gillnetter, chained to the
> dock so close in to shore she's high & dry on rocks, angularly
> beached, bleached, like some dying fish.
>
> where nothing belongs
> in all this absent morning, only sun who owns these shells of
> cannery housing, 'these unused footbridges, these brambles whose fruit
> no one picks. Silent boats. Docks serving only sun, & wind off the
> open waters. Moving. Down the track come 3 boys idle, looking for
> some - Wow, a boat.
>
> Her sullen cabin's locked, but two of them
> violate a side window. Hey, a searchlight! Does it work? Look at
> this! An empty bottle, flung in glittering arc across the sun,
> smashes into a thousand bits.

The life, decay and death of the fishermen and the cannery workers is symbiotic with that of their raw material, the fish themselves, while the violence of the three boys (notice the sexual overtones of "violate" above) is mirrored by the violent uprooting of the Japanese community for internment during the Second World War and at a more personal level by the female narrator's rebuffing of an attempted sexual liaison. Beyond that, the poet makes us very keenly aware that urbanity, civilization and luxury depend on the subhuman hardship and deprivation endured by the "hands," those who catch, mechanically kill and process the fish, their "harvest," "this death that must be kept cool, fresh."

In fact, however disparate and geographically removed the two settings of Toronto and Steveston may appear, many of Marlatt's preoccupations overlap with Lee's. The Section "Moon," for instance, ends:

> A few people drink in the Steveston, a few
> young men; stopt up, burning, slow, nowhere to go, no crowds to
> light, no strange women, no gambling games, no risk. Except the
> occasional storm outside, the rare failure of guaranteed equipment,
> the unexplained accident
> as shipwreck, or, only the *smaller* packers
> forced out, bought up.
>
> This corporate growth that monopolizes
> the sun, moon & tide, fish-run. So they see nothing remarkable
> in this, they know it like the back of their hands on a familiar
> table, like fish conveyed by belt to the steady chopping of steel
> blades. Beer to lips, end of a shift, end of another week. It
> sucks them dry, these men soaking in their beer (so many thousand
> cans today), these women in white, tired or wearily hopeful, drained
> by the ditches of their unsatisfied lives.

Implicitly as well as at times explicitly Marlatt equates the workers with their product; the cans of fish are also the cans of beer, for the men and women of Steveston, speaking of "this net we're caught in" or "the mesh of a net we refuse to see," are as helplessly controlled by the monopolies as the salmon are by the need to swim upriver to spawn; the "water swollen with its filth, with sewage, milldirt" does not just affect the fish but conditions their own lives also and can be extended to aspects other than the physical. As with *Civil Elegies* often the best that can be hoped for is mere survival:

Somehow they survive, this people, these fish,
survive the refuse bottom, filthy water, their choked lives
in a singular dance of survival, each from each.

Again, like Lee's poem, *Steveston* is characterized by a strong sense of process. This is indeed one of the built-in advantages of the modern long- (or documentary) poem. Not being tied to traditional narrative, but on the contrary in this case enacting the flux of the delta and the sea, as well as of the human lives, she evokes the sense of constant struggle by means of a shifting, usually incomplete syntax that involves the listing of objects, and a frequent use of present participle constructions. Thus the poem's tentative affirmations can arise from a cluster of images and references that have gathered resonance by repetition, merging and then separating and modulating, often via wordplay (flakes, flaky, flaked out or lines of wind, lines of power) over the course of the poem.

If there is a plea for moderation and balance – "to take no more than the requisite, *required* to grow, spawn, catch, die" – a sequence which neatly conflates the interests both of the fishermen and of the fish, – what is desired aims a little higher, as here in the third paragraph of the section "Or there is love:"

To live in a place. Immanent. In
place. Yet to feel at sea. To come from elsewhere & then to discover
love, has a house & name. Has land. Is landed, under the swaying
trees which bend so much in this wind like underwater weeds we think
self rises from . . .

In a sense, with such statements and the plethora of supporting detail that has accrued over the course of the poem, *Steveston* crosses all its t's and dots its i's. How successful this seems to the reader will depend on how much remains in his or her mind of the suggestions, the hinted associations, and to what extent these bolster and justify the repeated questioning of material wealth against a backdrop of waste and decay. Here as in *Civil Elegies* the recurring quest seems to be to establish a sense of self within a community, with that self partly but never wholly defined by and subsumed in that community.

Can even such a generalized pattern be read into the post-Independence poetry of India in English? If the politically or religiously motivated assassinations, riots and communal violence in Bombay, Delhi and elsewhere over the past fifty years are any indication, the chances would not seem to be high. Certainly if one looks at the few currently available anthologies of Indian poetry in English, although there is much in the poetry of, say, Nissim Ezekiel, A.K. Ramanujan, Keki Daruwalla or Gieve Patel to show that they have observed closely and compassionately the urban scene in all its ugliness, squalour and corruption, there is to my knowledge nothing that conveys the sense of a community that we get from the prose of, for instance, Rohinton Mistry or Amitav Ghosh. Perhaps these poets, along with Kamala Das and Eunice de Souza, have been too preoccupied with establishing a modernist tradition in Indo English poetry to have been able also to tackle this broader problem, especially when, as is the case with English uniquely among India's many official languages, there is no natural geographic base such as there would be with, say, Punjabi or Tamil.

All the more reason, then, to welcome at least the intention of Rukmini Bhaya Nair's sequence "The Ayodhya Cantos," which make up more than a third of her eponymous second volume. Not that this poem is "about" place even to the extent that this can be claimed for our three previous examples: everything leads up to, and then focuses on, an event, the destruction by a Hindu extremist mob of the Babri Masjid mosque in Ayodhya in December 1992, an act that still represents an unresolved problem for the wider Hindu and Moslem communities in India. In order to achieve this focus, however, Nair brings the Hindu gods Vishnu, Hanuman and Sita down to an everyday, human scale – Hanuman, for instance, has a *paan* stall at the crossroads in Ayodhya while Vishnu is shown "ready to produce his own B Grade movie" of the riots – and are portrayed recollecting events in Indian history. Thus in "August 15th, 1947" – the date of India's Independence –

> Hanuman's mind returns to August, 1947. Red streams,
>
> And from Red Fort ramparts, a double-headed country announced.
> Partition & Independence, these are twinned. No one knows better
> Than Hanuman, son of wind, what freedom is, what it can mean.
> Or servitude, come to that. Each other's shadows, Muslim&Hindu,
> Nehru&Jinnah, MathuraMecca, NamaazAarti, KoranGita, Pir&Sadhu.

United in 1957 against the Firang, which was which? Hanuman faces
A familiar confusion. His brain is likie his body, skipping places, his
Body, like his unquiet heart, holds an infinity of allegiances…

But in the next sonnet, "Fragments," Nair asks:

How can Hanuman, wild
Arsonist, he of the burnt chin, flame-tailed destroyer of Lanka
Atone? Creature of myth, how can he understand the torments
Of history? In history, everything costs. Myth is free.

The irreverent, often comic, knockabout quality of a work that Nair herself terms a "Comi-tragedy," in that it moves from light to darkness, also makes use of a very down-to-earth Chorus of the People, who respond to the Chorus of the Priests, producing, as Nair says, "their own versions of the Bhavani shlokas," as here, following "Parasurama":

The truth is that Ayodhya is a dump. Our
Economy is in a ghastly slump. Cowdung's
Sold at two rupees a lump. Religion's even
Cheaper! Guns, homemade like lemonade
Sold up and down the temple lanes. Ghandi
Locked in a cage on Ayodhya's ghats for fear
He'll be defaced. Immortality elixirs at fifty paisa –
Bargains! And leprosy cured with magic rings, O Eka!

Paradoxically, though perhaps inevitably at this stage of Indian history, The Ayodhya Cantos represent more a plea for community than a representation of a community, however flawed. This certainly seems to be the motivation of the concluding sonnet, "Finale: The Voiceless Chorus of the Gods" (*Addressed to the Priests and People of Ayodhya)*

The last word is never spoken. It is heard in the canyons
Of the heart and in the cry of Garuda, Vishnu's golden
Bird, grieving for Sitara, turned to stone, for Hanuman
Wounded and alone, for Ira, Naina, Deena, Indu, Asiya –
For India. A subcontinent so vast and old that it defeats
Memory, its story told in bits and jagged pieces. *When did*

It begin? Who dies when a mosque comes down? Who lifts a finger?
Not the gods, immortal and uninvolved. Unctuous officials
The politicians and their pudding-faced heirs, lethally armed
Forget them! *Whom can you trust?* Citizens of Ayodhya, pray
If you must but above all, act! You have powers greater than
Bhavani's, insights deeper than Vishnu's. Listen to Garuda!
Blood-red neck down, wheeling blue-taloned over the Sarayu
Agonized, agonized. India is yours! The last word belongs to you.

If Nair succeeds in this poem, and personally I believe she does, though the sequence is too long and many-faceted to demonstrate its full complexity, it is by drawing together and representing above all in the same context a diversity of contemporary and historical human and divine Indian characters and types in the matrix of a language that for all its allusiveness is direct, quirky, colloquial, dramatic and, above all, inclusive.

"Inclusive" is also the first word that comes to mind in my final example, the late Arun Kolatkar's *Kala Ghoda Poems* (Pras Prakashan, Bombay, 2004). The locale of the title is an area of central Bombay that is home to several art galleries, museums, libraries and institutes of learning, though these figure only peripherally as backdrop or as the butt of occasional sly humour.

Formally, the poem appears at first sight traditional, consisting of a series of discrete portraits, each in variable three line stanzas, while the action all takes place within a single twenty four hour period. But there is nothing traditional about his choice of portraits, for his real concern is with street people or, as is the case with the very first poem, "Pi-Dog," with street animals and birds and even inanimate objects. Unless we are ourselves involved in the social services, we tend to think of communities as settlements, groupings of people with regular incomes and fixed addresses. Not so Kolatkar. The personae and sometimes indeed also the narrators of this poem sequence are all itinerant. The street is their home. Thus the poem starts off before sunrise with a dog who has his set place in a parking lot where he is composing in his head a sonata based on three themes, one suggested by "a magpie robin/ another by the wail of an ambulance,/ and the third by a rock drill." Other denizens of this area include Parameshwari, "the pipe-smoking mama,/the old lavatory attendant" whom we find "sitting all by herself/ on the steps of a dark/ and deserted Jehangir Art Gallery." Although we are told that she "has lost/ her gift of prophesy," she can "see through the new day/and know it/ for the clever forgery that it is."

So too with Meera, "the sad-eyed feminine half/ of the municipal street-cleaning team/ in this part of town" which is, we are in formed, "a difficult enough job/ at the best of times,/ made well-nigh impossible/ by the fact/ that more and more of Bombay/ keeps mushrooming/ on land wrested from the sea,/the malarial swamps, /salt marshes/ and creeks that surround it and reclaimed by Sweepings,/ such as this trolley collects/ day after day;/ with the result that/ the more you clean Bombay/the more Bombay there is to clean."

Kolatkar's characters would be a reviewer's despair: there is so much wit and insight here that deserves quotation. For present purposes, however, suffice it to say that the poet runs the whole gamut of street people, singly and in groups. These include "The Ogress," one side of her face badly disfigured by scar tissue, who is "a kind/of auxiliary mother/ semiofficial nanny/ and baby-bather-in-chief/ to a whole chain of children/ born to the street." He deals too with an assortment of children – one small, unkempt and unwashed girl, addressed as "brat fatale" and "proto Jezebel," is "looking fine/ tumbleweed hair and all" – The Barefoot Queen of the Crossroads, The Blind Man Stringing a Cot, The Lepers' Band, and even an old bicycle tyre, and manages to take in such events as a young woman picking lice from the hair of her "dirty, no-good lover" who's just been released from jail, or another young woman eight months pregnant, running after a kerosene delivery truck with her jerry can. Then, too, there is the frail old fisherwoman sitting over her plate of peas; an awakened drunk talking to himself; the Rat Poison Man's Lunch Hour; the Potato Peelers: and finally, for good historical measure, the medallion head of David Sassoon, a nineteenth-century merchant-prince of Bombay. And so on, through the evening and into the night.

Although here, as also with the *Ayodhya Cantos*, some knowledge of Hindu religion and mythology would be helpful, firsthand acquaintance with Bombay could only add to one's pleasure. Even without prior knowledge the general tenor of the mock-heroic can be appreciated in such pieces as "A Note on the Reproductive Cycle of Rubbish" or the following passage where, thanks to the street sweeper outside the art gallery, "a fresh new series of installations/ goes on display/in front of the Jehangir Art Gallery . . . / with no fanfare, and unseen by any/ save a few discerning crows and a kitten,/ in the form of modest piles of rubbish/ all along the kerb/ at regular intervals of about/ fifteen paces perhaps,/ and consisting of dry leaves, scraps of paper,/ prawnshells, onion skins, potato peels,/ castoff condoms, dead flowers/ – mostly gulmohur and copper-pod./ The installations might as well have been/ titled 'Homage to Bombay, one',/'Homage to Bombay, two' and so on,/ since a good bit of the city stands/ on sweepings such as these./ All of Colaba, for example, or Khetwadi."

Collectively, then, these vignettes and the interactions of some at least of the participants add up to a tableau of incredible charm and vitality. But does this constitute a community? Why not? One might wonder whether the shared poverty of Kolatkar's dirt-poor characters does not also give them something in common that transcends, or short-circuits, religious and ethnic divisions, a conclusion supported at least anecdotally by Suketu Mehta's forays in *Maximum City* into the slums of Bombay . In any case, Kolatkar's inventiveness in this sequence raises the possibility of an Indian poet writing in English a long satiric poem that could be set alongside Shashi Tharoor's prose masterpiece *The Great Indian Novel.*

Conclusions are not easy to arrive at where both time and distance are contributory factors, as they are in the poems discussed, but I shall be content if I have at least drawn attention to five widely divergent examples of the modern long poem or poem sequence and have suggested its potential as a way of dealing with an issue, that of the individual in the community, whose importance can only increase as cities get ever larger and more impersonal. Poetry, whose characteristic mode is suggestion rather than statement, can never hope to *define* community and should not even try, but poets should surely see as one of their recurrent tasks, embodying aspects of community through image, symbol and cadence. This, I feel, is what Nair and Kolatkar have been able, at least partially, to achieve and in doing so they may have been able to extend the line and the viability of this form in a new context.

WORKS CITED

Grant, George. "Dennis Lee, Poetry and Philosophy." *Descant, 39.*

Jiles, Paulette. *The Jesse James Poems.* Winlaw, B.C: Polestar Press, 1988.

Kolatkar, Arun. *Kala Ghoda Poems.* Bombay: Pras Prakashan, 2004.

Lee, Dennis. *Civil Elegies and Other Poems.* Toronto, Ont.: Anansi, 1972.

Marlatt, Daphne. *Steveston.* In *The Long Poem Anthology.* Ed. Michael Ondaatje. Toronto, Ont.: Coach House Press, 1979.

McNeil, Florence. *Barkerville.* Saskatoon, Sask.: Thistledown Press, 1984.

Nair, Rukmini Bhaya. *The Ayodhya Cantos.* New Delhi: Viking/ Penguin, 1999.

Ondaatje, Michael. *The Collected Works of Billy the Kid.* Toronto, Ont: Anansi, 1970.

Rosenthal, M.L., and Sally M. Gall. *The Modern Poetic Sequence: The Genius of Modern Poetry.* New York, NY: Oxford University Press, 1983.

Williams, William Carlos. *Paterson.* New York, NY: New Directions, 1963.

Stephanie McKenzie

The Aesthetics of Some Aboriginal Poetry and Some Poetry from Newfoundland

I want to highlight three comments made by Daniel David Moses in the preface to his and Terry Goldie's *An Anthology of Native Canadian Literature,* a book published twelve years ago:

> 1) Our culture is so obsessed with everything making sense, being straightforward, being hooked into time lines and bottom lines(xvi).
>
> 2) A lot of Native people have been working with words without publishing. It's not this horrible painful need that so many white writers have when they spend a couple of years working on something and can't get published. If the material is working orally within the community, that's enough (xviii-xix).

3) I think our cultures probably allow us to be more autobiographical than the mainstream. In the mainstream markets editors want to know what one alienated individual thinks. Our culture is suspicious of that. We want to know where the opinion is coming from. Who are his people? (xxi)

The appellation "our" refers to a pan-Indian consciousness which was borne out of the social and political realties of the 1960s and 1970s in Canada (as well as the United States); as Barbara Burnaby further explains in her article "Policy on Aboriginal Languages in Canada: Notes on Status Planning," "the term 'Native' itself was adopted in the 1970s to refer to members of all . . . [different Aboriginal] groups" (306). This recognition reminds one that pan-Indianism is a relatively new construct within Canadian Aboriginal history; indeed, as research continues in the field of Aboriginal studies, it is necessary – and will be even more so in the years to come – to distinguish between different nationally determined Aboriginal voices, such as Cree and Ojibway, just as it is necessary to distinguish between voices as diverse as English and French, even though they may have shared the same homeland for over two hundred years. However, and as this article will go on to show, there is still value in allowing for a pan-Indian consciousness in the analysis of Aboriginal literature because there is a necessity to provide foundations for future scholarship. There is also worth in recognizing affinities between even more disparate voices; in this study, for example, the recognition of such affinities allows for a consideration of *aesthetics* – a much-needed focus in Aboriginal scholarship consumed, as the field is, with considerations of "images" and "desires" – a focus which detracts from such things as prosody and the *mechanics* of verbal arts.

My last claim, and the central interest of this article, is elucidated by turning first to a consideration of not Aboriginal poetry but the voice of one Newfoundland poet – Al Pittman. Born in St. Leonard's, Placentia, Newfoundland, Pittman was a playwright, short-story writer, children's author and poet who lived most of his life in Newfoundland; he is most remembered though, for being a poet. Pittman wrote six books of poetry and garnered a reputation during his lifetime as the people's poet of Newfoundland. Pittman was a dedicated Newfoundland nationalist, meaning that he understood Newfoundland to be its own cultural nation, separate in its consciousness from the mainland of Canada. This, in large part, defines his poetry. Pittman wrote for his community and, throughout his lifetime, worked to establish a rapport between himself – a poet responsible to community – and the people around him. Like those voices of whom Moses speaks when he refers to a community-driven art, Pittman's poetic voice is shaped by dedication to community – in this case, Newfoundland. It is his last collection, *Thirty-for-Sixty*, which illustrates the significance of these observations.

Community and its attendant reliance on a recognized relation between speaker and listener define *Thirty-for-Sixty*. The title of the book is the name of a Newfoundland card game, described in the book's last poem which bears the same name:

Newfoundland's national pastime
is a game of Growl (otherwise called
Auction or A Hundred and Twenties).
Thirty-for-sixty is the ultimate bid.
To make that bid without the five
of trumps in your hand is a foolish
thing to do. Chances are (nine times
out of ten) you'll end up in the hole. (62)

Equating Newfoundland with a nation in its own right, separate from that of Canada, and using a traditional Newfoundland "pastime" to provide the central metaphor of his collection, Pittman foregrounds a concern which will resonate throughout this book: a concern that Newfoundland identity be remembered and propagated without being subsumed by federalism. "The Pink, White and Green," a poem dedicated to fellow Newfoundland poet and nationalist Des Walsh, also underscores this sentiment. The last stanza of the poem romanticizes the flag of the poem's title (not the present-day provincial flag which underscores Newfoundland's entry into Canadian confederation) which has become a symbol for Newfoundland patriotism, if not separatism:

Back on to the house he's well aware
of his widow up there in the window
watching him sweep the summer's growth of grass
down to the ground, low below
the Pink, White and Green flag
flying high above the only nation
he and she have ever known. (12)

Not only is *Thirty-for-Sixty* immediately shaped by a sense of Newfoundland identity, but it is also dependant on a sense of belonging to conversational exchange. The voice of a storyteller shapes this collection. Sometimes this recognition is overt, as in "Lambs to the Slaughter" where the narrator begins by telling the reader "[s]he told me this twice" (34), and in "Thirty-for-Sixty" where readers listen to a story which has been passed down to the narrator by his father who, ostensibly describing a card game, "wasn't talking about cards" (62). The same is true of "Standing Room Only," where the narrator self-reflexively underscores his voice in the first two lines: "I tell this not as I would in Confession / but without a word of a lie" (21). There are also numerous, direct addresses to family members to whom Pittman consistently spoke over the years in his various books of poetry: "Home on the Heights," "A Bouquet for Emily," "To Kyran in Full Flight," "The Annunciation," and "The Homecoming." What is most notable, though, is the manner in which Pittman employs repetition in this collection of autobiographically inspired, communally dictated, aware, and dedicated verse.

Repetition defines *Thirty-for-Sixty*. The parents of the little girl in "The Citrus Sea" are " . . . intent on . . . intensity" (9). "The man mowing the meadow" in "The Pink, White and Green" "is no gardener of gardens" (11). The narrator of "Lupins" finds flowers "at a quick twist in the twisted road" in the " . . . morning's morning deluge" (13). " . . . I packed my pack" (15), the narrator of "Tuesday's Child" says, and "[t]he closest I came to coming close" (16) to Tuesday Weld was with " . . . her lover" (16). He will not try to find her again, though, unless he has time for " . . . going nowhere with / nowhere to go but here, holding / hands with the lone and lonesome" (17). The narrator in "Standing Room Only" once drove his father's "old Oldsmobile" to an "old quarry" where he and a lover "held on to each other like lovers / on the brink of love until it came / to toss-up time between time and Eternity" (21). This same man has also " . . . prayed a lot of prayers," but, as he also says, giving up the chance of ever going to heaven, even if that means hell, " . . . that's a promise I promise to keep" (23). The lover-speaker in "Touching You" promises his reader that "[t]ouching you is to touch . . . / The loveliest love" (25). "I strive for dreams to dream," the speaker says in "The Moon Also Rises," " . . . and the sun / ascends above a blank blanket of cloud" (26). In "This Side of Heaven," there are " . . . medicines / to . . . dull the dullest" (28). The girl robbed of a lifetime memory in "Lambs to the Slaughter" " . . . knew what little and as much / as she could (in her little age)," and "[c]ounting the days (without knowing / what day) she went to sleep each night / reciting the litany of the names / she had named the lambs" (34). "Whatever little time we live, time / in the end, / adds up to no time at all" (36) begins "Rites of Passage." Watching a woman, the narrator of "Sunshower After Dark" intones, "[y]ou go by in a slight sight / of time, but time and sight / enough to imagine you as I do" (38). "Ralph is tending bar and doing the bar's / business bookwork" in "Erin's Pub," and "[h]e's a singer of high degree and sings / his ancestral soul"

(40). In "Intruder," parents "do their best to turn their backs / back to the immediacy of their lives" (42). Describing his former wife in "Marilee on the Heights," Pittman writes:

> And you move inside
> as some lover might move
> in the arms of a lover ("Home on the Heights" 45)

"[L]ong before this beginning begins," writes Pittman for his daughter Emily, your "frail flowers will wilt," though he's quick to say she'll always be " . . . brighter than the brightest light" ("A Bouquet for Emily" 48). He observes:

> Most of my friends have children
> who have children. Some of their children
> have children . . . ("My Daughters Write Poems" 50)

"The borders you must cross to get to Mexico / are nothing compared to the borders / you've crossed to get to where you are" ("To Kyran in Full Flight" 51), Pittman writes for his other daughter, Kyran. "There, on the edge of eternity / by the eternal river," the narrator of "The Annunciation" muses, "we'd lie silent" (54). Pittman predicts that Alden, his grandson, will come home to Newfoundland one day, to " . . . the fairies, the ghosts and goblins" (57), a phrase he repeats three times in "Homecoming." The narrator of "The Fuller Brush Man" " . . . imagine[s] [his] fingers imagining" a bartender's hair as his father once imagined his mother's hair, "reach out of reach for all things lovely" (61).

These examples might seem excessive, but so, too, is the repetition in *Thirty-for-Sixty*. Or maybe excessive is not the right word. As an academic, and realizing that Pittman was also a professor of literature for over twenty years, I would say that this kind of repetition is influenced by the canons of English literature and that it might hearken back to Anglo-Saxon annals and the repetition upon which the *scop* depended for mnemonic aid when he was pressed to recount the history of the isles to a restless crowd. Having observed how much Newfoundland and its history meant to Pittman, I might say that Pittman turned back to his country's ancestors and that there is something Wadham-like about the way he navigates his ideas with repetition.[1] Understanding how much time Pittman spent talking with different people – and even more time listening to them – I might state that this repetition smacks of the way in which people talk honestly with each other, not editing repetitious phrases and words but emphasizing their points and their interests as the conversation naturally demands. Or is there something more to be considered here?

Pittman's poetry has always reminded me somewhat of the poetry of Chief Dan George, a Coast Salish orator, rhetorician, actor and poet from British Columbia. In particular, it is a collection of poetry published by Chief Dan George in 1974 that reminds me of *Thirty-for-Sixty* – *My Heart Soars*. Like Pittman, Chief Dan George wrote for and about community – in his case, though, a pan-Indian community. *My Heart Soars* is especially dedicated to community, published, as it was, during the Native Literary and Cultural Renaissance of the 1960s and 1970s in Canada. During this time period, there was an explosion of writing by Aboriginal peoples in Canada considered, by many, to be unprecedented because it came to the forefront of attention after a significant "period of silence" in Aboriginal publishing. Critics such as Greg Young-Ing and Penny Petrone note that between the mid-1910s and the mid-1960s in Canada, not many Native authors published literary works,[2] and while this recognition has created problems in the criticism of Aboriginal literature, it is true that in comparison to the 1960s and 1970s in Canada, the former six decades witnessed little in terms of conventional publishing. *My Heart Soars* belongs to a significant moment in Aboriginal publishing and literary history when different types of literature by Aboriginal authors surfaced in Canada within a relatively short time frame. Translations of traditional stories became available in print for the first time.[3] Collaborative projects between non-Native editors and First Peoples continued to appear,[4] but Aboriginal translations which did not bear the stamp of another culture's interpretation were also published.[5] A significant number of political works also characterized these years; they were written by those trained or self taught in legal and judicial matters and could be termed "legal" or "strategic" literature.[6] Autobiographies or life stories were also frequent (Maria Campbell's *Half-Breed* and Lee Maracle's *Bobbi Lee: Indian Rebel* are noteworthy examples), and they gained a considerable amount of respect for Aboriginal voices. As well, a notable number of First Nations *elders* and *chiefs* published their life stories and accounts of history at this time.[7] Like those manuscripts which had been revived and offered publication for the first time during these decades, such as Edward Ahenakew's *Voices of the Plains Cree* (1923),[8] Mike Mountain Horse's *My People the Bloods* (1936),[9] and Walter Wright and Will Robinson's *Men of Medeek* (1935-36),[10] these works incorporated recollections of a past and advice for present generations.

One of these writers, Chief Dan George, consistently drew attention to the fact that times had changed and that his nation and others would have to adapt to the demands of a new world. He made the following declaration in a soliloquy in the Playhouse Theatre, Vancouver, in the spring of 1968, words later recorded in *My Hearts Soars*: "I am a chief but my power to make war is gone, and the only weapon left me is my speech. It is only with tongue and speech that I can fight my people's war" (In Gooderham, *I Am an Indian* 18). In 1974, he would make emphasize this point, inscribing his assertions throughout his poetry:

> Soon there will be many books
> that will tell of our ways
> and perhaps will shame even those
> who think us inferior
> only because we are different.
> To those who believe in the power
> of the written word these books
> will proclaim our cultural worth.
> It has been done so for other races
> and their teachings.
> This is how our young people
> will bring to you the true image
> of our native people
> and destroy the distortion
> of which we have been the victims
> for so long.
> Then we will prosper in all things. (55)

Like other Native writers contemporary with him, Chief Dan George was underlining his conviction that history had many faces and that there were other stories telling different histories. He was also encouraging the younger generation to write and suggesting that the First Nations would have to partake in "mainstream" literary traditions in order to ensure that their voices would be heard and their traditions protected. To be sure, this should not detract from the recognition that Aboriginal traditions had been assiduously protected in both oral literatures and in inscripted sources for years, but as Chief Ken Harris also noted in *Visitors Who Never Left: The Origin of the People of Damelahamid*, published in 1974, so many changes had taken place in the previous fifty years that it was imperative that Aboriginal peoples write and engage with Canadian publishing practices: "There is no longer the time to tell the myths as we used to in the old days" (xxiii), he said. In *Legends of My People the Great Ojibway* (1965), Norval Morriseau appealed to Aboriginal peoples to foster the youth and encourage them to partake in the traditions being carved by his generation: "I wish as I am writing that you, my people, would try to preserve our precious knowledge by encouraging our younger people to take an interest in it" (55). Like political activists of the time, Chief Harris, Morriseau, Chief Dan George and others were recognizing that silence and separation were no longer effective reactions to recent history and that literary, like political, endeavors would have to be governed by a desire to inform those who were not educated about Aboriginal traditions. In *The Unjust Society*, a book published in 1969, Harold Cardinal appealed directly to non-Aboriginal peoples to learn about Aboriginal values: "We offer our culture; we offer our heritage. We know it is different from yours. We are interested in your culture and your heritage; we want you to discover ours" (79).

A proponent of these sentiments, Chief Dan George, in *My Heart Soars*, drew attention to the past and its continued importance in the future. Though shaped by the *zeitgeist* of the Native Renaissance, *My Heart Soars* shares characteristics with Pittman's Newfoundland verse in *Thirty-for-Sixty*. Both texts poetically underscore the need for the younger generation to be aware of their national histories and to maintain the traditions of their ancestors. As well, like *Thirty-for-Sixty, My Heart Soars, as* the book's opening verse reveals, is also dependent on the autobiographical:

THANKS:
TO MY FATHER!

For he gave me skill, stamina,
and the knowledge of my past.

TO MY MOTHER!
For she gave me the love for life
and taught me to respect it.

TO MY WIFE!
Because she shared my burden
when it threatened to slow my
pace and kept by my side when
we travelled lightly.

TO MY CHILDREN
AND THEIR CHILDREN!
Because in their eyes
I have seen myself.

THIS IS GOOD! (6)

Throughout *My Heart Soars*, the reader is reminded of the continuity between generations as is the reader of *Thirty-for-Sixty*. The narrator has learned from his mother, who " . . . had a kindness / that embraced all life" (9), just as Pittman's narrator has learned from his mother's love of the river that he "splash[es] in her blood like a fish" ("A River Runs Through Her," 59). The words of a father leave " a deep impression on [the] young mind" (37) of Chief Dan George, as do the stories of the father in Pittman's "Thirty-for-Sixty" " . . . leave / his son one last word of wisdom" (62). All poets inevitably derive poetic material from the autobiographical, but not all poets are incessantly reliant on the overtly autobiographical as are Pittman and Chief Dan George. I am reminded here of Regna Darnell's observations in an article entitled "Narrative Authority in the Storytelling of Native American Grandmothers." Darnell thematically compares plains Cree stories, recorded in Freda Ahenakew and H.C.Wolfart's *kôhkominawak otâcimowiniwâwa/Our Grandmothers' Lives as Told in Their Own Words*, and "southern Yukon life histories of three elderly women as told in English to Julie Cruikshank," recorded in *Life Lived Like a Story* (48). Darnell attempts to explain the significance of a narrative trait which I think can also be attributed to both Pittman and Chief Dan George:

> The template for telling a life story seeks coherence in relation to past stories, both history and myth, and a pedagogical model of what will resonate with the experiences of the audience. Storytellers "mobilize traditional dimensions of their culture . . . to explain and interpret their experiences" (Cruikshank 1990:x). Narrative authority rests precisely in reflecting on experience continuous to that of the next generation. (50)

There might be something interesting about the fact that both *Thirty-for-Sixty* and *My Heart Soars* nostalgically remember "traditional dimensions" in verse, "mobilizing" cultural signifiers to register the importance of continuing and maintaining cultural traditions. However, it is the combination of this trait with others in both Pittman's and Chief Dan George's collections that is most significant.

Like Pittman's verse, the poetry of Chief Dan George is not only shaped by an awareness of communal vitality but also a dependence on repetition and a strong foregrounding of the speaking voice:

> As I *see* beyond the days of now
> I see a vision:
> I *see* the faces of my people,
> *your* ***sons' sons***
> *your* ***daughters' daughters***,
> . . . .
> *It is good to live!*
> *It is good to die!* (my emphases, *My Heart Soars* 22)

Here, there is the repetition of words, the repetition of units (noun phrases) within larger structures, the repetition of lines, and the repetition of sentiments and generations (sons' sons, daughters' daughters). There is also the indication. at this point, that litany (albeit, a specific type of repetition not found in Pittman's work) will come to characterize Chief Dan George's poetry, as it does:

> No longer

can I give you a handful of berries as a gift,
no longer
are the roots I dig used as medicine,
no longer
can I sing a song to please the salmon,
no longer
does the pipe I smoke make others sit
with me in friendship,
no longer
does anyone want to walk with me to the
blue mountain to pray,
no longer
does the deer trust my footsteps . . . (30)

Here, the repetition of a structure ("no longer") serves to build momentum and pose consistency between the disparate considerations listed which are all to be defined by loss, and the reader is forcefully made aware, then, of what is "no longer." There are also other forms of repetition which manifest themselves quite frequently in Chief Dan George's poetry and which are quite remindful of the type found in Pittman's:

If **you** *talk* to animals they will *talk* with **you**
and ***you*** *will* ***know*** each other.
If ***you*** *do not* talk to them ***you*** *will not* ***know*** them,
and what ***you*** *do not* **know** ***you*** *will* **fear**.

What **one fear**s **one** destroys. (my emphases, *My Heart Soars* 33)

Within this brief excerpt, there are three different types of repetition:
1) the repetition of words ("you," "talk," "know," "fear," "one")
2) the repetition of phrases ("you will," "you do not")
3) insinuated repetition created out of the expression of an antithesis ("you will know," "you will not know")

Likewise, throughout *Thirty-for-Sixty,* one will find words, phrases, and, sometimes, complete lines repeated within the duration of one short space. The most memorable example I can offer is taken from "Brimstone Head":

From *here*, looking **north**, there's *nothing*
to *see* but the *sea*. And in winter, *nothing*
but blue-white ice glowing and flowing
from *here* to the polar ocean. It's a sight
to behold and a long way from *here* to
nowhere **north** of *here*. (37, my emphases)

"Brimstone Head" typically repeats words, but there is another repetition here with the repeated sound – "see" – a word expressed as both noun and verb.

In order to make sense of these comparisons, I find it useful to turn to another poetic storyteller whose work was also published during the Native Renaissance of the 1960s and 1970s, Mary Augusta Tappage. Born at Soda Creek in the Cariboo country of British Columbia in 1888, Tappage told her stories to Jean E. Speare in 1973, and these were recorded in *The Days of Augusta*. Here, Tappage would recall the days of the gold rush and Western settlement; she would also nostalgically recall her former work as a midwife, as well as other traditions she saw waning at the time she spoke her verse. Within the study of Aboriginal literature, as-told-to-narratives – the combined work of ethnographers, editors, and/or missionaries and first peoples – are incredibly suspect, but there are still rich works which much be considered, such as *The Days of Augusta*. Recorded in this collection is a repetitious quality which is infused throughout all of Tappage's poetic stories, as is the case with "The Holdup," the first poetic narrative in the collection:

My aunt told us. We were excited.

It was at *Three-mile* **Creek**
there at the Hundred-and-Fifty-Mile on the old **trail**;
well the same way you go to Ashcroft now;
well here is this **creek**,
they call it *Three-Mile*.

It was all **bushy**
right to the edge of the **trail** *it was **bush***;
the government didn't cut right-of-ways
in those days, no –

so *it was all* **bush**.

. . . .

Anyhow this place was **bushy**
and **here** the robbers must have waited
till the stage went by. "***Stop***!"
They told the **driver** *to* ***stop***
but he was hard-of-hearing.

. . . .

The **driver**, he *didn't stop*, no,
when ***they*** *told* him. ***They*** *shot* at him
above his horses. ***They*** *didn't kill* a soul.
They scared the horses.
I think **they scared** everyone.

My aunt told us everyone was **scared**. (my emphases, 11-12)

Tappage's use of repetition is intricate, and I have attempted to show the different types of repetition in this poetic narrative. There is the repetition of words ("Creek," "trail," "Three-mile," "bush," "bushy," "here," "stop," "driver," and "scared"), a phrase ("it was"), and clauses ("it was bush," "my aunt told us," "they scared"). However, there are other types of repetition, or insinuated repetition, created by syntax play.

The second stanza begins by employing a subject complement which is an adverb – "bushy"; by the second line, the subject complement has become a noun. By the end of the stanza, the subject complement is preceded by an adjective – "all" – which marks a significant change from the description at the beginning of the stanza. What was previously a description – "bushy" – has become a concrete noun – "all bush." By the first line of the next stanza, the subject complement has reverted to being an adverb, but it has a new association based on the crescendo of changes which took place in the previous stanza, and "bushy," therefore, takes on a more forceful meaning. The repetition of the word "stop" is not straightforward, either. It is invoked first as an imperative – "Stop!" It is then situated within a main clause – "They told the driver to stop" – and, in the next stanza, the verb appears in its negative form, though again in a main clause – "he didn't stop." There is some similar method being employed in the recounting of the passengers' actions – "they told," "they shot," "they didn't kill." And there is something similar in the poem's ending – "they scared the horses"; "they scared everyone"; "everyone was scared." By taking words out of the original context in which they appear in the poem and employing them in different ways throughout the poem, the reader is quickly, though subtly, led to the poem's emphasis. The active voice creates drama – "they scared" – and reminds one of the possibilities involved in the negation of an earlier use of the active voice – "they didn't kill" – which follows on the build up of the use of the active voice in two crucial instances of this narrative – "they told" and "they shot." By the time we get to the end of this poem, we realize that there has been great potential for danger, and we feel this not only because of what is said but, more importantly, *how* it is said; that is, it is largely the shifts in syntax which build momentum and drama. It is also both the repetition of syntax and the shift in syntax at the poem's beginning and end – "my aunt told us" – that creates effect. By the time we get to the end of the poem, we realize that the poem's opening "[m]y aunt told us" is an incomplete statement – that we have had to wait until the end of the poem for the significance of what the aunt has told: "everyone was scared." The focus of the poetic account, then, is not the fact that robbers stopped a stage and robbed the drivers of gold but that the event or act created fear: it is fear which is recorded and remembered.

Does the repetition in Pittman's and Chief Dan George's poetry function in a similar manner? In "This Side of Heaven," dedicated to the Cape Breton singers "Raylene and the rest of the Rankins," Pittman explores, as he explores so often in this collection, the value attached to "here" – the here and now of community:

> Nowhere beyond here are there medicines
> to mend the broken heart or dull the dullest
> pain. Nowhere else is known the flight
> of birds, the eclipse of ecstasy. . .
> . . . .
> As long as you live this side of Heaven
> forever fare thee well.
> Only here has Heaven any need of angels
> or any need of us to be their guardians.
>
> And here's only where we
> might do our best to be so. And be. (28)

This poem fits nicely into a collection which functions as a piece of advice and a warning. Throughout *Thirty-for-Sixty*, Pittman scorns heaven, or the idea that one would want to go there in the first place, and he tells us that the here and now – the communities of which we are a part during our everyday lives – are the only things that matter. These are the only true measures of value, and "here," as "Rites of Passage" suggests, is all that we have got:

> The ground beneath our feet
> is our foothold for as long as we
> can stand and hang on. The sky
> is where birds and angels dwell.
> We've all been visitors there and come
> back home to the back yards of Heaven. (36)

This is a sentiment, but what exactly can be said about the *aesthetics* which govern this collection, as well as those which shape *My Heart Soars* and the verse of Tappage?

Perhaps it is a significant piece of wisdom found in Chief Dan George's collection which suggests possible ways to approach this question:

> When a thought forms
> it needs much time to grow.
> Silence between spoken words
> has always been a sign of deliberation.
> In these new times of a modern world
> where everything has become of value
> silence has become time.
> Time unused has become time wasted.
> We are told: "Time is money". (54)

This excerpt functions very much in terms of units which build upon one another and which are separated by a demand to process the causal relations between units. In some ways, this excerpt reminds me of the manner in which neo-Augustan verse of the eighteenth century depended upon rhyming couplets – units in themselves – to work together to build a larger, cohesive narrative. In the above passage, lines 1-2, 3-4, 5-7 and

8-9 form units which first function independently to produce individual ideas and which must then be connected by the reader to provide a larger narrative, or message. To deliberate on the first unit (1-2) is to ponder the time taken to produce significant ideas. The second unit (3-4) leads one to consider the value of silence in conversation. The third unit (5-7) equates silence with the most significant measurement of the contemporary world – time. The fourth unit (8-9) emphasizes that time is a mercantilist value of the contemporary world. Together, these different considerations endorse the following suggesting which the poem then makes, again in incremental steps:

> It is harder to find somebody
> who will listen, but everybody reads.
> Therefore, we must write about our ways,
> our beliefs, our customs, our morals,
> how we look at things and why,
> how we lived, and how we live now. (55)

There is a consistency throughout the fifteen lines of the above passages and their different units which is fostered by repetition; most glaringly, perhaps, the reader is led to consider Chief Dan George's admonition that Aboriginal peoples write in order that the uneducated can learn about Aboriginal values. However, there are numerous other considerations here (as I have outlined above) – the reader is given pause in the space between ideas which, though they build upon one another, must be considered individually. Typographically, the reader must literally pause at end stops, and it is significant that, throughout the portrayal of separate units, strong verbs and nouns are employed, and few, if no, adjectives or adverbs; that is, the language does not play with itself as we have come to expect in postmodernist poetry which inevitably draws our attention as much to play as meaning itself. Rather, play, or ornamentation of language, is repetition which serves to endorse the separate maxims asserted. A lot is not said here, and that is one of the poetry's prime strengths.

In a significant amount of Aboriginal literature, as well as in the poetry of Al Pittman, there is not only a dependence on repetition but also a paring away of the unnecessary, the excessive, the not needed. This is not a quality which defines the contemporary, postmodern poetry of a Paul

Muldoon, Ken Babstock, or Erin Mouré, to name a few notable examples. Rather, this quality could be considered somewhat anachronistic in the contemporary publishing world. Notably, this quality has been spoken about by a number of different critical voices which engage in the analysis of Aboriginal literature, including, but not limited to poetry. In his foreword to Henry Pennier's *Chiefly Indian*: The *Warm and Witty Story of a British Columbia Half Breed Logger*, published in 1972, E. Wyn Roberts describes his reaction to researching Salish stories:

> [T]he stories or vignettes came pouring out and I began to anticipate more the composition of the stories than I did to my accumulation of vocabulary and grammar. . . . I began to love this subtle humour, the kind and optimistic nostalgia of the stories, their honesty and *lack of pretension* . . . (my emphasis)

What Roberts terms a "lack of pretension" has been called by Christina Mader, in her study of Bush Cree Stories, "Taking it Back, Passing it On: Reverence for the Ordinary in Bush Cree Teacher Education," a "reverence for the ordinary" (113). This quality is also spoken about at length by Darnell who relies upon the prior work of H.C. Wolfart and Freda Ahenakew:

> Wolfart's introduction to the grandmother stories emphasizes that "almost nothing" about the lives of Indian women has been known "outside their own communities" (Ahenakew and Wolfart, 17). Memories go back to the beginning of this century, through oral tradition and personal experience; the "value system" of those times is maintained in the narratives by virtue of their continued performance. Because women are speaking to other women, much can be taken for granted. . . . What Wolfart refers to as "*unadorned narrative*"(my emphasis, Ahenakew and Wolfart, 19) is indeed informal and conversational even in literal English translation – an oral style having much in common with that of the southern Yukon women speaking in English of their comparable experience. (Darnell 49-50)

It is true that in the poetry of Chief Dan George and Mary Augusta Tappage, as well as Rita Joe and, more recently, Daniel David Moses, Phillip Igloliorti, Jeannette Armstrong, Marie Pokue, Nympha Byrne,

Christine (Kisitinis) Poker, the prose of Lee Maracle, Maria Campbell, Henry Pennier, James Redsky and Tappage, as well as the later prose of Ruby Slipperjack (*Honour the Sun*) and Beatrice Culleton (*In Search of April Raintree*), the stories of George Clutesi, Basil Johnston and Norval Morriseau, the essays of Aboriginal writers of the 1960s and 1970s and the essays still written by Drew Hayden Taylor and Janice Acoose, that there is a "paring away," a sense of the "unadorned" (notably, there is also the flipside – the very spectacle of language – in the writing of another coterie of Aboriginal writers who share a pan-Indian identity). This same "unadorned" is also found in the Newfoundland poetry of Al Pittman, Tom Dawe, Boyd Chubbs, Robin McGrath, David Elliott, the early poetry of Des Walsh, Boyd Chubbs, and Enos Watts where readers are also given time to pause, think, process and reflect. Significantly, in both bodies of poetry, the unadorned is also carried by the repetitive.

When Agnes Grant contributed to the University of Manitoba's Monographs in Education series in 1986 with *Native Literature in the Curriculum*, Grant identified approximately thirteen characteristics of Native literature. Speaking of works founded on Aboriginal oral traditions, Grant noted that they were identified by a "reverence for words," or "words not spoken apart from meaning" (63). Grant also suggested that in Native literature "the good storyteller does not create words to relay his story; rather, he discovers words which have already created a story" (63-64). Furthermore, Grant suggested that much is "implied" in Native writing because "common understandings are assumed" (69). In his study of an American Native movement similar to and roughly approximate in the United States with the Aboriginal literary output in Canada in the 1960s and 1970s, Kenneth Lincoln, in *Native American Renaissance*, also addresses a similar, aesthetic phenomenon:

> In general, a storyteller does not interpret or gloss the tale or tell too much. Listeners imagine their participatory places in the story. Just as silence speaks primally to the mind, so space is fertile without objects. Everything counts. "Nothing" can be suggestive presence. (49)

The "white space," or uncluttered nature, of much Aboriginal literature and the poetry of Al Pittman (as well as a significant amount of Newfoundland poetry) leads one to consider the valuing of silence and speaking which should be considered not polar opposites but operators in the same system – participants in narrative exchange. There is room to pause, process and reflect when reading a significant amount of the literature I have been discussing as, at the same time, there is room to focus on repetitive words, phrases, and sentiments. In fact, these things are demanded of the reader.

What I am suggesting is that the repetition which defines, in large part, the prosody of Chief Dan George, Tappage and Pittman might be inextricable with a valuing of silence – registered on the physical page in a poetics recognizably "unadorned" or "unpretentious" – which, in turn, grows out an emphasis on the speaking voice which likewise dominates the verse of those discussed in this article. There seems to be some sort of relation between repetition and the valuing of breath, or pause, or space which is indicated not only by the visual layout of this poetry (if a keen editor or graphic designer has been cognizant of the importance of translation) but also in the "uncluttered" sentiment and sparseness of language. To make sense of this, one could consider what writers during the Native Literary Renaissance of the 1960s and 1970s said about one specific difference between non-Aboriginal and Aboriginal values. In Wilfred Pelletier (Baibomsay) and Ted Poole's collaborative work *No Foreign Land: The Biography of a North American Indian*, published in 1973, Wilfred Pelletier (Baibomsay) speaks of silence and its value in Aboriginal cultures by drawing attention to what he perceives as the lack of this same value in non-Aboriginal cultures:

> One of the differences I noticed was that they would talk and talk and *talk*. My father talked some too, but not as much as those guys would, and my mother didn't say anything. It was hard to get used to. . . . They'd come and talk, talk, talk, talk. And priests! Never shut their mouths, never. I used to hear priests ask a question and before anyone could answer they would ask another question and answer it themselves most of the time. It was like using us or having us there just so they could talk to themselves. They would just go on and on and on, and after they'd leave the people would say, "I wonder what they came here for? I wonder what they wanted?" I can see now . . . that all white institutions are based on talk. The structure always requires one person to get up in front of a lot of other people and talk . . . and talk . . . and talk. . . . [T]hey don't even know enough to

> shut up and listen. And I don't just mean listen to someone else talk. Indians know how to listen to silences. Whites are panicked by silences. (37-39)

Jeannette Armstrong speaks of this same ethos in her and Douglas Cardinal's *The Native Creative Process*:

> One of the central instructions to my people is to practice quietness, to listen and speak only if you know the full meaning of what you say. It is said that you cannot call your words back once they are uttered and so you are responsible for all which results from your words. It is said that, for those reasons, it is best to prepare very seriously and carefully to make public contributions. (90)

These are importance comments, but I do not think the differences point so neatly to "white" and "Indian."

Rather, it is the commensurate existence, I think, of a tribal, or national, voice, *ipso facto* urgent to be heard and nostalgic out of necessity, its parameters delineated by a collective consciousness that scorns its ownership by "other"; an attendant and heightened awareness of the importance of listening, often to leaders or elders; and a strong connection with formal, ceremonial orature and its living continuance within an immediate community that leads to repetition as a dominant aesthetic and the paring away of the not needed. Furthermore, prescience in this type of prosody controls the character of its deliverance, rather than the other way around. That is, beauty shifts to and always serves a message rather than message becoming subservient to beauty or aesthetic (though the two are equal both inside the poem and out). Almost a paradox, repetition – the excessive – supports and lends itself to pared-away aphorisms, and maxims, the marks of what could be called a wisdom literature.

NOTES

1. Wadham, a naval officer, is thought to have written, in 1756, the navigational song "Wadham's Song." "It is thought that the Wadham Islands, or Wadhams, a group of islands at the eastern entrance to Sir Charles Hamilton sound, southeast of Fogo Island, might have been named after him" (*Encyclopedia of Newfoundland & Labrador*, vol. 5, 495).

2. Greg Young-Ing notes that "[a]fter Pauline Johnston's untimely death in 1913, almost six decades were to pass before another Aboriginal author would be published in Canada" (182), and Penny Petrone states that "[t]he decades between the First World War and the 1969 government White Paper on Indian policy was a barren period for native writing in Canada" (*Native Literature in Canada* 95).

3. See, for example, Alex Grisdale and Nan Shipley's *Wild Drums: Tales and Legends of the Plains Indians* (1971) and James Redsky's and James R. Stevens's *Great Leader of the Ojibway: Mis-quona-queb* (1972).

4. Norman Lerman's collection of stories from the Lower Fraser area in British Columbia, *Legends of the River People* (1976), and Randy Bouchard and Dorothy I.D. Kennedy's collection of narratives, *Shuswap Stories* (1979), are notable examples.

5. Norval Morriseau's *Legends of My People: The Great Ojibway* (1965), George Clutesi's *Son of Raven, Son of Deer: Fables of the Tse-shaht People* (1967), Alma Greene's *Forbidden Voice: Reflections of a Mohawk Indian* (1971), Ken Harris's *Visitors Who Never Left: The Origin of the People of Damelahamid* (1974), and Basil Johnston's *Ojibway Heritage* (1976) all recorded, in written form, stories and legends which had been handed down to, or remembered by, the tellers of these works.

6. See Harold Cardinal's *The Unjust Society: The Tragedy of Canada's Indians* (1969) and *The Rebirth of Canada's Indians* (1977), William I.C. Wuttunnee's *Ruffled Feathers: Indians in Canadian Society* (1971), Wilfred Pelletier's *Two Articles* (1971) and the collection of essays contained in Pelletier and D.G. Poole's collaborative project *For Every North American Indian Who Begins to Disappear, I Also Begin to Disappear* (1971), and Harold Adams's *Prison of Grass: Canada from the Native Point of View* (1974).

7. Henry George Pennier published his life story, *Chiefly Indian: The Warm and Witty Story of a British Columbia Half-Breed Logger* (1972); Mary Augusta Tappage told her accounts of history to Jean E. Speare, recorded in *The Days of Augusta* (1973); Chief John Snow published *These Mountains Are Our Sacred Places* (1977), an outline of Stoney history which described this nation's negotiations with the Canadian government during the making of Treaty Six and Treaty Seven; and Chief George Barker published his life history, *Forty Years a Chief* (1979).

8. In her introduction to this text, Ruth Matheson Buck explains that while Ahenakew's text was written in 1923, "[i]t was [only] after the death of Edward Ahenakew in 1961 that the papers were found in a tattered and neglected state by his niece, Katherine Ahenakew Greyeyes, who sent them to [Buck] because of [her] own interest in western history and the long association and friendship between [their] families" (10).

9. There is no clear explanation why Mike Mountain Horse's story was not published earlier. In his introduction to this work, Hugh Dempsey explains that Mountain Horse's story was notably "prejudiced against the old-time pagan Indian," and Dempsey suggests that this was because the publishing industry was still very much prejudiced against Aboriginal authors and that Mountain Horse "believed he had to satisfy [certain expectations such as these] if he expected to get his manuscript published" (x).

10. Stan Rough explains that *Men of Medeek* was written during 1935-36 but that "[i]ts author, Will Robinson, submitted the manuscript to several publishing companies, whose editors felt that its appeal was too limited" (preface to text). Then, in 1953, following the death of Mr. Robinson, his wife "endeavored again to secure its publication, but while editors showed interest, no company was prepared to arrange for its publication." When Stan Rough became aware of the manuscript in 1960, he "submitted it to yet another publisher, and after holding the manuscript for a year, they returned it feeling that it had a limited sales potential." It was not until 1962 that the Kitimat Northern Sentinel Print Shop published the work.

WORKS CITED

Ahenakew, Edward. *Voices of the Plains Cree*. Ed. Ruth M. Buck. Toronto: McClelland and Stewart, 1973.

Ahenakew, Freda, and H.C. Wolfart, eds. *kôhkominawak otâcimowiniwâwa / Our Gradnmothers' Lives as Told in Their Own Words*. Saskatoon: Fifth House, 1992. In Darnell.

Burnaby, Barbara. "Policy on Aboriginal Languages in Canada: Notes on Status Planning." *Theorizing the Americanist Tradition*. Eds. Valentine, L. P. and Regna Darnell. Toronto: University of Toronto Press, 1999. 299-314.

Campbell, Maria. *Half-Breed*. Toronto: McClelland and Stewart, 1973.

Cardinal, Douglas and Jeannette Armstrong. *The Native Creative Process: A Collaborative Discourse between Douglas Cardinal and Jeannette Armstrong*. Penticton, BC: Theytus, 1991.

Cardinal, Harold. *The Unjust Society: The Tragedy of Canada's Indians*. Edmonton: Hurtig, 1969.

Darnell, Regna. "Narrative Authority in the Storytelling of Native American Grandmothers." *Papers of the Thirtieth Algonquian Conference*. Ed. David H. Pentland. Winnipeg, MB: University of Manitoba Press, 1999. 47-62.

George, Chief Dan. *My Heart Soars*. Saanichton, BC: Hancock House, 1974.

Grant, Agnes. *Native Literature in the Curriculum*. Monographs in Education Series 15. Eds. Alexander Gregor and Keith Wilson. Winnipeg, MB: University of Manitoba Press, 1986.

Moses, Daniel David. "Preface: Two Voices." *An Anthology of Native Literature in English*. Ed. Daniel David Moses and Terry Goldie. Toronto: Oxford University Press, 1992. xii-xxii.

Encyclopedia of Newfoundland and Labrador. Vol. 5. St. John's: Harry Cuff, 1994.

Gooderham, Kent, ed. *I Am An Indian*. Toronto: J.M. Dent & Sons, 1969.

Harris, Chief Kenneth B. In collaboration with Frances M. P. Robinson. *Visitors Who Never Left: The Origin of the People of Damelahamid*. Vancouver: University of British Columbia Press, 1974.

Mader, Christina. "Taking it Back, Passing it On: Reverence for the Ordinary in Bush Cree Teacher Education." *Canadian Journal of Native Studies* 19.1 (1999): 91-118.

Maracle, Lee. *Bobbi Lee: Indian Rebel*. Rec. and ed. Don Barnett and Rick Sterling. Richmond, BC: Liberation Support Movement P, 1975.

Morriseau, Norval. *Legends of My People: The Great Ojibway*. Ed. Selwyn Dewdney. Toronto: Ryerson Press, 1965.

Mountain Horse, Mike. *My People the Bloods*. Ed. Hugh A. Dempsey. Calgary: Glenbow-Alberta Institute, 1979.

Pelletier, Wilfred and Ted Poole. *No Foreign Land: The Biography of a North American Indian*. New York: Pantheon, 1973.

Petrone, Penny. *Native Literature in Canada: From the Oral Tradition to the Present*. Toronto: Oxford University Press, 1990.

Pittman, Al. *Thirty-for-Sixty*. St. John's: Breakwater, 1999.

Roberts, E. Wyn. Foreword. *Chiefly Indian: The Warm and Witty Story of a British Columbia Half Breed Logger*, by Henry George Pennier. Ed. Herbert L. McDonald. West Vancouver: Graydonald Graphics, 1972.

Wright. Walter. *Men of Medeek*. As told to by Will Robinson. 2nd ed. Kitimat, BC: Northern Sentinel P, 1962.

Tappage, Mary Augusta. *The Days of Augusta*. As told to Jean E. Speare, ed. Vancouver: J. J. Douglas, 1973.

Young-Ing, Greg. "Marginalization in the Publishing Industry." *Looking at the Words of Our People: First Nations Analysis of Literature*. Ed. Jeannette Armstrong. Penticton: Theytus, 1993. 177-87.

Daniel Heath Justice

The Necessity of Nationhood: Affirming the Sovereignty of Indigenous National Literatures

> The only obvious difference between the French and the Indians [in Canada] is that the French represent a formidable voting block, which can decide who come to power and who does not....So is the right of identity simply a privilege of power? THOMAS KING[1]

The relationship of Aboriginal literatures to the broader Canadian literary canon is not unlike that of Aboriginal peoples in relationship to the Canadian nation-state – in a word, it is vexed. As Kristina Fagan (Métis) points out, "Canadian critics of Aboriginal literature have tended to look through the lenses of culture and colonialism," therefore side-stepping the issue of nationhood, which stands as one of the most significant historical and contemporary concerns for Indigenous peoples worldwide.[2]

This essay is engaged with two primary questions, one prescriptive, the other descriptive: what should be the role of nationhood in the study of Indigenous literatures in Canada today, and what is the significance of political nationhood in broader Canadian contexts? Each question is deeply implicated in the consideration of the other, and it is necessary to address both in the context of thinking of a vibrant and ethical literary criticism in this land. But before commenting at length on the first question, it seems particularly useful to begin with a reflection on the latter.

The "Good of All?"

As I write this essay, the twenty-sixth Governor General of Canada, Adrienne Clarkson, has ended her term, one marked by her well-documented commitment to recognizing the continued presence of First Nations and other Aboriginal peoples. Her successor, Michaëlle Jean, has been officially installed into the position. As I have learned since coming to Toronto three years ago, the Governor General, as Head of State, stands as both representative of the Crown to the Canadian people, and the representative of Canada to the world. As such, Jean's inaugural address – much lauded in Anglophone Canada, much derided in Quebec – gives some idea of how the mercurial public sentiment toward other "solitudes" in Canada colours the relationship of Aboriginal nations to the Crown.

In her inaugural address, Jean made the following bold announcement:

> The time of the "two solitudes" that for too long described the character of this country is past. The narrow notion of "every person for himself" does not belong in today's world, which demands that we learn to see beyond our wounds, beyond our differences for the good of all. Quite the contrary: we must eliminate the spectre of all the solitudes and promote solidarity among all the citizens who make up the Canada of today.[3]

While ostensibly commenting on the competing sovereignties of Quebec and Anglophone Canada, Jean's installation speech casts a much wider net, one with implications that quite firmly and predictably displace Aboriginal nationhood. Her support for a single model of Canadian cultural and political supremacy expressly demands an erasure of Indigenous political or social autonomy. By placing immigrants and settlers as both the moral and physical inheritors of a political *terra nullis*, in which the only significance of Aboriginal peoples is their generous facilitation of colonization, Jean presents a multicultural feel-good Canadian Dream that is firmly ahistorical, unabashedly assimilationist, and genealogically dependent upon hundreds of years of brutally repressive public policy toward First Nations and other Aboriginal peoples.

While Jean provides token mentions of "the wisdom of the First Nations," whose great contribution to the Canadian nation-state has been to "pass on to . . . new settlers the essence of this generous land," her speech presents the place of Indigenousness in Canada as expressly *cultural*, not political. According to Jean, there are many quaint and colourful cultures in Canada, but they are all part of One Canada. National unity makes the dreams of a poor Haitian immigrant a reality, and through hard work and love of Queen and country, she found that she could even rise to the rank of Right Honourable Governor General. Any idea that the unified nation-state of Canada which fulfilled her dreams and ambitions might have been built ingloriously on the bodies of Indigenous peoples is displaced in favour of the more heart-warming and predictable narrative of the Nice Natives sitting down with the Sweet Settlers to weave the grand Canadian tapestry. All we seem to lack from this account is the turkey dinner.

I do not doubt Jean's sincerity, nor her love of the Dominion of Canada. Nor do I dismiss the very real struggles that she and millions of other Canadians have faced in making a place for themselves in this land; as an immigrant myself, I feel some measure of affinity for her quest to find a new home that is free of the constraints of the old one. Yet, as a *Cherokee* immigrant to Canada, I am also very well aware of the fact that my presence in this land is inevitably connected to histories and policies of displacement against the Indigenous nations who were here first, and who are here still. No matter how sympathetic we might be to the very real difficulties and traumas of immigrant experiences, we cannot ignore the fact that the opportunities for non-Natives in Canada come as a consequence of the land loss, resource expropriation, social upheaval, and political repression of Aboriginal peoples. The "good of all" is not, unfortunately, quite as simple as it sounds, nor is it quite true in this case.

Affirming Nationhood

This introductory analysis, though questioning the problematic patriotism of the Governor General's speech, should not be assumed to be either a sweeping dismissal or an unreflective celebration of nationalism. Cultural critics such as Benedict Anderson, Paul Gilroy, Homi K. Bhaba, and others have made clear the constructed nature of collectivized identities, but their most influential analyses are generally concerned with the dominating creeds of nation-states and racialized identities. The political specificities that define the kinship-based ethos of Indigenous nationhood are deserving of a separate consideration, one that engages with both the political concept and reality of Indigenous nations, particularly as those qualities are represented in the literatures of Aboriginal writers in Canada. By doing so, I want to argue not only the necessity of such nationhood in any consideration of Aboriginal peoples, but also, perhaps, the inevitability of such an idea when respectfully approaching Native issues, for the discourses of Indigenousness in North America have always been rooted in political assertions of collective identity through their ties to land, kinship, and history. To deny the centrality of politics from Indigenous identities and cultural and artistic expressions is to dismiss the centuries of armed and ideological struggle of Aboriginal peoples to retain their communal, self-determining sovereignty. Similarly, to be a member of an Indigenous nation in a colonized country is a political act in itself, as the existence of such a collective is an embodied denial of the power of the State to claim either historical or moral inheritance of the land or its memories.

Jean's insistence on the good of all Canadians over the "spectre of all the solitudes" – "all" being a significant modifier, as it unequivocally extends beyond the issue of Quebec separatism – links her words and their implications to a rhetorical tradition that claims Indigenous lands and resources for the appropriative priorities of the nation-state.[4] There is nothing neutral in this language. However well-intended it may have been, such language is ultimately hostile to the survival of Aboriginal peoples as anything other than dispersed and fragmented ethnic individuals, whose identities descend from the assimilative commercial multiculturalism of Canada rather than being rooted in the kinship rights and responsibilities that have defined Aboriginal values, knowledge, and politics for thousands of years.

Indigenousness is *not* ethnic difference; it is both cultural and political distinctiveness, defined by land-based genealogical connections and obligations to human and nonhuman bonds of kinship. "Aboriginal cultures," according to David Bedford and Danielle Irving, "are not simply one more strand of a multicultural tapestry. Their traditions, which probably most Aboriginal persons want to preserve, are not easily compatible with the bourgeois, liberal democracy to which the remainder of Canada is committed. Being treated as equal Canadians amounts to culture genocide."[5] Cultural and, I would argue, political, as the political has been consistently targeted in Canadian policies toward Aboriginal peoples.

Indeed, re-embedding the political in the analysis of culture is necessary in understanding Aboriginal issues, as Kanawake Mohawk political theorist Taiaiake Alfred demonstrates: "Indigenous governance systems embody distinctive political values, radically different from those of the mainstream. Western notions of dominion (human and natural) are noticeably absent; in their place we find harmony, autonomy, and respect."[6] Cooperative relationship is central to most Indigenous epistemologies, both contemporary and historical; coercion and racial compartmentalization as foundations for social and political control have little common currency in the vast majority of Aboriginal traditions. When humanity is one of many equal peoples in the world – sharing the right of consciousness and significance with the rest of creation – humility shapes both the individual and communal response to the world, and the values of balanced relationship are more important than any individual achievement, especially those that might threaten that balance.[7]

Kinship and community sit at the centre of Indigenous political and cultural expression worldwide. In contrast, individualist Eurowestern politics of majority-rule democracy, along with free trade capitalism, emphasize competition and coercion as fundamental social values, and the dangers posed by these systems to Indigenous peoples are not insignificant, as Maori scholar Graham Hingangaroa Smith notes:

> [We must move] beyond the focus on the type of individualism that comes out of the new economic ideologies. The new focus on individual rights and freedoms and on individual choice is at once in conflict with one of the fundamental values associated with Indigenous peoples: the recognition of our collective solidarity. Such collectivity is embedded in our notions of family, tribe, cultural traits, values, and practices.[8]

Yet collectivity is only one part of what has been called "the peoplehood matrix," in which collective Indigenous sovereignty is embedded. According to Tom Holm (Cherokee-Creek), J. Diane Pearson, and Ben Chavis (Lumbee), there are four common and interconnected elements in Indigenous politico-social structures: language, place/territory, sacred history, and ceremonial cycle, all of which are expressed through community in lived experience and socio-political expression. Such a conceptual model, the authors argue, "is a holistic matrix and reflects a much more accurate picture of the ways in which Native Americans act, react, pass along knowledge, and connect with the ordinary as well as the supernatural worlds."[9] This conceptual model of relationship and engagement is far more responsive to the adaptive dynamics of Indigenous epistemologies than are the antiquated progressivist models of "savagism" and "civilization" that still permeate law and popular culture, and which locate Aboriginal sovereignties solely as historical, culture-based structures rather than as expressions of both historical *and* contemporary political concerns.[10]

It is worth noting that the vast bulk of nation-state Indian policy regarding Aboriginal peoples in Canada and the U.S. has specifically targeted Indigenous peoples *as* peoples, not as individuals. The existence of other sovereignties within the territorial boundaries claimed by these nation-states has been an obsessive topic of concern for both, on both economic and political grounds. As Holm, Pearson, and Chavis note, "colonization is the attempt to dispossess indigenous groups by denying, undermining, or attacking their existence as peoples....colonizing powers, to further their own goals, attempt to strip from indigenous groups each of the four aspects of peoplehood through the means of territorial dispossession, assimilation, religious conversion, or outright extermination."[11] Even a casual glimpse at the policies of Canada and the U.S. demonstrate the perceived threat of Indigenous nationhood to the nation-state, with assimilation of the tribal body into the state population – and the associated extinguishment of communal cultural, spiritual, land, and resource rights – as the dominant concern of the colonizing enterprise.[12]

If the dynamics of kinship relationships are the political extension of sovereign Indigenous nationhood, as defined by communities by themselves in the context of a physical and spiritual relationship to one another and to a particular land, then it seems reasonable to posit the recognition of nation-to-nation relationship as a useful and ethical foundation for analyzing a wide range of Aboriginal and Canadian issues, from politics, and history to sociology, medicine, and literature. To dismiss nationhood from analysis, especially when it is such a concern of Indigenous peoples themselves, once more silences Native voices and perspectives and reinforces the dominative power of Canadian colonialism.

The acknowledgment of nationhood does not, however, require an oppositional relationship to other sovereignties, as numerous alliances, including that between the Six Nations of the Haudenosaunee Confederation, make clear.[13] Indeed, an inherently antagonistic sovereignty is counter to relational worldviews that emphasize cooperation; kinship requires an adaptability that can accommodate the integration of others into the kinship system, either through adoption or alliance, two much-honoured social and political traditions in Indigenous North America. Alliance can itself be a site of Indigenous political action, according to Malea Powell (Eastern Miami-Shawnee):

> We need a new language, one that doesn't convince us of our unutterable and ongoing differences, one that doesn't force us to see one another as competitors. We need a language that allows us to imagine respectful and reciprocal relationships that acknowledge the degree to which we need one another (have needed one another) in order to survive and flourish. We need, I would argue, an alliance based on the shared assumption that "surviving genocide and advocating sovereignty and survival" has been a focus for many of the people now on this continent for several centuries and, as such, should also be at the center of our scholarly and pedagogical practices enacted in these United States . . . I propose this reimagined alliance not out of idealism, but out of my historical understanding of the ways in which such practices were central to the earliest treaty-relationships between folks who would later be called "American Indians" and the European explorers, traders, and settlers who came to this continent.[14]

Aboriginal peoples need not be seen as inevitable opponents or enemies of those communities that make up the Canadian nation-states. However, for any alliance relationship to truly be successful, it must be built on a foundation of mutual respect and equality, where the sovereignty of each participant is substantively acknowledged and taken into consideration, no matter how large a disparity there may be in size or power between the associated sovereignties. Anything less than full reciprocity of respect – on shared terms and standing, not imposed assumptions – is inadequate to the task of an informed ethical understanding within or among peoples.

Literary Nationalism

Extending this idea of an alliance and respect based on equal sovereignty into the other structural theme of this essay, assimilative multiculturalism simply *cannot* be the assumed common ground for discussion if we are to engage in a responsible and meaningful study of Aboriginal literatures. Although Aboriginal writing has received increasing scholarly and mainstream attention since the 1973 publication of Maria Campbell's autobiography, *Halfbreed*, much of that engagement has been through this assimilative lens, through which Indigenous peoples are read primarily as colourful contributors to the great Canadian socio-cultural mosaic. While this reading is generally intended by scholars and teachers to affirm the human dignity of Aboriginal peoples, it ironically erases one of the most fundamental aspects of Indigenous survival: the status of nationhood.

As Kristina Fagan argues in her incisive literary analysis of Taiaiake Alfred's political treatise *Peace, Power, Righteousness: An Indigenous Manifesto*, the cultural study of Indigenous literatures, though common in academia, is divorced from being relevant to Indigenous lives, and is weakened by its avoidance of political concerns. Yet it is precisely this distance from Native realities that drives its popularity. She writes:

> The "cultural" approach (sometimes called "culturalism") has been the most popular way of thinking about Aboriginal literature and identifying particular aspects of Aboriginal cultures (such as tricksters or medicine wheels) in a text. Compared to "nation," however, "culture" can be a politically soft and shifty term. Our ideas about culture walk close to "folklore," associated with identifiable external symbols – distinctive clothing, food, housing, language, and so on. Canada has a long history of fascination with such symbols; they represent a non-challenging form of difference where Aboriginal peoples become yet another culture in the mosaic.[15]

Although culture is an important area of study, when it is separated from the political sphere, readers are distanced from both the uncomfortable personal implications of colonialism as well as decolonizing strategies of intervening in the colonizing processes. "Culture" alone is voyeuristic; it gives access without accountability, and it fetishizes the surface at the expense of deeper significance.

Such avoidance is understandable to a degree, as discussions of colonialism – just like discussions of race, gender, class, sexuality, and other political realities – can evoke feelings of guilt, blame, fear, anger, frustration, and hopelessness. Yet those discussions also open a space for silenced voices to be heard again; they can break open assumptions and expectations, reembody exorcised histories, and open our minds and hearts to other ways of seeing, knowing, and believing. They also provide us with the possibility of developing anticolonial strategies that empower both Native and non-Native peoples toward lasting social justice. Cultural readings, by themselves, distract us, and they fix our attention on shallow surfaces. Culture alone cannot change the world. The power – and danger – of nationhood is that it *can*. Fagan acknowledges this, stating that "Aboriginal nationalism involves specific political demands with which the critic must try to come to terms. If we choose to work with the concept of Aboriginal nationalism, we must consider to what extent we support Aboriginal nationalist claims. And if we do support those claims, what does that mean in terms of literary value?"[16] We are implicated in the ethical consequences of our readings no matter what we do, but only one option gives us the possibility of challenging the terms and effects of that implication.

The critical expression of nationhood in Native literatures – literary nationalism – is a powerful extension of Indigenous intellectual sovereignty, where, according to Robert Warrior (Osage), the purpose is "not a struggle to be free from the influence of anything outside ourselves, but a process of asserting the power we possess as communities and individuals to make decisions that affect our lives."[17] Literary nationalism looks first to Indigenous contexts for interpretive analysis, to social histories, intellectual values, ceremonial traditions, and lived experiences of being both tribal – as in one's specific nation – and being Indian/Native/Aboriginal/Indigenous, a broader category. The plurality of each of these categories is not accidental. There is no monolithic "Native way" of expressing national or individual ideas, no single "Aboriginal worldview" that encompasses the variety of Aboriginal perspectives. Just as there are many First Nations and Aboriginal communities, so too are there many sovereign understandings of all that it is to be Indigenous in Canada.

Placing Indigenous nationhood at the centre of analysis shifts the interpretive lens. Doing so does not assume that non-Natives have no place in the conversation; it does, however, privilege Indigenous sovereignty of expression. Terms such as "mediation," "cross-cultural," "hybridity," and "cosmopolitan" abound in critical studies of Aboriginal literature, and while some good work has been written with a focus on bridging Native and non-Native worlds, the underlying implication is almost always that non-Native understanding is central to the exercise of Indigenous literary criticism. Once again, non-Natives are given a privileged (and, ironically, often central) place in the discussion, and when that point of privilege explicitly displaces Aboriginal nationhood and priorities, it renews and replicates the mechanisms of colonialism that many of the writers claim to reject.[18]

With nationhood and respect as defining principles of analysis, all participants enter with an awareness of their subject positions, and non-Natives cannot assume to be the subject of concern. Rather than Indigenous writers, scholars, and readers being located as optional guests at the Canadian literary table, this shift places the meal firmly in Indigenous hands, where non-Natives understand themselves as guests, and where Native priorities determine the nature of the food and conversations. Such a shift is an idea very much in keeping with Muskogee Creek-Cherokee scholar Craig Womack's call for literary separatism, in which "tribal literatures are not some branch waiting to be grafted onto the main trunk. Tribal literatures are the *tree*, the oldest literatures in the Americas, the most American of American literatures. We *are* the canon."[19]

Engaging Native literary contexts on their own social and political terms is the aim of literary nationalism. How, then, might such an analysis function, and how would it be different from current culturalist readings, especially in Canada, where the critical voices advocating this position are relatively few? The literature itself is a good place to start. Too often we read authors and texts in isolation from any shared context aside from the general "Native Canadian" or "Native American" category. This can certainly give us an idea of the larger commonalities between colonized peoples in North America, but it is a necessarily meager result.

What if we either replace or add to that reading one that firmly locates multiple writers of a shared national tradition in conversation with one another?

My own theoretical approach to the question is by examining nation-specific literatures and readings; following the revolutionary Creek-centered work of Craig Womack, my first scholarly book is a study of Cherokee literature through Cherokee political and social history. Given that critics, politicians, and the general public so frequently collapse specific nations into a generalized pan-Native category that erases the distinctiveness of its constituent parts, an approach that privileges specific nations and traditions seems to me an important intervention in the field, and one that gives voice to peoples and worldviews that are often erased or homogenized. Such a model need not be reduced to ethnographic reportage; if done thoughtfully, it will be anything but, as its attention to the socio-political is rooted first in the voices and texts themselves, then radiates outward to encompass the full and varied contexts of internal meaning and significance. A nationhood focus, far from being myopic or parochial in scope, actually necessitates engagement with broader influences, as one cannot know the intimate without understanding the ways in which that intimacy has been shaped by exterior social and environmental forces. A literary nationalist is thus very well placed to study cosmopolitan concerns, and often on a much deeper level than those who take a more generalist approach to Native literatures.

For example, although the term "Aboriginal" in Canada encompasses First Nations, Inuit, and Métis writers, the perspectives, needs, and concerns of each broadly defined group are lost in the general category "Aboriginal," as are the specific impacts and influences of broader social and political pressures. A generalized course on Aboriginal literature has a necessarily limited amount of time and resources to give to these specificities, so any study posited on this model will inevitably provide a very limited understanding of both the cultural and political contexts of the literature, as well as their aesthetic dimensions and functions. Yet if we take a nationalist approach and examine one or a few nations in greater depth – and with it, a smaller body of texts on a more intimate level – we become connected to the lives, hopes, dreams, and imaginations of the people in profound ways.

The Métis literary tradition is a good example. When we read the work of Métis authors as part of a diverse but connected political, historical, and literary genealogy, as well as culture, we not only get a deeper understanding of the conditions under which this literature has been produced, advocated, challenged, and disseminated, we are also more thoughtfully immersed in the relationships between the texts, their times, and their authors *according to Métis priorities*. Although Maria Campbell, Gregory Scofield, Beatrice Culleton Mosionier, Marilyn Dumont, and other Métis writers each have individual voices and perspectives, their diverse works are part of broader expressions of specifically Métis subjectivities. As being Métis means to be in a distinctive political status, both in relation to other Aboriginal peoples and the Canadian nation-state, any literature that expresses Métis subjectivity is inevitably embedded in political questions and concerns. The peoplehood matrix of Métis nationalism provides context and depth that other reading strategies are inadequately situated to engage.

This is not, however, to say that nation-specific analyses are the only thoughtful way of approaching the concept of nationhood in Indigenous literature. A thematic or alliance-based model is also in keeping with Indigenous political priorities, while avoiding the pitfalls of pan-Native or hybridist criticism that displace Native specificities. Cherokee scholar Jace Weaver's 1997 critical study, *That the People Might Live: Native American Literatures and Native American Community*, examines peoplehood and nationalism across a wide range of texts, authors, and communities, which he links through the neologism of "communitism" ("community" plus "activism"). Looking for these shared links does not necessitate a politically- or culturally-divorced approach; if anything, those links demonstrate the moral imperative of integrating nationhood into the analysis. Weaver says it best when he writes: "Only when we relate literatures to, and situate them in, Native history and the changes in Native cultures can we begin to understand them....Criticism not focused on and rooted in Native communities only serves the myths of conquest and dominance that seek to subdue and conquer, render tame, our stories."[20]

Imagination

It is the aforementioned moral imperative of highlighting Indigenous nationhood that seems, to my mind, the most compelling justification for taking such an approach. In the end, literature is an extension of the dreams, hopes, fears, and visions of its creators, and imagination is an essential aspect of any community's survival. In every chapter of *The Truth About Stories: A Native Narrative*, Thomas King writes, "The truth about stories is that that's all we are."[21] In making this statement, King is not diminishing the power of stories; in fact, he is emphasizing their power to transform and shape the very reality in which we exist. Stories *are* our world; they give dimension and texture to our existence, give us a sense of both the possible and impossible.

Those of us concerned with the continued survival and dignity of Aboriginal peoples have an obligation to expand the imaginative reach of those things that are possible. To teach Aboriginal literature as only quaint cultural artifact is to limit the imagination, to say that nationhood is impossible, that the only way to endure after centuries of genocide and dispossession is by fragmenting and blending in to the very system that created the devastation in the first place. It is to deny Aboriginal peoples the opportunity to heal from the woundings of history, to seek mutually respectful alliances with or strategic separations from non-Natives as they best see fit. It is also to deny non-Aboriginal peoples the chance to intervene in the consequences of their own participation in the colonialist enterprise, to seek a just and equitable future that is mindful of the past.

Imagining new realities is inevitable; it is part of being human. However, the terms of that imagining are always in flux, and here again we come to the moral imperative of doing this work. If, as David Newhouse (Onondaga) asserts, "the creation of the Indian was an act of political imagination," where "Europeans took a thousand different communities and created something that did not exist before: a new people," then it serves to reason that "the created who were made without imagination now have imaginations and are using these imaginations to create a new world and challenge the creators."[22] We can choose to replicate the impotent Indians of public policy and popular stereotype, or we can affirm the new world to which Newhouse refers, one which represents Aboriginal peoples on their own terms, according to their own diverse and varied histories, priorities, rights, and responsibilities.

Indigenous nationhood, in all its messy uncertainties, inconsistencies, and complications, is an integral part of that challenge, as it places our struggle at the heart of our survival. It is not simply blind jingoism in redface and feathers; if anything, it demands of its practitioners strength, patience, and humility, for it places us firmly in a reciprocal relationship of obligations to living peoples and the kinship networks of which we are all a part. And it posits an understanding where process is more important than product, as kinship is a living system, a set of actions and responses that change and impact others, not a static state of being. Nationhood – the political expression of kinship – is a constant act of creation, one that affirms the lives, dreams, and commitments of Indigenous peoples.

The affirmation of "One Canada" – or even one French Canada and one English Canada – cannot be said to be for the "good of all" when it relegates Aboriginal peoples to the position of bystanders in a land that they have inhabited since time immemorial. To engage honestly, sincerely, and deeply with Aboriginal concerns is to take into account the significance of nationhood to those concerns. Indigenous nations are not now, nor have they ever been, satellites of the nation-state. Yes, they stand as solitudes – not by choice, but by necessity. Colonization has given Aboriginal peoples and their literatures two ultimately untenable options: assimilation, or tokenism. Neither choice acknowledges Native humanity and agency, for both relegate Indigenousness to a secondary consideration in relation to the ambitions and interests of the Dominion of Canada.

Yet there *are* other alternatives, options that come from Aboriginal peoples themselves and grow strong in Native soil, options that open the imaginative possibilities beyond the Hobson's choice of assimilation and objectification. As a political, intellectual, and cultural expression of Indigenous realities and sovereignties, literary nationalism offers a much-needed intellectual and ethical corrective to the colonialist study of Indigenous literatures.

NOTES

1. Thomas King, *The Truth About Stories: A Native Narrative* (Toronto: House of Anansi Press, 2003) 149.

2. Kristina Fagan, "Tewatatha:wi: Aboriginal Nationalism in Taiaiake Alfred's *Peace, Power, Righteousness: An Indigenous Manifeso*," in *American Indian Quarterly* 28.1 (Winter 2004) 12.

3. Michaëlle Jean, installation speech, 27 September 2005, Governor General of Canada website, <http://www.gg.ca/media/doc.asp?lang=e&DocID =4574>,

18 October 2005.

4. This statement should not be read as supportive of the Quebec sovereignty movement. Just as the "states-rights" movement in the United States has been consistently anti-Native, often advocating the termination of tribal land and resource rights and the abrogation of treaties between American Indian tribes and the U.S. government, so too has Quebec continually demonstrated its quite selective approach to sovereignty. The Quebec separatist movement is firmly embedded in the hyper-assimilative patriotism model of exclusion, and is thus as compromised as that of the nation-state of Canada. Although Quebec sovereigntists are quite articulate about their own desire for sovereignty, their dismissal of similar Indigenous assertions – which has a much longer genealogy that significantly predates that of Quebec – amounts to an ultimately indefensible hypocrisy.

5. David Bedford and Danielle Irving, *The Tragedy of Progress: Marxism, Modernity, and the Aboriginal Question* (Halifax: Fernwood Publishing, 2001) 11-12.

6. Taiaiake Alfred, *Peace, Power, Righteousness: An Indigenous Manifesto* (Toronto: Oxford University Press, 1999) 5.

7. In *Honour Earth Mother/Mino-Audjaudauh Mizzu-Kummik-Quae* (Wiarton, ON: Kegedonce Press, 2003), Anishinaabe writer Basil Johnston explores this relationship, noting that "What our ancestors found out about the world was sacred; everything was sacred by virtue of its creation by Kitchi-Manitou, and everything was sacred because every form of life had an element of mystery" (148). Much of the book explores the nature of this mystery, in which all peoples – human, plant, animal, mineral, elemental – have consciousness and personalities, and all express themselves in various ways.

8. Graham Hingangaroa Smith, "Protecting and Respecting Indigenous Knowledge," in *Reclaiming Indigenous Voice and Vision*, edited by Marie Battiste (Vancouver: University of British Columbia Press, 2000) 214-215.

9. Tom Holm, J. Diane Pearson, and Ben Chavis, "The Peoplehood Matrix: A Model for the Extension of Sovereignty in American Indian Studies," *Wicazo Sa Review* 18.1 (Spring 2003) 15.

10. See again *The Tragedy of Progress*, where coauthors Bedford and Irving analyze the progressivist biases of modernity that have stood as one of the central conceptual underpinnings of social science, and with it public policy toward Aboriginal peoples. Progressivism, as part of the Enlightenment project of infinite human perfectability, implies social evolution from primitive (or savage) states to more advanced and "civilized" ones. In this model, Indigenous nations (as "tribes") have traditionally been seen at the bottom of the evolutionary scale, with free-market Eurowestern nation-states at the top.

11. Holm, Pearson, and Chavis, "The Peoplehood Matrix," 17.

12. In Canada, examples include: the Indian Act regime and the selective use

of Indian status to disenfranchise significant numbers of Native women; Métis exclusion from treaty rights and land protections; the residential school system and the role of religious proselytism, education, and abuse to coercively separate Native children from home, family, language, and culture; the "sixties scoop," in which provincial governments targeted Aboriginal children for removal from their communities and subsequent adoption into Eurowestern families; the proposed White Paper of 1969, which aimed to fully terminate Indian status and land rights and which has, in subsequent years, been a model for incremental implementation, as with the recent controversy regarding the failed First Nations Governance Act. In the U.S., examples include: the Grant Civilization Policy that paralleled the Canadian residential school system in many regards; allotment of tribal land holdings; termination of federal recognition in the middle of the twentieth century; and relocation of Indian families to urban areas with the express purpose of breaking up reservations.

13. In Iroquois tradition, the Haudenosaunee Confederation – or the Iroquois League – was founded by the Peacemaker along a philosophical and political structure known as the Great Law of Peace, in which warring communities were brought together in a common cause. Although they were bound together in alliance, the distinctiveness of each nation of the Confederation – Onondaga, Mohawk, Seneca, Oneida, Cayuga, and, later, Tuscarora – was recognized as being vital to the totality's success. The Great Law was an expansionist philosophy that encompassed other nations but, unlike Eurowestern expansionism, recognized the sovereignty of those nations that were integrated into the League. See "They Are the Soul of the Councils," chapter three of *Iroquoian Women: The Gantowisas*, by Barbara Alice Mann (Seneca), for an insightful analysis of the Confederation's political and cultural expansionism.

14. Malea Powell, "Down by the River, or How Susan La Flesche Picotte Can Teach Us about Alliance as a Practice of Survivance," *College English* 67.1 (September 2004) 41-42.

15. Fagan, "Tewatatha:wi," 13-14.

16. Fagan, "Tewatatha:wi," 17.

17. Robert Allen Warrior, *Tribal Secrets: Recovering American Indian Intellectual Traditions* (Minneapolis: University of Minnesota Press, 1995), p. 124. Warrior, along with Jace Weaver (Cherokee) and Craig Womack (Muskogee Creek-Cherokee) use the term "literary nationalism" as both the conceptual centre and title of their forthcoming book, *American Indian Literary Nationalism*, and it is from this and their other varied works that I draw my own understanding of the term.

18. For a very troubling example of such displacement and appropriation, see Elvira Pulitano's *Toward a Native American Critical Theory* (Lincoln: University of Nebraska Press, 2003). Womack has written an extended response to her book in the manuscript of *American Indian Literary Nationalism* (see above); I have

also discussed the book at length in "Rhetorical Removals: A Review Essay," forthcoming from *Studies in American Indian Literatures*. Pulitano's book is an extended attack on literary nationalism, drawn from the underlying perspective that colonization in the Americas has compromised Indigenous "purity" to such a degree that no one can really speak with legitimacy as an Indigenous person – except, of course, for non-Native scholars whose "cosmopolitan" perspective places them in an informed and authoritative position to do so. Needless to say, such a claim flies in the face of Indigenous survival.

19. Craig S. Womack, *Red on Red: Native American Literary Separatism* (Minneapolis: University of Minnesota Press, 1999) 6-7.

20. Jace Weaver, *That the People Might Live: Native American Literatures and Native American Community* (New York: Oxford University Press, 1997) 165.

21. King, *The Truth About Stories*, 122.

22. David Newhouse, "Imagining New Worlds: The Aboriginal Imagination," in *Aboriginal Cultural Landscapes*, edited by Oakes, Riewe, Belanger, et al. (Aboriginal Issues Press, 2004), 84.

Chelva Kanaganayakam

Spattering Dung over Canadian Lawns: Immigrant Writing and Literary History

In a comment that is both provocative and controversial, Irving Layton draws a comparison between Rienzi Crusz and Michael Ondaatje, and finds the poetry of Ondaatje less appealing than that of Crusz. "I think your poems have much more magic and substance to them than those of your countryman Ondaatje" (Mansbridge 337) says Layton in a letter dated 9 December 1981. Layton's preference, one assumes, is for the exuberance and passion of Crusz than for the more minimalist and understated work of Ondaatje. In a further comment, Layton, in a letter written to Crusz on 1 July 1985, comments that Crusz, unlike so many contemporary poets, has something significant to say about "the crude geography of east and west." He adds: "I especially like the way you spatter Ceylonese dung over the trim Canadian lawns. I have an urge to water each time I find myself passing one. Your poem "Conversations with God" holds cow dung and lawn in perfect poetic suspension."[1]

Strangely enough, the metaphor conjures up images of disruption and contamination that Crusz for the most part did not attempt in his work. His poetry expresses the despair of a new immigrant who is unable to bear the harsh weather of Southern Ontario; at times he encounters overt or thinly veiled racism at literary readings or even in church. He does not find the consumerism of the West particularly attractive. But these, in the whole corpus, do not amount to much, and his poetry does not possess the kind of resistance that is found in the writings of many others. Irony rather than anger or vituperative denunciation is his chosen mode. Nonetheless, Layton's comment has a particular significance in that it draws attention to the notion of intervention, of engagement with the Canadian literary scene. Crusz's poetry introduces, to use Bill Manhire's felicitous phrase, a "dirty silence" that Canadian literature so desperately needs. [2]

Critical response to Crusz's work is less willing to accommodate the Canadian dimension of his writing. While there is some acknowledgement that he works with relatively straightforward binaries of sun and ice, the main thrust of criticism has been to look at whether or not he essentializes the Sri Lankan landscape. Craig Tapping, for example, faults Crusz for indulging in what he calls "a colonial's dangerous nostalgia" (147), while Suwanda Sugunasiri castigates him for his betrayal of the country of his birth.[3] Very little attention has been paid to the fact that Crusz was forty when he came to Canada in 1965 and had written no poetry until he became an immigrant in Canada. His first collection entitled *Flesh and Thorn* appeared in 1974. He is, in that sense, very much a Canadian poet, although the themes that fascinate him are, admittedly, Sri Lankan.

Crusz's case is, in many ways, a representative one of the immigrant writer whose work is predominantly about "home" and only minimally about Canada. A number of writers, including Neil Bissoondath, Cyril Dabydeen, Lorna Goodison, Arnold Itwaru, Austin Clarke, Anita Rau Badami, Rohinton Mistry, M.G. Vassanji, and Shyam Selvadurai would fall into this category. They write about the lands that ostensibly nurtured their consciousness. And yet they remain Canadian writers, identified as such in the lands they left behind, or in the countries they go to for literary readings. The term "hyphenated-Canadians" sometimes gets used as a way of circumventing the issue of cultural identity, although writers continue to resist such labels that are ostensibly inclusive but in fact tend to marginalize writers.

The issue, then, remains something of a problem particularly when there is need to create a sustained literary history of Canada. Where literary history slides into a history of literature it is possible to claim that a multicultural Canada has nurtured a large number of immigrant writers who write about the lands they left rather than the ones that they have become a part of. Literary history, on the other hand, needs a continuity that explains the complex process by which conditions determine how works are written. There is a necessary link between the conditions – political, economic, and social – in which writers find themselves and the kinds of stories they choose to tell. The space they inhabit and the accrued meanings of space and time play a constitutive role in the narratives that are grouped within the framework of a nation. Equally important is the sense of continuity, of establishing connections that demonstrate the movement from one phase to another.

It is possible to argue that immigrant authors writing about lands other than Canada have a legitimate reason for being included as Canadian. At some level it can be argued that there is little difference from a writer who lives in Ontario and writes about the prairies and one who lives in Toronto and writes about Bombay. Both suffer displacement and rely on memory to create their imaginary worlds. The difference, however, might well be that one still deals with a landscape and context that is identifiably Canadian while the other does not. A response to this would be that the notion of Canadian as it is defined here is narrowly referential and is largely applicable to certain kinds of writing. None of these makes definitions or definitive categories easy to establish. It is hardly surprising that Monika Kaup, in a comprehensive essay on West Indian Canadian writing is led to ask: "When does a particular West Indian immigrant's writing stop being expatriate literature and join the Canadian narrative?" She goes on to maintain that the existence of a group of West Indian Canadian authors is a fact, but also concedes: "West Indian Canadian authors have also offered conflicting definitions of their group" (175).

This process of making distinctions and establishing a classificatory system, then, comes under stress when it deals with immigrant writing. Since it is hardly possible to ignore the writing that locates itself in places other than Canada, one option would be to offer a critique that claims that what is ostensibly about another country has an allegorical significance for Canada. Thus the preoccupations of a work such as *Such a Long Journey* (1991) would resonate with concerns in Canada. What occurs here, then, is a form of deliberate displacement that enables the writer to achieve a dual purpose. Often with realist novels, there is enough material to justify a latent Canadianness, despite the ostensible concern with unrelated matters. Particularly with Mistry, whose work focuses so heavily on the family as a metonym for the nation, the claim of universality is neither difficult nor entirely far-fetched.

Alternatively – and this is often easier to accomplish – it can be asserted that what is offered in such immigrant writing is precisely what is not available in Canada, but one that either evokes a measure of nostalgia or righteous self-satisfaction. Thus if Mistry's novel conjures up notions of family or community, that might well be a world that is no longer available to Canada in quite the same way. By the same token, the corruption or political upheaval that one encounters in Mistry might well serve as a reminder of the political and social stability that Canada enjoys. In short, the immigrant writer's narrative becomes the "other" and paradoxically, becomes Canadian by virtue of not being Canadian.

These are justificatory myths that are necessary and useful. But they still pose difficulties, particularly for literary historians, for the kinds of connections one makes with lived experience in Canada is often not reflected in immigrant writing. Even when the writing draws attention specifically to Canada, the thematic focus tends to be circumscribed in ways that are predictable. That they exist in such formulations is important, largely because that is part of the lived experience of immigrant life in a multicultural Canada, but they address specific aspects – cultural conflict, racism, and hybridity, to name the most popular ones. It is a matter of some interest that when M. G. Vassanji's *No New Land* (1991) appeared, not only did the CBC's *Journal* do a special segment on it, but also had a discussion involving three Canadians – one from the West, one from the East, and one from Ontario to discuss the merits of the novel. That it could be done is in itself a matter of some interest, for no other text by Vassanji brought up such interest. In short, a book such at *The Book of Secrets* (1994) or *The In-Between World of Vikram Lall* (2003) might be significant enough to win the Giller Prize, but it is presumably not *relevant* enough to create a discussion about its Canadianness.[4]

The fact that some of the finest books written by immigrant writers are not necessarily about Canada makes the enterprise of focusing solely on Canadian content problematic. Exceptions do exist, such as Ondaatje's *In the Skin of the Lion* (1987) and Sky Lee's *Disappearing Moon Café* (1990), but they are, quantitatively, a smaller number than those set elsewhere. And even when emphasis falls on those that are set in Canada, to reiterate the immigrant theme would be to further underscore the exilic condition of the immigrant writers. Within this framework, mainstream writers thus constitute those who write about the land, the landscape, and what it means to claim a sense of belonging, while immigrant writing is about not belonging.

Curiously enough, writing in languages other than English appear to be far more comfortable invoking the land and the people with much greater confidence and authority. Both in fiction and in poetry the literature that deals specifically with Canada accounts for a substantial body of vernacular writing. And they are not necessarily about race or ethnicity or forms of discrimination. Rather, they are about the land and its effect on the world view of the immigrant. Space, for instance, is an enduring theme in local literatures, where the private and the public, the sacred and the secular intersect in ways that alter social relations in a significant manner.[5] A short story written in the vernacular, translated into English, is likely to display a texture that is more recognizably "Canadian" than texts written in English.

Some of this is explained by the propensity of ethnic groups that do not speak English fluently to stay together. The English-educated seem far more willing to move into mixed or even white neighborhoods where they have little difficulty in interacting with the people or using social facilities. For those who do not belong to this category, the reverse is true. They remain insistently ethnic. But their ethnic loyalty also provides them with the assurance to look around and to absorb the new world that is made available to them. They see Canada on their own terms, but not as outsiders. The sense of being on the inside enables a sense of belonging and empowerment. Thus caste affiliations and gender relations undergo profound changes in Canada. The curious combination of witnessing a rapidly changing world together with the security of living among their own enables writers from these communities to respond more directly to Canada. While literary history hardly takes into account the contribution of this writing, it remains an important body of work, quite centrally Canadian. And this is precisely why in the "home" countries, such writing is more often considered "diasporic" in ways that English writing is not.

That said, in relation to sales and marketing, there is a much greater need for authors who write in English to ensure a Canadian dimension. Vernacular writers often publish their books themselves, and their readership is primarily their own community. A narrow system gives them the exposure they need. With writing in English, the stakes are high, and mainstream publishers are mindful of their readership and its needs. While it is true that the readership is not averse to material that they do not recognize as Canadian, it is likely that at some level they would endorse works that speak to them. It is also true that several writers, such as Rienzi Crusz and Cyril Dabydeen have not relied on mainstream publishers.[6] Smaller publishers with a limited print run give them the latitude to write more freely about matters that may not mean much to the "average" Canadian reader. For the most part, the "successful" writers such Ondaatje, Shyam Selvadurai, Vassanji or Mistry rely on mainstream publishers, and their readership is certainly not their ethnic community. They need a Canadian readership to establish a measure of connection.

This of course raises an interesting question about the possibility of detecting differences among those who consistently prefer major publishers and those seem content with smaller publishers. Ondaatje and Crusz are both Sri Lankan Canadian authors and both have been prolific as writers. But while the former has published with major publishers, the latter has published with smaller companies. This may not always be a matter of choice, but the fact that publishers have preferred one and not another might have something to do with the kind of writing that is likely to have mainstream appeal. Here again neat conclusions are difficult to offer since someone like Crusz has much greater Canadian content in his work than, say, Mistry who, apart from a few short stories, has chosen to write only about India. Genre may be a factor, since Crusz writes only poetry whereas Mistry writes fiction. Nonetheless, any formulation that seeks an easy correspondence between subject matter and mainstream publishing is bound to flounder when it comes to writers such as Mistry.

The issue of who belongs and who remains marginalized has been broached tangentially at various times and in various ways. One is the well-publicized Writing Thru Race conference that happened in Vancouver in 1994 and excluded all whites from participation. The rationale was that since the mainstream did not include non-white writers, it was important for minority writers to come together to discuss matters that were pertinent to them. How the drama unfolded will be of some interest to both cultural and literary historians, but the fact remains that such a gesture establishes a clear divide between white and non-white. The fact that some mainstream writers supported the gesture as necessary and significant and that some major immigrant writers chose not to attend the conference are equally important in establishing the absence of a clear binary in such matters. That such a conference did occur is, however, of considerable importance.[7]

Another attempt to look at the issue somewhat tangentially is in the collection of essays entitled *Is Canada Postcolonial?* edited by Laura Moss and published in 2003. The editor's introductory essay and the articles and responses written by a number of scholars are a testimony to the complexity of the question. An underlying assumption behind the collection is that if we were to agree on the notion that Canada is postcolonial in the same way that, say, India or Nigeria is, then it is possible to claim that resistance to colonial hegemony not only unites Canadian literature with other postcolonial literatures, but also establishes a grid for accommodating all immigrant literatures within a Canadian umbrella. According to this argument, all literatures are in some measure concerned with shedding the influence of colonialism, and differences in content are less important than the overarching preoccupation.

A corollary to this line of thinking would be that Canadian writing has been always concerned with interrogating the complex issue of identity. Given the historical context of migration and the very different ways in which in each region developed its literature, it is hardly surprising that all writers are concerned, at some level, with the troubling issue of identity. In that sense, it is possible to assert that Mistry trying to work out the complexity of Parsi identity in Bombay is no different from, say, Sky Lee working out the nuances of a Chinese identity in Vancouver or another writer exploring what it means to write from the prairies. Identity thus becomes one of the many motifs that serve the function of uniting what might otherwise be a disparate body of work.

Making this claim can be seen as an attempt to use a form of universalism to overcome the difficulty of establishing clear lines of connection. And yet, they might not always be far-fetched. Shyam Selvadurai writes an essay in which he not only draws attention to his hyphenated status, but also justifies such labels by stating that living in Canada had a profound impact on the writing of *Funny Boy* (1995), a novel set almost entirely in Sri Lanka. What he has to say is in many senses paradoxical. On the one hand, he states quite clearly that, regardless of the publisher and the audience targeted by the publisher, the readership he had in mind was Sri Lankan. Having learned about the contribution of Edward Said, he was determined to make sure that the tale he told about Sri Lanka needed the stamp of approval from Sri Lankans. The only way in which a writer could avoid the trap of essentialism is by making sure that a Sri Lankan readership recognizes that his objective was not to appropriate Sri Lanka. Writing about Sri Lanka from the perspective of a Sri Lankan was a way of ensuring that Sri Lanka would not be appropriated by the West.

As he puts it: "For someone to compare writing through the voice of another culture to that of writing through the voice of a tea cosy was, to me, dismissive and Eurocentric, and ultimately showed a failure to take into account the complexity of the world and its numerous peoples" (5-6).

But there was more to it than that. He refers to an international conference organized by PEN in 1989 and the protest launched by a group of non-white artists who called themselves Vision 21, and who were appalled that the program had very little immigrant content. In short, the whole episode sharpened his consciousness about conditions in Canada and in Sri Lanka. Canada thus provided the kind of context in which it was possible to write about Sri Lanka. Canada might not figure directly in the novel, but it made the writing possible and necessary. The argument here is a complex one in that it claims that being a Canadian writers entails a responsibility to ensure that the representation of Sri Lanka is accurate. In that sense Canada and Sri Lanka have a symbiotic relation to each other, but the essay does not quite address the problem of *Funny Boy* not being a Canadian work.

It is thus possible to argue that when literary history provides the social or cultural conditions necessary for a particular kind of writing, it does not matter that the subject matter does not have a direct bearing on the immediate landscape. Thus Shakespeare writing about a prince in Denmark or Tennyson writing about King Arthur does not make their writing any less British. They both responded to local conditions that made them write about countries that were not immediately relevant. Readers accepted them as legitimately British in the same way that readers of Cyril Dabydeen or Austin Clarke might accept their writing as Canadian. Such reasoning attempts to do away with subject matter as a constitutive aspect of Canadian writing.

In writing about culture and space in India, the anthropologist Dipankar Gupta draws attention to the idea of root metaphors that are central to the consciousness of a people. Root metaphors are subtextual, and they arise from a long period of living in a landscape where certain values become immanent. Root metaphors do not require definition but they remain central to the epistemology of a people. What remains unstated is the root metaphor. The notion of root metaphors is thus central to defining the conventions that shape the ontology of a culture. If one were to see that as a possible paradigm, then it becomes clear that for the immigrant writer, the subtext, if it exists at all, lies outside Canada or is limited to immigrants in Canada.[8] Such a stance might be viewed as essentialist, but it is not without a measure of validity. The very profusion of "vernacular" terms in immigrant writing flaunts the presence of an untranslatable dimension in the texts.

This assumption works better in a context where the population is either relatively homogenous or static. Gupta draws attention to regions in India that have not experienced much change in several centuries. The same is hardly true of Canada, where immigration accounts for a substantial body of the population. While certain areas have a few centuries of unbroken tradition, for the most part, certainly in larger cities, the more characteristic pattern is one of change. A literary history that looks for root metaphors is likely to falter in Canada.

That said, literary histories do no need patterns of continuity. W.H. New in his introduction to *Literary History of Canada* (1990) draws attention to a number of events that shaped the thinking and political climate of Canada in the last four decades. These conditions, including the Vietnam War, the changes in economy, the struggle over Native rights etc. are central to the way that Canadians saw themselves. And the literature, in many ways, works with these conditions as the backdrop. New quite rightly points out that increased immigration too was part of the experience of recent Canada. Having drawn attention to historical events that have had a shaping influence on Canadian writing, he also insists that any attempt to impose specific grids in order to unify Canadian writing will be be misleading. Although he does not devote a great deal of time to immigrant writing, he demonstrates that "few writers can adequately be contained by a single classification" (296). He elaborates:

> In the last two decades following 1960, while many writers continued to reach beyond national borders for parallels, personal interest and measurements of difference, more and more writers in both official languages were responding directly to traditions inside their own country … To acknowledge a tradition, however, is not to be bound by it. Contemporary writers have reinterpreted their literary inheritance in their own terms, for their own time. They have shaped the words of speech and history into the malleable forms of contemporary art. (296)

The notion of plurality thus becomes a way of embracing a body of literature that refuses to be contained in any single classification. The issue, then, is not whether there is something called "Canadian" so much as deciding on what constitutes such a label. This of course is a far cry from what Dorothy Livesay said in 1969 when she commented that "our narratives reflect our environment profoundly; they are subtly used to cast light on the landscape, the topography, the flora and fauna as well as the social structure of the country" (269).[9]

The distance between the two is not simply one of insularity and inclusivity. In his book on the Anglophone Canadian novel, published in 1993, Frank Davey offers an insightful commentary on the different stances that make any monolithic reading on Canadian literature problematic. The texts he selects insist on their multiplicity. And yet the sixteen novels that he considers in his book do offer some measure of unity. He admits that "all the novels considered in this book assume Canada in their assuming of the recognizability of a body of Canadian signs – geographical, historical, cultural – from Eaton's catalogue to the Hudson's Bay Company, from Ypres, Anne Wilkinson, Billy Bishop, the kidnapping of James Cross to the names of arctic explorers" (252). Post-national arguments, according to Davey, are varied, but they seem to possess markers that point to a recognizable Canadian identity. The manner in which he concludes his book reiterates his conviction that thematic unity rather than *weltanschauung* is likely to have greater success within a Canadian framework. Says Davey: "Specific novels may argue for a humanist Canada, a more feminist Canada, a more sophisticated and worldly Canada, an individualist Canada, a Canada more responsive to the values of its aboriginal citizens, but collectively they suggest a world and a nation in which social structures no longer link regions or communities, political process is doubted, and individual alienation has become normal" (266).

In his recent work on the history of literary histories, E.D. Blodgett is careful to veer away from positions that are "exclusionary, essentialist, and reifying" (18). He realizes that "the generic function of a national literary history is to construct the nation" (4) but makes the observation that a single stream does not constitute literary history, particularly in countries such as Canada. That said, he recognizes that Anglophone literature in Canada uses space rather than time as an originary and unifying trope. Metaphors of landscape may lead to stereotypes, but they do recur, and they shape literary forms and subjectivities. While Anglophone writing relies on space, Francophone literature, for various historical reasons, emphasizes time as a way or ordering its literary history. First Nations writing subscribes to neither and looks to a sense of collectivity in order to chart its oral and written traditions. Blodgett then adds: "Ethnic minority literary history, moreover, bears a complementary relationship to First Nations and Inuit literary history. Although their role as immigrants and settlers puts them the same general camp as that of the French and English of earlier centuries, they also carry with them the shadow of catastrophe" (13).

The notion of catastrophe is an important one, and it certainly applies to certain communities – Sri Lankans being a case in point – but not to others. And even when catastrophe or disaster serves as a common thread, it still does not necessarily make it any different from Sri Lankan writing written in Sri Lanka or elsewhere. Blodgett's classificatory model works well for Anglophone, Francophone and First Nations writing, but when it attempts to include immigrant writing, it relies on thematic preoccupation rather than inherent structural properties.

Ultimately, the notion and land and space, in their broadest terms, become central markers of national literatures. New points out in *Land Sliding* (1997) quite rightly that these are contested terms, and one needs to be cautious about the ways in which the trope of land is used as a way of comprehending a tradition of writing. He makes it clear at the very outset that his "intention here is not to produce a linear history of a national culture or a new geography of social relations, but to provide a discontinuous analysis of some textual practices, to indicate how, inside a social context, land-language *slides*" (17). How land is introduced, represented or configured depends on how authors choose to position themselves. But almost all the authors discussed by New have something to say about the land. It is true that the book does not provide a rationale for all literatures written in Canada. In fact when he attempts to be comprehensive in *A History of Canadian Literature* (1989) he admits: "In Canadian literature the language is plural, the network of associations (both within the country and beyond its political boundaries) complex. Few writers can be adequately contained by a single classification" (296). Nonetheless, the argument in *Land Sliding* is a compelling one, and its implications for literary history can hardly be dismissed.

In various ways, immigrant writers too have a great deal to say about the land. Crusz's "After the Snowfall" is precisely about the changes in the appearance of the land. The poem captures the author's perception with remarkable clarity:

> Through garage door lockouts,
> winter-hazed:
>
> bleached bones   the catalpa
> (without   its green crinoline head)
>
> King Maple   so humbled
> frail white arms   skying
>
> a tree
> praying for its life
>
> Driveway   divided
> snow walls   on either side
>
> the Red Sea   parted again
> and Moses   nowhere in sight
>
> But Pharaoh   on his snowplough
> continues history: walls the last exit,
>
> laughs: there shall be no diaspora today!
>
> O Lord, mine are summer eyes –
> tomorrow   the promised land?
>
> your Egypt   still shimmers and shines
> in its white   misery
>
> (*Beatitudes*, 4)

Here the poem is both about representing the real – the physical shape of the poem itself is significant – but also about transforming the image into something that is mythical and religious. The perspective is that of the outsider whose imagination alters the referential into something abstract and spiritual. The inability to adapt transforms the reality of snow into an image of exile. The landscape is hostile, and since it is also alien, the poet's consciousness shapes it in order to reflect a religious myth.

The landscape is also central to Ramabai Espinet's recent novel *The Swinging Bridge* (2003), in which the narrator keeps moving from Montreal to Toronto, and from Toronto to Trinidad. The novel is concerned with reclaiming land and renegotiating the effects of time. The juxtaposition of Canada and Trinidad is deliberate and often significant in the way it reveals the manner in which land in Trinidad is much more than property. Its associations are personal and communal, and distances merge with time in ways that determine experience. Losing or reclaiming one's land is about positioning oneself in a complex system of community life. In relation to the episodes that are set in Trinidad, the sections in Toronto and Montreal reveal space to be functional. Time determines distances, but not much more. As the narrator undertakes a journey from Montreal to Toronto, the landscape matters very little and the time it takes to travel matters even less. The only incident that is recorded during the journey is one that deals with racial prejudice. In some senses, the novel is about the failure to grow roots in Canada.

The notion of absence that the novel deals with finds expression in an essay written by Selvadurai in an essay that laments the absence of meaning in the landscape that surrounds him in Ontario. At the beginning, each trip to the cottage reminds him that his partner "belongs" in a way that is not available to him. His memories reside in Sri Lanka, where the landscape is inextricably linked with a way of life. The author is deeply conscious of the injustice of not having any claim to the land, but each year the perception changes: "With each year, I saw the progress of my entries from unfamiliar to familiar to taken-for-granted; a growing knowledge of my landscape." He concludes with lines that are optimistic about seeing the land not merely in functional terms, but in ways that affirm a sense of belonging: "The sun had climbed high in the sky and its rays stretched in great bars across the lawn. A loon was calling on the lake, a motorboat had started up in the distance, children were playing on swings in the neighboring garden. It was time to go swimming."

The fact that Vassanji won the Giller Prize on two occasions drives home the danger of attempting to use the nation as a frame to comprehend a land in which even pervasive mythologies have undergone profound changes. Fluidity rather than stasis explains the processes at work in Canada. J. Edward Chamberlin's book on First Nation's writing has the marvelously suggestive title: *If This is Your Land, Where Are Your Stories?* (2003) In his introduction the author asks: "Can one land ever really be home to more than one people? To native and newcomer, for instance? . . . Can the world ever be home to all of us? I think so. But not until we have reimagined Them and Us" (4). Reimagining is difficult when we persist in asking the wrong questions and expecting the wrong answers. If we insist on using the nation or even a circumscribed version of space as exclusive markers of belonging, then immigrant writing will remain marginalized. The stories that immigrant writers bring with them and choose to tell, or the manner in which they choose to structure their narratives, may not conform to the rules of conventional Canadian literature. The alternative might be to interrogate the literary categories themselves, since the richness and multiplicity of immigrant writing cannot be ignored without diminishing the scope and breadth of Canadian literature.

NOTES

1 The archives at the University of Waterloo.

2 Manhire's comment is made in relation to the poetry of New Zealand. He uses the phrase "dirty silence" to suggest the kind of intervention that he thinks is necessary to broaden the scope of New Zealand poetry.

3 Says Sugunasiri: "While Rienzi Crusz may not have hidden his immigrant status and seemingly identified with blackness, at least metaphorically, he is no closer to being Sinhalese or Sri Lankan, than Ondaatje, in his sensibility or rootedness. However nostalgic he may sound now, he is indeed the bourgeoisie who fled the revolution" (67).

4 For a valuable discussion of the implications of the coverage, see *Closed Entrances* (1994) by Arnold Itwaru and Natasha Ksonzek, pages 67-68.

5 My comments are based on the large number of literary works written in Tamil in Canada. While several of them deal with "home" or with some version of in-between existence, there are many that respond to the new conditions in ways that do not draw attention to marginality.

6 Crusz has consistently used TSAR in Toronto to publish his books while Dabydeen has dealt with a number of small publishers.

7 For a comprehensive account of the background to the conference, Angela

Hryniuk's essay that appeared in *The Toronto Review* in 1994.

8 Says Gupta: "A multivocal *regnant set of meanings* of root metaphors allows us a perspective on culture that is neither individualistic nor consensual. The multiple saliences in the regnant set of meanings arise from varying locations of actors and groups in society" (18).

9 Quoted in an article by Andrew Stubbs on Canadian Long Poetics, 18.

WORKS CITED

Blodgett, E.D. *Five-Part Invention: A History of Literary History in Canada.* Toronto: University of Toronto Press, 2003.

Chamberlin, J. Edward. If *This is Your Land, Where are Your Stories?* Toronto: Alfred Knopf, 2003.

Crusz, Rienzi. *Flesh and Thorn.* Stratford, Ont.: Pasdeloup Press, 1974.

Crusz, Rienzi. *Beatitudes of Ice.* Toronto: TSAR, 1995.

Davey, Frank. *Post-National Arguments: The Politics of the Anglophone-Canadian Novel Since 1967.* Toronto: University of Toronto Press, 1993.

Espinet, Ramabai. *The Swinging Bridge.* Toronto: HarperCollins, 2003.

Gupta, Dipankar. *Culture, Space and the Nation State: From Sentiment to Structure.* New Delhi: Sage, 2000.

Hryniuk, Angela. "'Writing Thru Race' and the Mainstream Backlash." *The Toronto Review of Contemporary Writing Abroad,* 12. 3 (1994): 1-6.

Itwaru, Arnold Harrichand and Natasha Ksonzek. *Closed Entrances: Canadian Culture and Imperialism.* Toronto: TSAR, 1994.

Kaup, Monika. "West Indian Canadian Writing: Crossing the Border from Exile to Immigration." *Essays on Canadian Writing* 57 (Winter 1995): 171-193.

Lee, Sky. *Disappearing Moon Café.* Vancouver: Douglas & McIntyre, 1990.

Manhire, Bill. "Dirty Silence: Impure Sounds in New Zealand Poetry." *Dirty Silence: Aspects of Language and Literature in New Zealand.* Ed. Graham McGregor and Mark Williams. Auckland: Oxford University Press, 1991: 143-57.

Mansbridge, Francis. Ed. *Wild Gooseberries: The Selected Letters of Irving Layton.* Toronto: Macmillan, 1989.

Mistry, Rohinton. *Such a Long Journey.* Toronto: McClelland and Stewart, 1991.

Moss, Laura. *Is Canada Postcolonial? Unsettling Canadian Literature.* Waterloo: Wilfrid Laurier University Press, 2003.

New, W.H. *A History of Canadian Literature.* New York: New Amsterdam Books, 1989.

New, W.H. Land *Sliding: Imagining Space, Presence, and Power in Canadian Writing.* Toronto: University of Toronto Press, 1997.

New, W.H. Ed. *Literary History of Canada. Canadian Literature in English.*

Toronto; Univeristy of Toronto Press, 1990.
Ondaatje, Michael. *In the Skin of a Lion*. Toronto: McClelland and Stewart, 1987.
Selvadurai, Shyam. *Funny Boy*. Toronto: McClelland and Stewart, 1994.
Selvadurai, Shyam. "The Influence of Canada in *Funny Boy*." *Across Cultures: Issues of Identity in Contemporary British and Sri Lankan Writing*. Ed. Neluka Silva and Rajiva Wijesinha. Colombo: The British Council, 2001: 4-10.
Selvadurai, Shyam. "A Vacation from My Past." *The New York Times*, July 5, 2004.
Stubbs, Andrew. "Forensic Rhetoric in Epiphanic Space: Crime as an 'Idea of Order' in Canadian Long Poetics." *The Brock Review* 8 (2004): 17-44.
Sugunasiri, Suwanda. "`Sri Lankan' Canadian Poets: The Bourgeoisie that Fled the Revolution." *Canadian Literature* 132 (Spring 1992): 60-79.
Tapping, Craig. "Front Lines." Rev. Hedi Bouraoui, *Echosmos*, Rienzi Crusz, *A Time for Loving*, C.H. Gervais, *Letters from the Equator*. *Canadian Literature* 117 (Summer 1988): 145-47.
Vassanji, M.G. *No New Land*. Toronto: McClelland and Stewart, 1991.
Vassanji, M.G. *The Book of Secrets*. Toronto: McClelland and Stewart, 1994.
Vassanji, M.G. *The In-Between World of Vikram Lall*. Toronto: Doubleday, 2003.

Cynthia Sugars

(Dis)inheriting the Nation: Contemporary Canadian Memoirs and the Anxiety of Origins

> The question of origins, then, is the central secret of our anxiety and anguish.
>
> OCTAVIO PAZ, *The Labyrinth of Solitude* 80

> Perhaps if one goes back far enough all our ancestors are adopted. . .
>
> ROBERT POGUE HARRISON, "Choosing Your Ancestors" 105

In the Fall of 2005, there was an exhibition at the Ottawa City Hall of maps and other documents related to the region's history. At the front of the room was a guest book within which an irate visitor criticized the exhibit's sparseness and identified himself as a descendant of one of the first settlers in the Ottawa Valley. The writer went so far as to include a genealogy providing proof of his august lineage. This urge for genealogy should perhaps not surprise us given the central role played by the United Empire Loyalists' Association and the International Order of the Daughters of the Empire (IODE) in Canadian culture. While the former association grants membership to people who are not of Loyalist descent, one of its main services is an authentification of Loyalist roots, submitted to the "Dominion Genealogist," and the issuing of a "certificate attesting to your Loyalist ancestry" (UEL website 1). Comparable attempts to identify Canadian "firsts" include the ongoing discussions, particularly among popular historians, to isolate the moment of first contact between aboriginals and Europeans. If critics have identified the indigenization process as one means of forging a legitimate presence in Canadian space, what Thomas King identifies as "the only antiquity that North America would ever have" (*Truth* 56), there has also been an attempt to go "behind" the aboriginal to chart the antiquity of the white presence in North America.[1]

Such attempts, while informed by a politically correct awareness of the history of imperialism, nonetheless seek a founding moment for Canada's white origins – an ab-originality that is not aboriginal. Competitions rage, therefore, about which people were the first to "discover" Canada, as if the land itself were still being claimed by vying imperial powers: before General Wolfe (1759) there was Samuel de Champlain and Jacques Cartier (1534), before Cartier there was John Cabot (1497), before Cabot there were Portuguese, Basque, and Celtic fishermen, before them, the Welshman Madoc (1170 AD), before him the Norse Vikings (~1000 AD), and before them the Irish Saint Brendan travelling to Newfoundland atop a whale (~560 AD).[2] All are contenders for the distinction as a prime European ancestor. Historians have even gone so far as to identify the first European born in North America, a Norseman Snorri Thorfinnsson, as a kind of symbolic ancestor for white Canada.[3]

The urge for origins has long been an obsession in Canadian cultural history, perhaps because such origins are a chimera. According to Stuart Hall, it is because the New World is constituted "as place" and hence invokes "a narrative of displacement" that it recreates "the endless desire to return to 'lost origins'" (402). Richard Cavell takes this one step further in his analysis of Northrop Frye's figuration of the Canadian landscape as "an originary space" (116), a colonialist abstraction premised on a felt absence and disjunction.[4]

Lois Parkinson Zamora has identified this as the "anxiety of origins" that characterizes New World cultures, what she defines as "a contrasting impulse to create precursors rather than cancel them" (ix).[5] Lacking anything as definitive as the Mayflower landing of the United States, or the convict ships of Australia, Canada's colonial origins, the moment when the nation (as a white nation-state) was catalyzed into being (even in a proto-national form) is impossible to pinpoint. While Benedict Anderson identifies one of the prime characteristics of nationhood to be the invention of a mythical "immemorial past" that "glide[s] into a limitless future" (11-12), there is no immemorial past for colonial Canada. Instead, Canadian nationhood is affirmed by attempting to identify a clear beginning from which one can chart the genealogical progress and validity of national identity. Yet not only is there no "moment" that one can fix upon to achieve this end, but there is also no single people that one can identify as the ancestors of the contemporary Canadian populace. If the absence of clear origins can be said to be something that defines the contemporary Canadian state, albeit in different modalities, it also contributes to a shared obsession with origins and ancestors. Where is here?, the archetypal words of the settler-invader, is transformed into How did I/we get here?, where the "here" can refer to the speaker's unsettled emplacement in contemporary Canadian space, and his/her presence in the contemporary colonial/postcolonial now. Such explorations not only seek an identifying point of conception, but are also compelled by a desire for a chain of inheritance, in some form, that can enable the present-day populace to make sense of itself. As Julian Thomas puts it, "The repeated suggestion is that the truth about the nation may be found concentrated, like a genetic code, in its homunculus" (118).

Zamora identifies this compulsion as the "Ancestral impulse" in New World texts (x). In her account, this historical consciousness is governed by metaphors that are spatial or existential. I would add to her list biological metaphors that invoke notions of genealogy. Indeed, genealogy represents a particular version of the quest for origins. However, while Zamora identifies the dominant mode of American (i.e., US) and Latin American cultural texts to be the creation of ancestors rather than the cancelling of them, I would argue that many contemporary Canadian texts create precursors expressly in order to "cancel" them. These texts operate under a dual compulsion: a desire to conjure legitimating ancestors, and a recognition that the authentification sought for in the attempt is illusory. In this sense, the "compulsion for antiquity" (Armstrong) is grounded not in "the fear of known precursors" but in "the obscurity or absence of precursors and a historicizing urge to identify and include them" (Zamora 8).

The classic notion of nationhood being rooted in a single people, sharing a common, if untraceable, bloodline, is obviated in a Canadian context because of the mixture of peoples that were present at the nation's beginnings and the compromised colonialist foundations of the nation-state. Despite appeals to such rhetorical figures as the founding nations/peoples of Canada, or the founding fathers of Confederation, or even, in feminist terms, the pioneering "foremothers" of Canadian culture,[6] it has historically been impossible to define the nation in such genealogical terms. The frequent anthropomorphizing of Canada's development as the offspring of Britain and/or France maturing "from colony to nation," which implies some notion of biological continuity, taps into this desire for and anxiety about origins. Nevertheless, appeals to a foundational genealogy (be it Loyalist, settler, voyageur, acadian, etc.) provide a way of circumventing the illegitimacy of the colonial occupation of Canadian land.[7]

Of course, this insistence on proven national bloodline is dubious on any number of levels, not the least of which is the inherent exclusiveness and racism of the endeavour. Himani Bannerji's analysis of the compromised foundations of the Canadian nation-state, and the exclusivity of the "Canadian imaginary," ties in with this through her analysis of the foundations of Canada as a liberal democracy imposed atop an exclusionary White settler colonial state (292-93).[8]Moreover, even as it undertakes a mediated turn toward history, the genealogical mission is premised on an inherent forgetting of history. According to Stephen Turner and others, this is especially true of settler-invader cultures which are premised on "a constitutive occlusion of the trauma of dislocation and unsettlement" (20).

Yet as Hall puts it, "If identity does not proceed, in a straight unbroken line, from some fixed origin, how are we to understand its formation?" (395). How does the past contribute to a sense of inheritance, what we might see as a sense of historical continuity and present identity? What happens when it is the continuum itself that is ruptured in some way, when history or ancestry, as conceptual terms, are placed under erasure? And what does this say about the "post" in postcolonial, which purports to signal an internalization, if not a negation, of the colonial ancestor? Are we witnessing the advent of a postcolonial ancestry, or, as Clark Blaise puts it, a "post-modern" ancestry, in the sense that ancestry itself is called into question even as it is evoked?

This interest in genealogical disruption and legitimation is a recurrent theme in many postcolonial fictions, from Sky Lee's *Disappearing Moon Cafe*, to Peter Carey's *Oscar and Lucinda*, to Salman Rushdie's *Midnight's Children.* In each case, the genealogical bloodline, and the quest for that bloodline, is rendered illegitimate or questionable through its having been tainted or disrupted by imperial history. As a result, the drive for genealogy, perhaps even the drive for a postcolonial genealogy, is rendered suspect. This is clearly articulated in the debate between Maria

Campbell and Linda Griffiths in *The Book of Jessica*, when Linda states that "Canadians know all kinds of stories about their ancestors. . . . But ask them about their own bloody grandfather that lived right here and it's, 'He was born, he lived and he died.' . . . I think the big gap is in our history here, not there" (95). This is a central question in many postcolonial literatures where cultural identity has been integrally unsettled by histories of dissemination.

A number of recent Canadian writers have explored their sense of disjunction and unhomeliness in contemporary Canadian space by meditating on the quandary of genealogy. Seeking "genetic consolation" (Blaise 140) in order to remedy this gap of identity, what they discover is that genealogical inheritance is necessarily deferred. Impelled by a combined urge for genealogy and an anxiety of origins, they demonstrate how such genealogies are disallowed due to the disruptions of colonial history, and explore the ways colonialism had a diverse range of disinheriting effects on different peoples in Canada. In some instances, the emphasis is on a paradox of origins, where the origins "are themselves oftentimes 'alien'" (Zamora 9). If the end result is a series of bastard children or orphans, the effect is to undermine the validity of genealogical accounts as in any way pointing to the coherence of Canadian identity today while at the same time contributing to a sense of shared (dis)inheritance. This paper will focus on a series of contemporary memoirs which contain such troubled genealogies: Clark Blaise's *I Had a Father*, Dionne Brand's *A Map to the Door of No Return*, Warren Cariou's *Lake of the Prairies*, Wayson Choy's *Paper Shadows*, Wayne Johnston's *Baltimore's Mansion*, and Thomas King's *The Truth About Stories*. In each instance, an interrogation of the purported origins/bloodline of the national populace occurs alongside a personal inquiry into origins. Yet the genealogical quest is disallowed even as it charts a process of discovery, which means that ultimately it does not satisfy the urge for genealogy. Each is marked by an elusive ancestry, defined by a mystery or secret that was repressed or untold. This may be the effect of diasporic migration, where cultural identities lose their purchase as continuous, homogeneous narratives. As these narrators discover, identity "is not a fixed origin to which we can make some final and absolute Return" (Hall 395).

What each of these writers is exploring, albeit in different regional and ethno-cultural contexts, is the impossibility of the postcolonial quest for legitimating ancestors in Canada. If these writers are linked by the impossibility of a decolonized Canadian identity, it may be their awareness of the unhomeliness of postcolonial identity that unifies them as a community of writers. Indeed, many contemporary writers in Canada have expressed anger and frustration in the face of an inherited historical disenfranchisement, both in terms of who has been omitted from official historical metanarratives, and in the sense of having been deprived of an understanding of the foundations of Canada's colonial history and its contribution to the present. Rudy Wiebe speaks of his anger upon learning that he was "memory ignorant" about the very land he occupied (134); Warren Cariou expresses his "remarkable ignorance" of his hometown on the Canadian prairies, which he believed was "a place of the new, a place of memories but not history" (40, 41). If contemporary Canada appears "unhomely," it is because it exists as a "site of unassimilable history" (Turner 22). This unhomeliness is charted alongside the unhomeliness of genealogical family lines that are constitutively aporetic. In each instance this aporia results from the irruption and/or suppression of colonial history.

On July 1, 2001, an extended article by Jack Aubry appeared in the *Ottawa Citizen* entitled "Diving into the Gene Pool." The article, featured as "A Citizen reporter's ancestral search," described the author's discovery of his "authentic" Canadian roots. A ninth-generation Canadian, Aubry's numerous and welcome discoveries include the revelation that he is descended from "this country's first Irish settler" who was everything to everyone: a settler/farmer, a coureur des bois, a trapper, and a survivor of captivity by the Iroquois (D3). If this were not enough, Aubry is also descended from one of the filles du roi, Canada's version of the First Fleet, the poverty-stricken women who were sent to New France in the late 1600s to serve as wives for the French settlers. A founding Anglo Irish father thus meets a founding mother of Quebec, merging to form an ancestral and inheritable "Canadianness" which is passed down through the centuries and surfaces in the person of Aubry in present-day Ottawa. This lineage is corroborated by a genealogical outline, running down the left-hand margin of the page, of the "Aubry Family Line" complete with coat of arms. That the *Ottawa Citizen* chose this article to mark the "Citizen's Weekly" section of its Canada Day issue is a testament to its sense of its readership, not to mention the constituency of "citizenship" itself. The article, written as a heroic tale of legitimating origins, while humorous in tone, is altogether unironic in its assertion of a continuous and authenticating ancestry. I begin with it because it provides a useful point of comparison for the meditations on genealogy that form the focus of this essay. The narratives by Clark Blaise, Dionne Brand, Thomas King, Wayne Johnston, Wayson Choy, and Warren Cariou are as tormented by an anxiety of origins as Aubry is untroubled by it.

Clark Blaise's 1993 memoir, *I Had a Father*, is, he says, "an exploration of my own sense of incompleteness" (ix). Blaise is haunted by what he sees to be a gap in his genealogical inheritance: "I had an ethnic father," he states, "but not an ethnic childhood" (ix). His book is a meditation on the allure of genealogy, pointing him "backward to the mystery of origins" (ix) only to draw him up short before a wall of unintelligibility. Significantly, it is not just his personal ancestry that obsesses him, but his sense of not belonging to a clearly identifiable place and community. As he himself states, he seeks a form of "genetic consolation" (140) in the face of ethnic and national disorientation. The narrative centres around the question that plagues Blaise: what would have happened had he chosen "le chemin de mon pPre" (ix). This phrase carries multiple meanings. Had he chosen the vagabond's path of restlessness and shape-shifting that marked his father's life, a fate that it is in him to have mimicked, his life would have turned out quite differently. However, he is also haunted by the distance he feels from his father's French Canadian ancestry. English-speaking and American-born, and tormented by his father's many absences and infidelities, Blaise nevertheless feels himself to be French Canadian the more the possibility of identifying as French Canadian eludes him. He experiences the ultimate form of unrequitable nostalgia, "nostalgia for this world I never saw" (29).

Blaise's peripatetic childhood contributes to his sense of homelessness, yet the narrative keeps circling back to the question of his father with whom he wants to see genetic links even though he worries that such links are an illusion. His memories are unreliable, yet resonant. Throughout the text, he writes about his genealogy in paradoxical terms: it is what he does not know about his ancestry (what he is not) that compels him most. More precisely, it is the paradox of genetic inheritance that most stymies him. Are we at the mercy of our genes/ancestors, or can we choose who we become? And what if we don't want that element of choice? On the one hand, he is not French Canadian because he has not lived the culture (not even through his father, who has tried to erase his

French ancestry, even going so far as to change his name). Nor does he feel himself to be at all like his father: "it seemed to me our bodies were enacting some comic inversion of inheritance, some ultimate joke on the gene pool" (127). "[O]ne of the few certainties in my life," Blaise writes, "[is that] I'm not like him" (153). On the other hand, it is in his blood since he feels the persistence of his ancestors in all facets of his life. His father "is my link to a tribe" (114). "I was my mother's son," Blaise states, "so why . . . should I feel only his encoding?" (10). If Blaise could identify "the vestigial structures he willed me" (180), he would be able to claim his "ethnicity," and by extension, a sense of belonging.

Yet any simple sense of national belonging is disallowed by his quest. French Canadians, he insists, are the "sons of the soil" (187), a "tribe" and "ancient culture" (114, 102), "the oldest North Americans" (26), and hence provide a form of authentic "indigenized" ancestry that is at once Canadian and diasporic, "mainstream and ethnic" (113). Yet any sense of authenticity is belied by the very impossibility of claiming it as inheritable. Even as Blaise invokes the rhetoric of heroic founding French Canadians, and identifies himself as "the grandson of sharecroppers and homesteaders" (86), his ability to conjure this national community as a homely space/people is disallowed: "It's comforting to know there's a place for me and embarrassing to me that I have no claim upon it" (176).

It is this ambivalence of inheritance that contributes to his sense of homelessness, and yet, this is the only home he has ever known, the only one he can claim as his "homeland": "Despite the fact that I was never a French Canadian, never spoke the language as a child . . . Québec is in a profound sense my home" (101). Blaise realizes this to be a kind of perversity: a desire for Québec that is always self-fulfilling through its very elusiveness. "[T]he only home I feel comfortable claiming is the only one I can never possess" (126), just as the ancestor he feels closest to is the one he never really knew. Without a home, there is no possibility of genealogical connection; without the ancestors, nowhere is home. And yet, for Blaise, any attempt at national distinctions based on ancestry and place is exploded through his awareness of the cross-border French Canadian diaspora. His ancestors are unlocateable; they are everywhere; this, in turn makes him neither French Canadian nor American but part of the globalized traffic of wanderers. Lumping himself among "history's castaways" (63), subject to "the world's identity-torn consciousness" (65), Blaise is a border crosser who comprehends the allure of national/

genealogical distinctions while realizing the illusion of such constructs. Nevertheless, he continues to invoke French North Americans as an identifiable "people." In the end, there is no resolution offered by the genealogical quest. If it offers the consolation of a kind of continuance – the final image of the book is a field of pumpkins that have all been sowed by one parent – he must forfeit the reassuring egotism of the quest and its location within national boundaries. Ultimately this renders the nation-space, as a conductor of genetic inheritance, nonsensical.

Like Blaise's memoir, Dionne Brand's *A Map to the Door of No Return* provides a meditation on the ambivalence of origins. Both works are discourses "on ancestral estrangement and filial longing" (Brand 61), and both engage with an irrevocable rupture of the diasporic genealogical line. As a child, Brand yearns to identify her African ancestral origins. Her grandfather teases her with a promise of a future moment of revelation, though he, like her, does not know the answer to the question of "what people we came from" (3). Nevertheless, she perseveres, drawn to the "Door of No Return," an origin that is not one, the place/moment of the rupture between Africa and the New World. If she can identify the people, she believes, she can locate "the home and nation" that she might claim as an ancestral homeland and, more importantly, assert some links between there/then and here/now, evoking continuity "as a touchstone to our present" (22). According to Edward Said, the identification of such origins offers a way of defeating the contingency of history, in this case a history that is marred by the horrors of imperial violence. The fixing of a definable point of origin, writes Said, is an illusion that "compensates us for the tumbling disorder of brute reality" (50). Likewise, Brand longs for "some continuous thread of biological or communal association, some bloodline or legacy" (67), which she invokes as a kind of cell memory that lingers at the edge of consciousness yet ultimately remains just beyond articulation.

Not surprisingly, the quest for origins yields up only "a rupture in history" (5). The "Door" is one to which no return is possible, neither for the slaves who were shipped off to the Americas, nor for their descendants who cannot locate that "Door" in any clear geographical or psychological sense. There is no possibility of getting back to the "before" of the Door's existence, which means that her ancestry is built upon a void. Nor, of course, is it possible to return to the Africa that existed then. It is not just a matter of not knowing who your ancestors are, but a question of there being no possibility of ever uncovering this. For Brand, unlike Choy, there are no "paper shadows" to provide a trace of genetic inheritance. There is no space behind the door to which one can appeal, even in the imagination. If Blaise lives in his imagined world of his father's and grandfather's Québec, Brand's African ancestors are beyond invention. *The Door of No Return*, then, is "no place at all but a metaphor for place" (18). As an imagined beginning, it is also a foundational non-beginning, a termination point. In Said's terms, this makes of the Door both an "intransitive" beginning (a "pure" point of origin) and a "transitive" one (one which has a teleological momentum) (50). The Door is the transcendental absence.

As a child, Brand hopes that genealogical identity will secure her a place, not only in some mythical ancestral homeland, but in the present, "cement[ing] our rights in the place we live" (67). In reality, however, this can never be, since the idea of Canada is officially premised on particular genealogical bloodlines. Brand's critique echoes Bannerji's analysis of the exclusivity of the Canadian imaginary: "Europeanness as 'whiteness' thus translates into 'Canada' and provides it with its 'imagined community'" (290). Brand, likewise, interrogates the notion of genealogical inheritance: "from the earliest Black presence to the present it would be easy, given the terms of entry for white settlers and immigrants, to presume that these same terms can be legitimately used to cement . . . [t]he right to nation. What we have to ask ourselves is . . . nation predicated on what?" (68). However, rather than appealing to the exclusivity of African origins, Brand is led to question the very concept of and desire for origins itself. "Too much has been made of origins," she argues (69). In this she echoes Hall's account of the two simultaneous axes of identity, "the vector of similarity and continuity; and the vector of difference and rupture" (395). Appeals to origins, she realizes, are responsible for racism and nation-based exclusions. "Nation-states are configurations of origins as exclusionary power structures," she states (64), which makes her own quest for origins suspect. And yet, to let go of the concept of origins is to let go of a key area of empowerment as well: "if I reject this notion of origins I have also to reject its mirror, which is the sense of origins used by the powerless to contest power in a society" (69).

Embracing this paradox at the base of identity politics, Brand's anxiety of origins transforms into a discourse on the shared experience of the contradictions of New World origins. If the Canadian nation-state is based on "a manufactured origin" (64), a "legitimacy based solely on conquest and acquisition" (64), this is an inheritance that all Canadians are answerable to, since it "play[s] to our need for home" (64). Whatever our ancestry, we all desire to fit in. If on the one hand Brand sees it as her mission to "narrat[e] the African-American presence that underpins the official story" (128), her goal is also to interweave this history with the inheritance of Canada's colonial history: "on the first floor of all our consciousness, all our imaginations in the Americas, there are these particular bones, shells carvings, arrowheads, broken amulets of the first peoples who inhabited this New World" (197-98). Interestingly, her interrogation of appeals to genetic origination folds back on itself. She cannot not be haunted by a desire for an authenticating bloodline: if the Door remains forever closed, she turns to New World aboriginals for authentification Hence Brand engages in her own version of indigenizing legitimation by asserting her aboriginal (Carib) ancestry through her grandfather. More than this, the grandfather is figured as a kind of genetic lifeline for the vanished Caribs: "They shared a common history. The Carib part grateful for its small survival in my grandfather's face" (222). If the African here takes precedence over the Carib, it is nonetheless the case that the aboriginal is necessary to effect a kind of authenticating ancestral line in the Americas (if not between Africa and America). Indeed, it was "the Carib in him" that saved her grandfather, and, by extension, his future descendants, by propelling him away from remembered catastrophe (a volcano that erupts on the island of Montserrat). The Carib in him is what makes him securely of the New World. Yet Brand problematizes this in an earlier episode when she describes a Salish woman asking directions of a Black bus driver in Vancouver. The irony of colonialism has scrambled things so that the "woman from this land walks as one blindfolded," asking "the driver through lost paths to conduct her through her own country" (220).[9] Ultimately, ancestry can offer no security against "the fissure between the past and the present" (5), and no security in the quest for national belonging.

For Wayne Johnston, the moment of Confederation functions as a kind of "Door of No Return" for Newfoundlanders: a beginning that also marks an end, and becomes a symbol for the haunting contingency of familial and national inheritance. If Brand can identify no clear family origins or place to effect a sense of belonging, Johnston's account is unsettled by too much family history and too poignant a sense of place, which in turn contributes to a nostalgia that becomes debilitating. In effect, it is the ties to Newfoundland that haunt and hold back its supporters, who "keep vigil for a destiny that will never be resumed" (227). In Johnston's memoir about his father and grandfather, *Baltimore's Mansion*, the ruptures in his genealogical history are laid atop the disrupted fate of Newfoundland following Confederation. The book is at once a lament for a lost Newfoundland and an interrogation of national/regional identity politics, which highlights an ambivalence in the book's treatment of Confederation.

At the beginning, Johnston describes a kind of nativized genealogy by establishing a link between the subjects of Newfoundland and the place itself. Johnston can trace his family name back into history, a kind of mise-en-abyme of sons of sons of sons (1), comparable to Anderson's notion of the "immemorial past" that marks national histories. Part of the family mythology is the genealogy of blacksmiths, "descended if not by blood then by trade" (30). He charts this genealogy of trade back to the time of the founding of the town of Ferryland by Lord Baltimore, who described the building of the first forge in 1622 (30). The founding of the forge is also aligned with a series of significant dates in the history of Newfoundland, all of which took place on the 24th of June: the founding of the first forge, John Cabot's landing, and the blessing of his grandfather's house and blacksmith's shop by the melted water of the "Virgin Berg," an iceberg in the shape of the Virgin Mary that passed along the coast in 1905. If this series of events charts a kind of mystic genealogy for Newfoundland itself, there is a slippage that occurs between the founding settlers of Newfoundland and the Johnston family line. In part this is because the grandfather's property shares its location with the ruins of Baltimore's buried mansion, yet Johnston also establishes his family line as one of the founding groups in Newfoundland's history: there were those "who referred to themselves as 'natives' because they were born in Newfoundland" and the "newly arrived Irish immigrant Roman Catholics like my ancestors" (66). The two groups merge their flags to form the eventual pink, white, and green flag of Newfoundland and hence become the founding European peoples of the colony. Years later, there is an equation made between the anticonfederates (those who voted against Confederation) and the first settlers, as though loyalty to Newfoundland is a genetic trace. The words of "The Lament for Newfoundland," which Wayne's Uncle Harold recites at a family gathering, effects this link between "the men who built our island" and "[t]hose who lost the fight for freedom" (68), a link that is further established through the aligning of Peter Cashin (the leader of the antconfederate campaign) and the Irish freedom fighter Parnell. The connection is also laid via Baltimore's naming of the Avalon peninsula after King Arthur's resting place, and the name of Wayne's father (Arthur), so that his father's destiny takes on mystical resonance and is somehow implicated in the destiny of Newfoundland as a whole. In a sense, King Arthur becomes a kind of transcendental ancestor for the Johnston family line, invoked by Lord Baltimore, and revived in Wayne's father, who, like his namesake, suffers a "grievous wound" from which he must be healed.

From the outset, the genetic chain transmitted from grandfather (Charlie), to son (Arthur), to grandson (Wayne) is established, an effect that is exaggerated by the frequent use of the third person "He," so that it is sometimes unclear which Johnston is being described at any given time. However, early on Wayne gleans that all does not meet the eye in this family sequence. Not only is a rift is introduced between Arthur and Charlie when Charlie reveals that the blacksmith trade is dying out and he will be the last of the Johnston blacksmiths (37), but it soon becomes clear that there is a more serious rupture when Arthur discovers that his father had been one of the "closet confederates," those who pretended to support independence but in fact voted for Confederation. The notion of genealogical links between people and place/nation is thus undercut, since it is clear that Charlie still loves Newfoundland even though he has voted in favour of union with Canada. This renders the one-to-one alignment of independence politics with an "inherited" link to the land/place problematic. This dilemma is further compounded when Charlie becomes figured as a kind of founding father in his betrayal of Newfoundland, a betrayal or curse that will be handed down to his son and grandson when they decide that they, too, must abandon Newfoundland for Canada.

In this way, the family genealogy, and its rupture, is charted alongside the destiny of Newfoundland. Indeed, it is during the counting of the votes that Charlie dies, as though he and Newfoundland are dying at the same moment. Arthur's vociferous antipathy to the Confederate cause becomes understandable when we realize his sense of betrayal by his father. Yet even Arthur's Newfoundland nationalism has been passed down from father to son. While Arthur identifies Confederation as the beginning of the end for the "country" (i.e., Newfoundland), Charlie speaks of the British takeover of the island in 1934 in similar terms: "will we ever get the country back," he asks his son (43). Both are plagued by a desire to return Newfoundland to its untainted origins, a yearning that proves impossible and destructive.

Confederation stands as the pivotal de-originary moment in the book – for Newfoundland, and for Johnston's ancestors. If the memoir charts the simultaneous founding and unfounding of a country, it also traces the derailing of a family history. In the process, the text deconstructs the teleological and ancestral drive of national narratives. Here the point of "origin," Newfoundland's entry into Confederation and the beginning of Canada as we know it today, marks the end of a nation, the moment when Newfoundland's potential, as an independent country, was obviated. The point of origin is thus construed as a foundational trauma. While Johnston's father obsesses about the referendum and its outcome, he is not so much deconstructing the event as insisting upon it. Indeed, the author notes how after Joey Smallwood's resignation and death, his family felt an immense loss, as though their raison d'Ltre had been stolen from them. This is emblematized in the father's insistence on referring to Newfoundland as a "country" rather than a "province," even years after Confederation. And yet, he tells his son that "'[t]he land . . . is more important than the country'" (227), realizing that "nationality was obsolete" (229). As "[c]itizens of no country" (228), Newfoundlanders come to feel themselves displaced in their own land. This is emblematized not only in the accelerated pace of exile from the island to the mainland, but also in the forced emptying of the outports in the 1960s, which left behind a series of ghost towns. Significantly, the book concludes with three departures: Wayne's leave-taking of Newfoundland to pursue a writing career; his father's departure to Alberta to follow his family; and Charlie's death in 1948/9, leaving the real world of Newfoundland's Avalon peninsula and crossing over into the mythical Avalon after death. While the genealogical foundations of a regional identity may afford some kind of antidote to the "crisis of belonging" (Cariou 11), Johnston's poignant memoir reveals that quest to be fraught. If the insistence on national, genealogical destiny is suspect, so is the commitment to regional stasis and identity, transforming the experience of belonging – to a clan, a region, or a nation – into a definitive, yet insatiable, haunting.

Wayson Choy's 1999 memoir, *Paper Shadows*, describes an entire community that is constituted by a disruption of origins, not only because of its diasporic nature, but because of state interventions that necessitated a system of intergenerational secrecy. While Choy's narrative documents his personal discovery of a rupture in his genealogical line, his account echoes the experience of innumerable Chinese families who were split apart as a result of emigration and were eventually sundered when the Canadian state issued its strictures against further Chinese immigration. Choy identifies his family as among the last wave of immigrants from China prior to the institution of the Chinese Exclusion Act in 1923, an attempt on the part of the Canadian government to ensure that Chinese immigrants did not alter the supposed genealogical purity of the Canadian nation. Choy's account not only highlights the racism and denial underlying government policy, but it also uncovers the damaging effects of such intolerance on a community that was historically defined by taxonomies of ancestral descent.

From the outset, Choy's memoir delineates an anxiety of origins, not only in terms of its protagonist's ruptured genealogical ancestry, but also in terms of any clear definition of New World/Canadian identity. If many of his "Uncles" are descended from a more established Chinese Canadian line, the railway men who arrived in Canada in the late 1800s, they too are kept apart from their relatives and become artificial members of surrogate Chinatown families. Hence, in a very daily sense Choy's relatives are "fake," relatives in name only. Choy's family are more recent arrivals who struggle with the split between generations of Old-World Chinese and New. The "mo-no" or local born generation embodies that split between worlds, marking both a point of origination and termination: "A mo-no was what the elders called a local-born like myself, someone raised in Gold Mountain who was thoughtless and mindless of the Old China traditions. A mo-no was Chinese and not-Chinese at the same time" (78). If this in-between generation is defined by a kind of divided ancestry, it is also this generation that confronts the enigma of genealogy in its particular incarnation in the Chinese Canadian community.

Choy's personal discovery, therefore, is not a singular one, as it emblematizes the experience of an entire community that has suffered genealogical rupture. Living under the illusion that his parents and grandparents are his biological family, Choy accidentally discovers that he was adopted, a discovery that renders him "a kind of orphan" (278). Most of the narrative is devoted to a loving and detailed account of his life with his adoptive parents, "the Chinatown childhood" of the book's title. Yet the impetus for the book is the intrusion of his "real" mother's ghost, an ancestor who both is and is not one. The book describes the haunting effect of genealogical contingency. Choy is tormented by the niggling sense that there is something hidden from him; more specifically, he charts a series of uncanny memories associated with his mother, all of which are based on an intangible awareness of the inevitability of his mother's (but which one's?) absence/death.

Choy was one of many children who were adopted in pre-1945 Chinatown. If the "boys were bought by childless couples to continue the family name" (282), what they provide is in fact an illusion of genealogy, a genealogy that is based on nothing but "paper shadows," official documents that testify to one's heritage. What Choy soon discovers, however, is that the entire community is grounded in assumed identities. Indeed, Choy learns that he has three mothers: Nellie Hop Wah (his paper mother, the false name on his mother's documents; her assumed identity); Lillian Choy (the mother who raises him); and an unknown woman who remains nameless yet is the one who gave birth to him. Even the name "Choy," he discovers, is a false one since it is an anglicized version of his grandfather's name "Tuey." Ironically, the paper names come to assume more reality than the people themselves, since in some cases paper trails are the only links between Old World and New. When Choy tries to trace his father's and grandfather's emigration to Canada, he cannot find the documentation because he does not know what paper names they were using, and these are the only ones that will be documented. "[T]he secrets of Old Chinatown families," he notes, "are buried among these hundreds of assumed names" (289).

Still, Choy grasps at genealogical inheritance, even as he knows it to be deceptive, a retroactive desire for some kind of teleology. He is reassured, for instance, to learn that his biological father was a member of the Cantonese Opera Company because he recalls his own enthrallment with the opera when he was a boy. However, the circumstances of his birth and adoption are never made clear, nor is the identity of his mother ever divulged. The quest for genealogical security is thus rendered an inherently unhomely one: "how does anyone come to think of parents and family and home, as if there were no mysteries, really?" (337-38). Genealogy is like the "endless knot" that Choy salvages from a set of Chinese wind chimes when he is a boy, "seemingly without a beginning or an end" (248). It thereby defies the logic of ancestry and descent, emblematizing, instead, a form of continuity plus rupture. This may be the allure of genealogy: that it is shrouded in mystery and is therefore haunting, while it also offers an illusion of reassurance and continuity. Absolute origins, such as Choy seeks, are necessarily absent origins. This renders the entire genealogical enterprise an inherently unhomely one: "It's surprising we know anything" (338). The error is to expect clear continuity, to expect there to be no mysteries. The Chinatown families, while ostensibly committed to the continuance of bloodline, are also matter-of-fact in the face of the realities that the illusion of such continuity depends on: "let old days rest" (280). Choy is surprised at the silence of an entire community because it takes him time to accept that the story of his life is not unique. Indeed, at the same time as he learns the details of his adoption, he also learns the truth of his father's traumatic separation from his own mother when he was forcibly removed from her and taken to Canada. By the end, Choy realizes that all ancestors are necessarily nothing but "paper shadows," names on paper that are inherently deceptive since they lure one into believing in the possibility of inheritability. If anything unites contemporary Canadians, it is this. "Whose life," he concludes, "is not an endless knot?" (338).

"Where do I come from?" (3) is the question that opens Warren Cariou's 2002 memoir, Lake of the Prairies. Throughout, Cariou is tormented by the niggling feeling that he is not who he thinks he is. The problem with origins, he suggests, is that they are always storied: "We always have to take someone's word for it, that mystery of origins" (4). And the problem with this is that inevitably things have been omitted. It is this ambiguity of origins that haunts the pages of Lake of the Prairies, that "ubiquitous childhood question" that demands to be answered yet remains unfulfilled: "origins must be questioned deeply and continually if we are to be at home in the world in a meaningful way. The closer we look at our stories of origin, the more likely we are to find other and sometimes contradictory stories beneath them" (12). More than simply identifying his ancestors, which turns out to be difficult enough, Cariou is obsessed with the paths of inheritance: how we become who we are, what debt we owe to our ancestors, how to tabulate what it is that is transmitted down the centuries.

As a boy growing up in Meadow Lake, Saskatchewan, the demarcations of belonging appear to be clear. Cariou belongs among the privileged by virtue of his white skin. The claiming of place is achieved through bullying: "We claimed places arbitrarily, simply by occupying them" (89). This version of colonial (il)legitimacy is expressed in the bastardized version of "This Land Is Your Land" that the boys sing: "This land is my land/ This land ain't your land/ I got a shotgun/ And you ain't got one/ . . . / This land is PRIvate property" (88-89). While making a mockery of the popular nationalist Canadian/American anthem, the rude version of the song in fact highlights a truth secreted beneath the text of the original. The celebrant chanting "This land is my land" in the song is able to chant this refrain because he/she has been on the winning side of history. As a member of this "winning side," or so he thinks, Cariou links his ancestry to the history of original homesteaders on the Canadian prairies. On his mother's side he is descended from German and Norwegian grandparents who "took up homesteads" on the western prairies among other "immigrants from various parts of Europe" (246). Likewise, on his father's side he comes from a long line of homesteaders and voyageurs. "[H]omesteading stories," he writes, "were the closest thing to our creation myths" (42).

Yet ultimately, Cariou confronts a dilemma: he is tied to these people, yet he feels that something is missing. On the one hand, he is without the "test of belonging," the experience of hard work (136); he has not suffered enough, he believes, to lay claim to the land. On the other hand, he recognizes these origins to be compromised. He hails from an ancestral line of European Canadian settlers, and yet he notes their implication in colonial history: "this thought puts me in an uncomfortable position. If those people hadn't come and hadn't brought those changes, then I could never have called this place home" (19). In a kind of reversal of chronology, he is who they have become, as if his existence has, in retrospect, been predetermined. If one can't choose one's ancestors, they do, in a sense, choose you – simply by leaving their intangible legacy in the genes and by their existence as historical subjects. "[H]ow [had I] been created in the shape of their lives," Cariou asks himself (245). In what sense was his existence predetermined? Haunted by the contingency of ancestry, Cariou wants to identify his own point of intransitive origination; he wants it to be his choice, not something that history, and destiny, has thrust upon him: "I wanted . . . to plant my own flag on my chosen place and claim it as my point of origin" (75-76).

When called upon, he can name his ancestry – French, German,

Norwegian, (English)[10] – but this "magnetism of the blood," while compelling, seems somehow false, "some collective delusion of tribal affiliation" (78). Because he cannot claim such places as his ancestral homelands, he feels a clear rupture in the genealogical continuum: "At family functions I listened to them, bewildered. I came from this?" (77). Sensing that something is missing, and perhaps longing for something that will give him a clear sense of ancestral identity in Canada, he imagines that there is a hidden family secret, that he is not who he thinks he is, that his parents are not his parents. Ironically, his wish is granted when it is revealed that his paternal grandparents were Metis.

The discovery of his aboriginal ancestry, however, is not easily assimilated. Not because there is any shame in the reveleation; on the contrary, Cariou fears that his embracing of the Metis bloodline could only be opportunistic. The indigenized identity, ironically, makes him feel more unsettled than ever. Because the demarcations between Natives and Whites in Meadow Lake have always been carefully policed, and because Cariou has always located himself on the White/winning side of the divide, the discovery of his mixed ancestry disorients him: "having grown up in a community that was hypersensitive about the divisions between Native and white, this information was unsettling . . . I found myself in a between-space, a location that the logic of Meadow Lake didn't allow. It was impossible to be both a Native person and a non-Native person; the two notions were mutually exclusive" (220, 222). On the one hand, Cariou experiences guilt at "the possibility that I had unknowingly benefited from that secrecy" (222). He also fears becoming appropriative, using his aboriginal ancestors, in retrospect, "to supplement some missing aspect of [himself]" (222). Ultimately, he can't claim to be Metis, because he hasn't grown up with himself as such. Nor can he return to his easy sense of himself as French/German/ Norwegian/English. "I am instead a little of this and a little of that; a child of the heterogeneous multitudes" (224).

This realization impinges on Cariou's relation to state-identified notions of ancestry which, he notes, "are still largely incapable of understanding and accepting hybridity" (224). As "a hybrid of a hybrid"(224), Cariou is destabilized by what could otherwise be construed as a more rooted/indigenized ancestry, yet the knowledge has made him less comfortable with the notion of genealogical inheritance rather than more so. Arguably, it may be that the Metis heritage was never really a family secret, but was simply not thought to be an issue. Asking himself why his grandmother would have kept her Metis identity from him, he wonders if it was a strategic move, and therefore one made in the interest of her descendants (her silence bought his privilege), or whether she simply did not consider it something that beared remarking on. In which case, her grandson's obsession with ancestral secrets, "the Indian in the woodpile" (220), may say more about his fixation on identity and inheritance than hers. Having for so long identified as a member of the Canadian mainstream, his devotion to ancestral genealogy has in some sense been a given, notwithstanding his doubts about the efficacy of such genetically determined national identifications.

In the end, because of the impossibility of establishing a clear-cut and singular genealogical line that could account for the vicissitudes of inheritance, Cariou falls back on the ties between land and story. Place becomes the means by which ancestry is given voice. We inherit our ancestors' livingness in place: "I like to think that the land doesn't forget, that our stories echo somewhere around our places" (313). While this notion undercuts the Canadian state's insistence on historical bloodlines, it is still committed to a kind of historical-regional determinism, which in turn is only possible if one can chart one's ancestry within a particular location. While this may be an option for Johnston, Choy, and Cariou, for Blaise and Brand, this is not possible.

One might expect Thomas King's meditation on genealogy to be equally deconstructive given his various send-ups of authentic "Indian" identity throughout his work. King's jokes about the supposed genetically based characteristics of "real Indians" are widely known, from his parodies of the notion in *Green Grass, Running Water*, to the humour, launched at King's expense, in the Dead Dog Café Comedy Hour CBC radio series. "[T]he real value of authenticity," King writes in *The Truth About Stories*, "is in the rarity of a thing" (56). This in itself would suggest that King's meditation on an authenticating ancestry, for himself and for Native peoples more generally, would be fraught with ambivalence. On the one hand, the fixing of clear aboriginal bloodline has been an oppressive venture, used by the state to subject Native peoples to regulated supervision. In recent years, the mystique of everything aboriginal had led to obsessive searches on the part of non-Natives for authenticating aboriginal roots. Such quests have been rightfully criticized as appropriative and indigenizing. On the other hand, King's interrogation of ancestral origins counters widely held conceptions of Native peoples' respect for and identification with their genealogical ancestry.[11] This dilemma echoes Brand's awareness of the simultaneous danger and usefulness of the commitment to origins. As King himself states, "There's no magic in the blood that provides us with an ethnic memory" (118), however one might be lured to search for such a link.

With these points in mind, it is interesting that King's 2003 Massey Lectures, *The Truth About Stories*, engage with the question of the ancestral past in a discussion of his Cherokee father who abandoned the family when King was three or four years old. Embedded within King's discussion of colonial history and Native storytelling is a deeply personal exploration of contingency and atonement, and it is his aboriginal ancestor who is the focus of his anxiety. While superficially humourous, the book is in part an investigation of origins and inheritance, and the making of amends. The "truth" about stories is that we all need them and use them to link us to our ancestors and make sense of ourselves; the other "truth" is that they need not necessarily be "true." The quest for or invention of a significant ancestor, then, would seem to be an inherently dialogical process, made all the more concrete in King's case in that his father has been an absent presence for most of his life.

The book begins with the tale of absolute, "intransitive" origins, a beginning point beyond which there is no other. Hence the title of this section of the book: "'You'll never believe what happened' is always a great way to start" (1). Echoing the format of *Green Grass, Running Water*, King begins each of the five lectures in the collection with a story about the origins of Turtle Island/North America. In an image that evokes those quests for a receding genealogy into an immemorial past, the story posits that the earth was built on top of the back of a turtle, which sits atop another turtle, etc., so that "it's turtles all the way down" (2). This inquiry into origins points to a kind of Quaker Oat box mise-en-abyme, and proves analogous to the personal investigation into origins and genealogy that is embedded within the book.

"The truth about stories," King writes, "is that that's all we are" (2), begging the question of whose stories contribute to who we become. While King attests to "seeing the world through my mother's eyes" (2), it is his father who ruptures the security of these tales of origins, and yet also his father who clearly motivates his quest. As King writes, "My father is a different story" (5), which would seem to imply that the story of his father, unlike other stories, is not what has contributed to who King has become. And yet, of course, it is the absence of this figure that propels King's quest to discover his significance. Even his memories of his father are not trustworthy: "I have one memory of a man who took me to a small café that had wooden booths with high backs and a green parrot that pulled at my hair. I don't think this was my father. But it might have been" (5). As Cariou writes of the storied nature of one's ancestry, "We always have to take someone's word for it" (4). If stories are elusive, ancestors are as well, a fact that is compounded when King admits to having lied to his friends about his father's desertion of the family: "For a long time I told my friends that my father had died" (5). In a scene that evokes Choy's account of the mysterious revival of his mother's ghost, King's family is startled by a phone call that comes some six years later; his father asks to come back, his mother agrees, and "that was the last we ever heard from him" (5). The mother assumes that her husband has been killed. Ironically, however, King and his brother only discover the "truth" about their father once he is dead, and the truth is that the father is not their father alone, but has had a whole other life and family apart from them all these years. This renders King's revenge fantasy all the more poignant. In his fantasy, he sees himself sitting beside his father in a bar, opening up a friendly conversation, and when his father realizes who he (King) is, the son will walk out on him. Yet in the end, the quest for the father only magnifies the son's sense of disinheritance. The father, he finds out, all but forgot King, and the fantasy scenario remains a "story," nothing more.

If, on the one hand, King "has never been able to move past these stories" of his father's desertion and remarriage (9), it is also the case that in a very obvious sense his father's absence has contributed to who he has become, since in effect it is his aboriginal ancestry that has most informed King's writing career and public persona. While questions are often raised about the legitimacy of his claims to aboriginality, given that he is only half Native, it is the absent Native in his past that has most affected his present, and which has in turn contributed to his cogent critiques of Canadian nationalism, racial oppression, white-Native relations, postcolonial theory, etc. The absent genealogical father has in this case perpetuated a store of anger in the son, which in this text is poised alongside aboriginal creation stories, as if to suggest links between personal and communal history. If the family one inherits is a matter of mere contingency, what Blaise refers to as "the insolence of fate" (16), one's origins are both what elude one (the memories are irretrievable) and haunt one ("[I] will be chained to these stories as long as I live" [9]). Interestingly, the text is book-ended by this evocation of the father. The final section of the book relates a story of a family whose experience bears remarkable similarities to King's family saga. Struggling with an adopted child suffering from fetal alcohol syndrome, the father abandons the mother and daughter with the not very comforting line: "They're better off without me" (165). While the event echoes the story of King's father, it is King himself here who feels that he has abandoned his friends by not helping them when they needed him, and it is his own ethics, along with those of North American society in general, that he finds suspect. If the book is a condemnation of North Americans' continued insistence on othering the Native, King's personal meditation suggests that he is little better. What might have been an authenticating or reconciling narrative, or even a story of communal ethics, reveals itself to be just another story. The discovery of his inheritance serves little more than to reinforce his sense of disinheritance: by his father, by society, by himself.

"We can't do anything about the ancestors we have inherited," states the blurb on the UEL website (1), as if to say that we can't all be lucky enough to have Loyalist ancestors. What the statement assumes, however, is that some version of linear inheritance is accessible to everyone. Yet what if the genealogical line connecting past with present is not so clear-cut? The writers I've been discussing reveal, however reluctantly, the difficulty of charting any clear line of genetic/psychic descent. Ancestors are either not whom they were believed to be, or they have been erased in the passage of colonial time. At one point in Lake of the Prairies, Cariou wonders what it was, exactly, that his ancestors "intended to pass down to later generations" (245). The truth is that ancestry, in the moment, does not work with such teleological drive. We may want to believe that our existence has been predetermined, we may want to insist on blood-line inheritance and "ethnic memory" (King 118), the sense that our ancestors made us who we are today. This is the elusive "genetic consolation" that Blaise speaks of. And there is certainly some truth to these stories of historical indebtedness. Nevertheless, what each of these writers also considers is the danger of such commitment to genealogy, a commitment to "a manufactured origin" (Brand 64) that generally results in disinheriting others. While these writers each describe a specific context of postcolonial disinheritance, they share an anxiety of origins founded on an unhomely sense of their emplacement in the New World.

(I would like to acknowledge the support of a SSHRC Standard Research Grant in the preparation of this essay.)

NOTES

1. I take this phrasing from James P. Howley's 1915 study *The Beothuks or Red Indians* in which he writes of the Beothuk people of Newfoundland as enabling us "to go behind the Indians in looking for the earliest inhabitants of North America" (quoted xvii). According to Howley and others, the Beothuk were distinct from continental Native peoples (many commentators described them as having "pale" skin) and were thought to be the "remnant of the Norsemen who attempted colonization in the tenth century" (xix). They were thus bracketed off from contemporary Native groupings and thought to represent a more archaic people. For my exploration of this topic, see my unpublished essay "Original Sin, or, The Last of the First Ancestors: Michael Crummey's *River Thieves*." According to Victoria Freeman, the legend of the Welsh colony established in Newfoundland by Madoc in 1170 was used to establish the Beothuk as "descendants of twelfth-century Welshmen" (30).

2. There has also been speculation that the fifth-century Chinese monk, Hoel Shin, may have visited what is now British Columbia, though this story has garnered far less currency than the accounts of European ancestors.

3. A statue commemorating the birth of Snorri in Vinland (modern-day Newfoundland) stands in the lobby of the National Archives in Ottawa, highlighting his significance as a symbolic Canadian first ancestor.

4. According to Cavell, Frye's famous "Where is here?" question represents the settler-invader's figuration of Canada as a "space without place" (114), in other words, a location that has been emptied out of the social or "real-life" dimension and posited in terms of a fantasy space. The same might apply to genealogical configurations of the Canadian nation, where bloodline functions as an abstraction that is divorced from social realities.

5. I wish to thank Sarah Phillips Casteel for directing me to Zamora's fascinating study.

6. See Jennifer Henderson's Settler Feminism for an incisive critique of this trope in discourse of Canadian cultural history and identity.

7. As recently as 2003, Georges-Hébert Germain applied the label of "white Indians" to the voyageurs. See his Les Coureurs des bois: la saga des indiens blancs (Outremont: Libre Expression, 2003).

8. See also Eva Mackey's *The House of Difference* and Sherene Razack's *Race,*

Space, and the Law for accounts of the racist foundations of Canadian national culture.

9. I am indebted here to a discussion that took place following the "Canada and Its Americas" session at the August 2005 International American Studies Association conference in Ottawa. In particular, I'd like to thank David Leahy for his incisive discussion of Brand's text.

10. I place "English" in parentheses because, as Cariou states, he is not of English ancestry but rather, as boy, felt that he must identify as "English" because he spoke the language (76).

11. The difference in Western and Aboriginal understandings of genealogy might be that Western notions of relations are based on a linear and hierarchical model, while aboriginal conceptions of interrelatedness are envisioned in terms of simultaneity, allowing ancestral spirits (human and nonhuman) to coexist with the living.

WORKS CITED

Anderson, Benedict. *Imagined Communities: Reflections on the Origin and Spread of Nationalism.* Rev. ed. London: Verso, 1991.

Armstrong, Richard H. *A Compulsion for Antiquity: Freud and the Ancient World.* Ithaca: Cornell University Press, 2005.

Aubry, Jack. "Diving into the Gene Pool." *Ottawa Citizen* 1 July 2001: D3-D5.

Bannerji, Himani. "Geography Lessons: On Being an Insider/Outsider to the Canadian Nation." *Unhomely States: Theorizing English-Canadian Postcolonialism.* Ed. Cynthia Sugars. Peterborough: Broadview, 2004. 289-300.

Blaise, Clark. I Had a Father: *A Post-Modern Autobiography.* Toronto: HarperCollins, 1993.

Brand, Dionne. *A Map to the Door of No Return: Notes to Belonging.* Toronto: Doubleday Canada, 2001.

Cariou, Warren. *Lake of the Prairies.* Toronto: Random House-Anchor, 2003.

Cavell, Richard. "Where Is Frye? Or, Theorizing Postcolonial Space." *Essays on Canadian Writing* 56 (1995): 110-34.

Choy, Wayson. *Paper Shadows: A Chinatown Childhood.* Toronto: Viking, 1999.

Corbett, Ron. "Where the New World Begins." *Ottawa Citizen* 16 July 2005: E1, E6-E7.

Freeman, Victoria. *Distant Relations: How My Ancestors Colonized North America.* Toronto: McClelland, 2000.

Griffiths, Linda, and Maria Campbell. *The Book of Jessica: A Theatrical Transformation.* Toronto: Coach House, 1989.

Hall, Stuart. "Cultural Identity and Diaspora." *Colonial Discourse and Post-Colonial Theory: A Reader.* Ed. Patrick Williams and Laura Chrisman. New

York: Harvester Wheatsheaf, 1993. 392-403.

Harrison, Robert Pogue. *The Dominion of the Dead.* Chicago: University of Chicago Press, 2003.

Henderson, Jennifer. *Settler Feminism and Race Making in Canada.* Toronto: University of Toronto Press, 2003.

Howley, James P. *The Beothuks or Red Indians: The Aboriginal Inhabitants of Newfoundland.* 1915. Toronto: Prospero, 2000.

Johnston, Wayne. *Baltimore's Mansion: A Memoir.* Toronto: Vintage, 2000.

King, Thomas. *The Truth About Stories: A Native Narrative.* CBC Massey Lecture Series. Toronto: Anansi, 2003.

Mackey, Eva. *The House of Difference: Cultural Politics and National Identity in Canada.* Toronto: University of Toronto Press, 2002.

Paz, Octavio. *The Labyrinth of Solitude: Life and Thought in Mexico.* Trans. Lysander Kemp. New York: Grove, 1961.

Razack, Sherene H., ed. *Race, Space, and the Law: Unmapping a White Settler Society.* Toronto: Between the Lines, 2002.

Said, Edward. *Beginnings.* New York: Columbia University Press, 1975.

Thomas, Julian. "A History of Beginnings." *Quicksands: Foundational Histories in Australia and Aotearoa* New Zealand. Ed. Klaus Veumann, et al. Sydney: University of New South Wales Press, 1999. 115-31.

Turner, Stephen. "Settlement as Forgetting." *Quicksands: Foundational Histories in Australia and Aotearoa* New Zealand. Ed. Klaus Veumann, et al. Sydney: University of New South Wales Press, 1999. 20-38.

The United Empire Loyalists' Association of Canada. Website. "Membership in the United Empire Loyalists' Association of Canada."

Wiebe, Rudy. "On the Trail of Big Bear." *A Voice in the Land: Essays By and About Rudy Wiebe.* Ed. W.J. Keith. Edmonton: NeWest, 1981. 132-41.

Zamora, Lois Parkinson. *The Usable Past: The Imagination of History in Recent Fiction of the Americas.* Cambridge: Cambridge University Press, 1997.

Contributors

John Clement Ball is professor of English at the University of New Brunswick in Fredericton and coeditor of the journal Studies in Canadian Literature. His most recent book is Imagining London: Postcolonial Fiction and the Transnational Metropolis (University of Toronto Press, 2004).

Donna Bennett teaches Canadian literature at the University of Toronto at Scarborough and is a member of the Department of English graduate faculty. Currently a coeditor of the University of Toronto Quarterly, she is also coeditor of Canadian Short Stories (2005), and An Anthology of Canadian Literature in English (2002).

Sally Blundell is a graduate student at the University of Canterbury, Christchurch, New Zealand. She is currently working on her doctorate on elective mutism as a response to terror and trauma in contemporary fiction. Over the last fifteen years she has also worked as a freelance journalist and editor.

Diana Brydon teaches Canadian and postcolonial literary studies at the University of Western Ontario. She has published on Canadian literary texts and postcolonial theory. Her current research examines the cluster of meanings attached to concepts of home under the pressures of globalizing processes within the contexts of postcolonial cultural studies and discourses around globalization.

George Elliott Clarke is the E.J. Pratt Professor of Canadian Literature at the University of Toronto. An expert in Black African-Canadian literature, his chief academic book is Odysseys Home: Mapping African-Canadian Literature (University of Toronto Press, 2002). The recipient of the 2001 Governor-General's Award for Poetry, Clarke received the prestigious Trudeau Fellowship Prize in 2005.

Dr. Paulo Lemos Horta (Ph.D., Toronto) is Assistant Professor of Humanities at Simon Fraser University and an associate of the Future of Minority Studies Project at Cornell University and the Cultural History and Literary Life research group based at the Universidade do Estado do Rio de Janeiro. He teaches world literature.

DANIEL HEATH JUSTICE is an enrolled citizen of the Cherokee Nation and teaches Aboriginal literatures and Aboriginal Studies at the University of Toronto. His book, Our Fire Survives the Storm: A Cherokee Literary History, is forthcoming from University of Minnesota Press in Spring 2006.

CHELVA KANAGANAYAKAM is professor of English and director of the Centre for South Asian Studies at the University of Toronto. His publications include Structures of Negation: The Writings of Zulfikar Ghose (1993), Dark Antonyms and Paradise: The Poetry of Rienzi Crusz (1997) and Counterrealism and Indo-Anglian Fiction (2002).

CHRISTOPHER LEVENSON, born in London, England, came to Canada in 1968 and taught English at Carleton University until 1999. The author of ten books of poetry, most recently The Bridge (Buschek Books, Ottawa, 2000), he has travelled extensively in India and has increasingly specialized in South Asian poetry and fiction in English.

STEPHANIE MCKENZIE (PhD in English, University of Toronto). She is a poetry editor, and poet. President of Scop Productions, McKenzie has copublished and coedited two anthologies of poetry from Ireland and Newfoundland & Labrador: The Backyards of Heaven (2003) and However Blow the Winds (2004). Her first book of poetry, Cutting My Mother's Hair, will be published by Salmon Poetry (Galway, Ireland).

JESSICA SCHAGERL specializes in Canadian Literature at The University of Western Ontario.

CYNTHIA SUGARS is an Associate Professor in the Department of English at the University of Ottawa. She is the author of numerous articles on postcolonialism and Canadian literature, and is the editor of two essay collections: Unhomely States: Theorizing English-Canadian Postcolonialism (2004) and Home-Work: Postcolonialism, Pedagogy, and Canadian Literature (2004).